AD-HOC NETWORKING

IFIP – The International Federation for Information Processing

IFIP was founded in 1960 under the auspices of UNESCO, following the First World Computer Congress held in Paris the previous year. An umbrella organization for societies working in information processing, IFIP's aim is two-fold: to support information processing within its member countries and to encourage technology transfer to developing nations. As its mission statement clearly states,

> *IFIP's mission is to be the leading, truly international, apolitical organization which encourages and assists in the development, exploitation and application of information technology for the benefit of all people.*

IFIP is a non-profitmaking organization, run almost solely by 2500 volunteers. It operates through a number of technical committees, which organize events and publications. IFIP's events range from an international congress to local seminars, but the most important are:

- The IFIP World Computer Congress, held every second year;
- Open conferences;
- Working conferences.

The flagship event is the IFIP World Computer Congress, at which both invited and contributed papers are presented. Contributed papers are rigorously refereed and the rejection rate is high.

As with the Congress, participation in the open conferences is open to all and papers may be invited or submitted. Again, submitted papers are stringently refereed.

The working conferences are structured differently. They are usually run by a working group and attendance is small and by invitation only. Their purpose is to create an atmosphere conducive to innovation and development. Refereeing is less rigorous and papers are subjected to extensive group discussion.

Publications arising from IFIP events vary. The papers presented at the IFIP World Computer Congress and at open conferences are published as conference proceedings, while the results of the working conferences are often published as collections of selected and edited papers.

Any national society whose primary activity is in information may apply to become a full member of IFIP, although full membership is restricted to one society per country. Full members are entitled to vote at the annual General Assembly, National societies preferring a less committed involvement may apply for associate or corresponding membership. Associate members enjoy the same benefits as full members, but without voting rights. Corresponding members are not represented in IFIP bodies. Affiliated membership is open to non-national societies, and individual and honorary membership schemes are also offered.

AD-HOC NETWORKING

IFIP 19th World Computer Congress, TC-6, IFIP Interactive Conference on Ad-Hoc Networking, August 20-25, 2006, Santiago, Chile

Edited by

Khaldoun Al Agha
LRI, Paris XI University, France

Ad-Hoc Networking

Edited by K. Al Agha

p. cm. (IFIP International Federation for Information Processing, a Springer Series in Computer Science)

ISSN: 1571-5736 / 1861-2288 (Internet)

ISBN: 13: 978-1-4419-4186-2
Printed on acid-free paper

eISBN: 10: 0-387-34738-0
eISBN: 13: 978-0-387-34738-7

9 8 7 6 5 4 3 2 1
springer.com

Table of Contents

TCP over Geo-routing for High Mobility: Vehicle Grids and Airborne Swarms

Jiwei Chen, Mario Gerla and Yeng-Zhong Lee

University of California, Los Angeles, CA 90095, USA
cjw@ee.ucla.edu, {gerla,yenglee}@cs.ucla.edu

Summary. Ad hoc wireless networks have become the architecture of choice for peer to peer communications in areas where the telecommunications infrastructure is inadequate or has failed. A major challenge is the reliable delivery of data when nodes move. The reliable Internet protocol is TCP. However, TCP performs poorly in mobile ad hoc networks, mainly because of route breakage. To overcome this problem, a robust routing protocol must be used. To this effect, Geo-routing has recently received attention in large scale, mobile systems as it does not require end-to-end path establishment and pre-computed packet forwarding routing structure at nodes. These properties make Geo-routing robust to highly dynamic route changes. For best performance, however, several parameters must be carefully tuned.

In this paper we study the joint optimization of TCP and Geo-routing parameters to handle high speeds. We first introduce two highly mobile ad hoc scenarios that require reliable delivery, namely the vehicle urban grid and the airborne swarms. Then, we study the impact of critical system parameters (e.g., hello message exchange rate, delay timer in TCP for out-of-order delivery, etc) on the performance of both UDP and TCP. We improve hello message efficiency in Geo-routing by using an adaptive hello exchange scheme. Then, we fix the out-of-order problem in TCP by using a receiver-side out-of-order detection and delayed ack strategy. We show that these parameter adjustments are critical for efficient TCP over Geo-routing in highly mobile applications. With these enhancements our TCP with Geo-routing solution easily outperforms TCP over traditional ad hoc routing schemes, such as AODV.

1 Introduction

Transport Control Protocol (TCP) is unquestionably one of the most widely used protocols in the Internet. TCP was originally designed for a wired network where congestion and buffer overflow account for most packet losses. Unlike wired networks, TCP performance in wireless ad hoc networks is affected by several new factors. These factors include unpredictable channels error, medium contention which may lead to capture, and frequent route breakage

Please use the following format when citing this chapter:

Chen, J., Gerla, M., Lee, Y.-Z., 2006, in International Federation for Information Processing (IFIP), Volume 212, Ad-Hoc Networking, ed. Al Agha, K., (Boston: Springer), pp. 1–15.

due to node mobility. All these factors challenge TCP to provide efficient and reliable end-to-end communications in mobile ad hoc networks.

Two recent developments have stimulated great interest for TCP in highly mobile scenarios: car to car communications, file sharing and content distribution during highway driving; and tactical communications between Apache helicopters and UAVs (manned and unmanned). The latter "airborne" situation is common in battlefield, homeland defense and search and rescue scenarios. In these scenarios, mobility can be characterized by the inverse of "contact time" with neighbors. The lower the contact time, the more challenging the routing. For example, an aircraft flying at 360Km/hr with transmission range of 300m will maintain contact with neighbors flying in random directions for an interval of the order of seconds. Thus, neighbor acquisition and route computation must be completed well below the second. Notice that "contact time" is proportional to the ratio of transmission range over speed, thus, what counts is the "relative" speed. For instance, people walking in a shopping mall (at 3m/s) with Bluetooth or Zigbee radios with 10 m range, say, would also lead to "high mobility" ad hoc net scenarios.

To overcome the problems posed by vehicular and aircraft speeds, a robust routing protocol must be used. To this effect, Geo-routing has recently received attention in large scale, mobile systems as it does not require end-to-end path establishment and pre-computed packet forwarding routing structure at nodes. These properties make Geo-routing robust to highly dynamic route changes. For best performance, however, several parameters must be carefully tuned.

In this paper we study the joint optimization of TCP and Geo-routing parameters to handle high speeds. We first introduce two highly mobile ad hoc scenarios that require reliable delivery, namely the vehicle urban grid and the airborne swarms. Then, we study the impact of critical system parameters (e.g., hello message exchange rate, delay timer in TCP for out-of-order delivery, etc) on the performance of both UDP and TCP. We improve hello message efficiency in Geo-routing by using an adaptive hello exchange scheme. We also fix the out-of-order problem in TCP by using a receiver-side out-of-order detection and delayed ack strategy. We show that these parameter adjustments are critical for efficient TCP over Geo-routing in highly mobile applications.

The remainder of this paper is organized as follows. Section 2 describes the urban vehicle ad hoc wireless environment. Next, Section 3 describes the use of clusters of small unmanned aircrafts for search, rescue and scouting applications. Section 4 reviews prior work on TCP for mobile ad hoc scenarios. Following this, Section 5.1 presents an impact study of various Geo-routing parameters and comparison of UDP and TCP over Geo-routing versus traditional ad hoc routing in a carefully controlled, deterministic motion scenario. An adaptive hello exchange scheme for GPSR is introduced. In Section 5.2 we consider the more general scenario with random motion. With random motion we show that out-of-order detection and recovery is required for efficient TCP performance. We conclude our work in Section 6.

2 The Vehicle Grid

2.1 Background

Safe navigation support through wireless car to car and car to curb communications has become an important priority for Car Manufacturers as well as Municipal Transportation Authorities and Communications Standards Organizations. New standards are emerging for car to car communications (DSRC and more recently IEEE 802.11p). There have been several well publicized testbeds aimed at demonstrating the feasibility and effectiveness of car to car communication safety. For instance, the ability to rapidly propagate accident reports back to oncoming cars on the highway, the awareness of unsafe drivers around you and the prevention of intersection crashes. The availability of powerful radios on board of vehicles, and of abundant spectrum (when not used for emergencies) will pave the way to a host of new applications for the "vehicle car to car grid".

These emerging applications span many fields: from office-on-wheels to entertainment, mobile internet games, mobile - shopping, crime investigation, civic defense, etc. Some of these applications are conventional "mobile internet access" applications, say, downloading files, reading e-mail while on the move. Others involve the discovery of services in the neighborhood (e.g., restaurants, movie theaters, etc) using the vehicle grid as an ad hoc network. In addition, a brand new type of applications can be envisioned which will involve a much closer "cooperation" among cars including maintenance of distributed indices, creation and "temporary" storage of sharable content, "epidemic" distribution of content and index. Examples include the collection of "sensor data" by cars as seen as "mobile sensor platforms", the sharing and streaming of files in a Bit-torrent fashion, and the creation/maintenance of massively distributed data bases with locally relevant commercial, entertainment and culture information (e.g., movies, hotels, museums, etc). Typically, these applications are totally distributed and follow a P2P collaboration model among cars. Fig.1 depicts a possible Urban Vehicle Grid scenario.

2.2 VANET Design

In designing protocols for the next generation vehicular network, we recognize that nodes in these networks have significantly different characteristics and demands from those in traditional wireless ad hoc networks deployed in infrastructureless environments (e.g. sensor field, battlefield, etc). Speed is one such difference. Automobiles travel at speeds up to one hundred miles per hour, making sustained vehicle-to-vehicle communication difficult. However, existing statistics of vehicular motion, such as traffic patterns during commute hours, can be used to develop sophisticated mobility models much more realistic than the current random waypoint models. By accurately characterizing

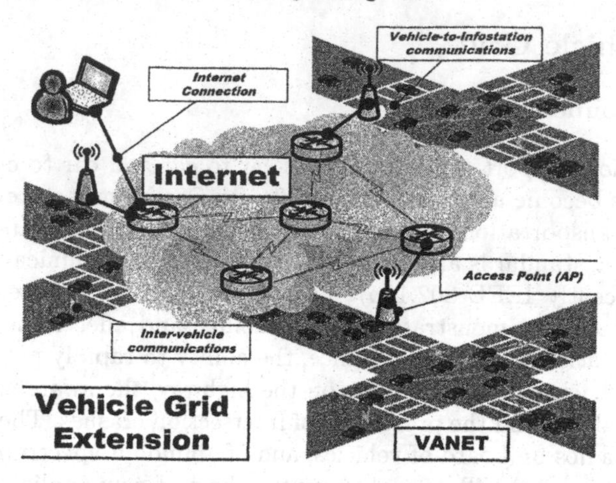

Fig. 1. A Urban Vehicle Grid scenario

vehicles' tendencies to travel together, these models can help maintain connectivity across mobile vehicular groups. Another important departure of vehicle networks from conventional ad hoc networks is the opportunity to deploy, in addition to traditional applications, a broad range of innovative content sharing applications (typically referred to as Peer-to-Peer applications). While their popularity has been well documented, they have been thus far confined to the fixed Internet (e.g., Bit Torrent, etc). The storage and processing capacity of VANET nodes make such applications feasible. Moreover, the fact that car passengers are a captive audience provides incentive for content distribution and sharing applications that would be unsuitable to other ad hoc network contexts. Examples include locality-aware information (map based directions) and content for entertainment (streaming movies, music and ads) [1, 2, 3]. These applications require high throughput network connectivity and fast access to desired data. Vehicles can also be producers of content. Examples include services that report on road conditions and accidents, traffic congestion monitoring, and emergency neighbor alerts. These applications require real-time and location-aware data gathering and dissemination [4].

The demands of these applications give us a list of requirements and challenges for vehicular applications including:

- Location awareness: both data gathered from vehicles and data consumed by vehicles are highly location-dependent.
- Time-sensitive dissemination of data to and from vehicles.
- Reliable communications in the presence of high vehicular mobility, intermittent connectivity and lossy channels.

The Geo-routing solution discussed in this paper and the associated Geo Location Service are ideally suited to support location awareness. The proposed robust TCP solution is a good match for the time-sensitive, reliable communications requirements in high mobility.

3 Airborne Swarms

Another example of highly mobile ad hoc network is the swarm of unmanned aircraft. A possible application scenario is a disaster area that requires the intervention of police, firemen, paramedics etc, but where the unfriendly environment bars direct access. The swarm operates in a completely distributed, autonomous manner, establishing a communications network between the rescue teams and all critical fixed and mobile sensors and actuators in the disaster area. It allows the police to "see", probe and manipulate the environment remotely before they can safely enter. Possible emergency scenarios include: chemical, nuclear plant disaster/sabotage; fire on a ship; explosion/fire on high rise building, etc. Other non-emergency application domains can benefit from the proposed swarm technology. For instance, space and planetary exploration (e.g., Mars), collection of scientific data in remote, sparsely instrumented regions, etc.

In the aftermath of a disaster we may assume that some "networked islands" of sensors, monitors and actuators have survived in the plant. For example, sensors may have been installed in strategic locations in the plant, building, ship etc; they had been preplanned for such an emergency. However, full sensor coverage and networking are generally not available after the accident, either because it was not practical or too costly to establish a complete infrastructure or because the infrastructure has been partially destroyed. Consequently, the entire area becomes partitioned into islands.

The rapid deployment of a swarm of air/ground agents will reestablish network connectivity, restore access to critical sensor probes, install new probes as necessary and help the collection and filtering of relevant data. Fig.2 shows a mobile backbone network of UAVs that reestablishes connectivity.

Airborne swarms find important applications also in the battlefield. Autonomous agents such Unmanned Airborne Vehicles (UAVs) are projected to the forefront for intelligence, surveillance, strike, enemy antiaircraft suppression, damage assessment, search and rescue and other tactical operations [5]. UAVs are organized in clusters to launch complex missions that include: coordinated aerial sweep of vast urban/suburban areas to track suspects; search and rescue operations in unfriendly areas (e.g., chemical spills, fires, etc), exploration of remote planets, and; reconnaissance of enemy field in the battle theater. The successful, distributed management of the mission will require efficient, reliable, low latency communications within members of each team, across teams and to a manned command post. Again, an efficient TCP implementation capable to survive aircraft mobility is essential. In the sequel we review current ad hoc TCP implementations and then propose a robust solution that will work up to vehicle and aircraft speeds.

Fig. 2. Maintaining connectivity with a mobile backbone

4 Related Work

Many research efforts in recent years[6, 7, 8] have directed to making TCP robust to all sorts of wireless network disruptions including mobility. In mobile ad hoc networks, in fact, most of the packet losses are due to route breakage [7]. Mobility causes frequent route interruptions. If the routing algorithm cannot track node motion and packets enroute cannot be salvaged until a new route is found, TCP goes into exponentially increasing timeout intervals with severe performance hit.

How to improve TCP performance in such mobile networks has been a hot area for years. Routing of course is one key factor, thus the interaction between TCP and routing has been thoroughly investigated in the past. Unfortunately, traditional on-demand routing schemes, such as DSR and AODV, cannot efficiently address the frequent route breakage and packet loss due to high mobility. These schemes pre-compute the route at call setup time. Every node has a predefined next-hop for the designated destination. When this next-hop node moves away (or dies), the routing scheme must find another path. Unfortunately, finding another path takes time (and generally leads to TCP to time out). To avoid this delay, multi-path routing could be adopted, allowing multiple candidate next hops for packet forwarding. However the overhead of multi-path routing grows fast and becomes intolerable as node mobility increases [9]. Another solution is to exploit routing layer feedback (eg, route broken/route repaired) to TCP. In [10, 11], TCP's state is frozen when the sender receives the route failure signal from intermediate nodes. TCP exits the frozen state when route is re-established. Fixed-RTO was proposed in [12] with selective and delayed ack to help constraining the damage when packet loss is known to come from path breakage.

Even Fixed-RTO has only limited effect (as we will show in our experiments). When nodes are moving very fast, no traditional (proactive or on demand) routing structure can adjust rapidly enough. For these extreme situations, Geo-routing [13, 14] has recently shown remarkable promise. Geo-routing uses the destination location as the "routable" address, and forwards packets (when possible) in a greedy manner towards it. Geo-routing is highly scalable, as nodes only keep geo-locations for their local neighbors. No explicit end to end route establishment is required. Since there is no pre-computed next hop to destination at set up time (as in all traditional schemes), rather the next hop is selected opportunistically "on the fly", Geo-routing promises to be robust to path breakage and short term channel failure if the network is sufficiently dense (ie, there are always nodes in the "right" direction).

Geo-routing also places some extra costs on the network. It relies on information that is not needed in conventional routing schemes (eg, GPS positioning, Geo Location Server, accurate knowledge of neighbor locations). Moreover, if the basic Geo-routing "greedy" approach fails when the packet is trapped in a "cul de sac" (sort of a local "maximum" in the greedy search), it adopts perimeter (face) mode to go around the void area.

Many of the above issues (eg, location determination without GPS, Geo Location server, perimeter routing to circumvent local maxima) have already been studied extensively in the literature [15, 16, 17] and will not be addressed here. However, previous studies were mostly based on UDP and lightly loaded networks. We recall that Geo-routing uses hello messages to update neighbor information. In light load, the issues of hello message O/H and of interference between hellos and data packet did not emerge. TCP is rather aggressive in increasing network load, thus, it is important to "tune" the hello message rate taking into account not only speed but also load. Regarding hello messages, the careful reader will recall that some schemes [18] discover the best next hop dynamically, with an election and thus are not encumbered with background hello message maintenance all together. However, such schemes require a change in the MAC protocol (and thus in 802.11 firmware) which we exclude in this study. Moreover, they introduce the extra election overhead. Thus, one of the important contributions of this study is the hello rate optimization. Other useful contributions are the analysis and solution of the out of order delivery problem in the specific Geo-routing context.

5 TCP Performance over Geo-routing in Mobile Ad Hoc

In this section, we analyze GPSR [13], the most popular implementation of Geo-routing. We first study the impact of high mobility on UDP and TCP over GPSR and tune GPSR parameters to optimize performance. Then, we compare UDP and TCP performance on GPSR with AODV. We do not compare GPSR with other routing schemes (eg, DSR, DSDV, OLSR etc) for lack of space. Besides, the latter schemes tend to perform worse than AODV in mobile scenarios [8].

5.1 Case Study: Deterministic Motion

The first motion scenario, deterministic motion model, is carefully crafted to allow high mobility in a controlled way, yet maintaining end to end topology connectivity all the time. In this scenario, shown in Fig.3, the sender and the receiver are fixed. A total of 12 intermediate nodes arranged in 3 columns are moving vertically up and down in constant but opposite velocity. We place the nodes at 200m interval of each other in each column. Neighboring columns have opposite moving directions so the relative motion is twice the node speed. Recalling that the transmission range is 250m, in this scenario a path is always available from the sender to the receiver in spite of motion throughout the experiments. This is a very important detail of this experiment that we will exploit later.

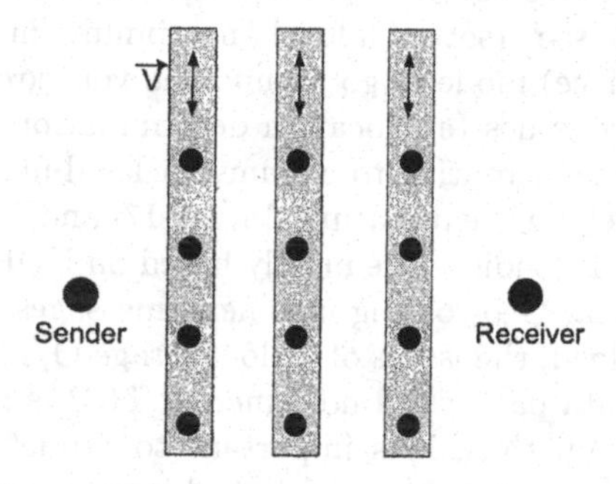

Fig. 3. Deterministic Movement Topology

In our experiments, radio rate is set to 2Mbps. Standard TCP (TCP NewReno) is used. Data packet size (for both UDP and TCP traffic) is 1000 bytes. GPSR hello packet refresh interval is initially set to 1s. All the results are averaged over 5 simulation runs with different random seeds. We vary mobility speed from 0m/s to 100m/s.

In the first experiment, UDP delivery ratio is presented in Fig.4. Fig.4(a) shows the delivery ratio with low CBR date rate (1 packet per second), The UDP delivery ratio in GPSR is quite good, almost 100%. This performance is indeed remarkable given the relatively high speed. Eventually, at top speed (100m/s) some packets are lost because of lack of a forwarding neighbor. This problem is easy to explain. Simple geometry shows that two nodes in neighbor columns moving at relative speed 200m/s are in contact at most for 1.5s. Recalling that hello refresh rate is 1s, and that some hellos may be lost because of interference, it is very possible that for some small fraction of the time a node has no forwarding neighbors. The packet is then lost! AODV in contrast does not work well, and the UDP delivery ratio deteriorates monotonically with the increased mobility, with more than 30% loss at 100 m/s . This is expected because of repeated path breakage and failure to find a route.

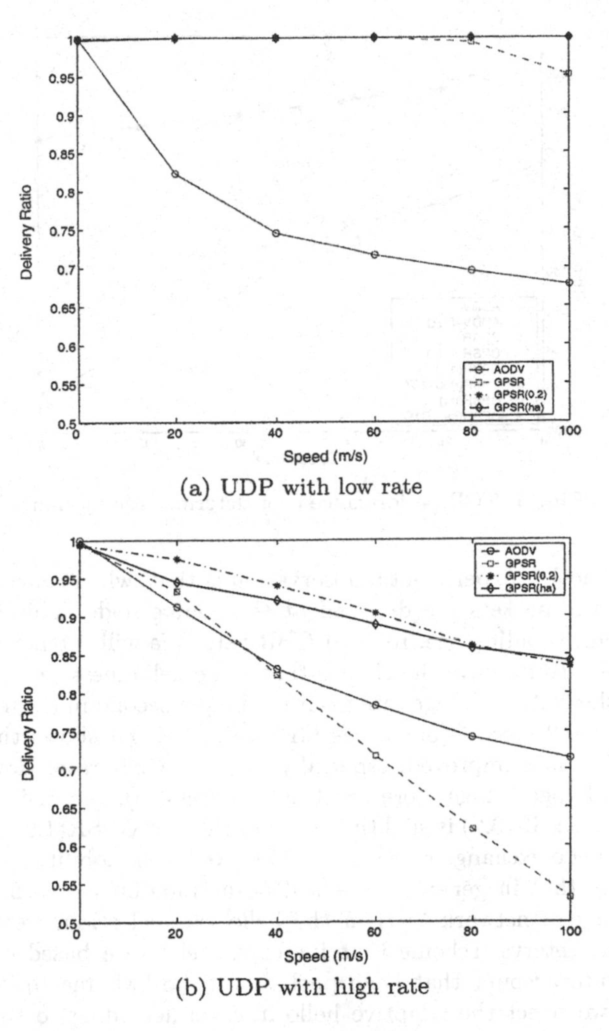

(a) UDP with low rate

(b) UDP with high rate

Fig. 4. UDP performance over deterministic motion

Fig.4(b) shows the delivery ratio for high rate UDP (40 packets per second). Surprisingly, GPSR collapses! The delivery ratio is even worse than in AODV for speed larger than 40m/s. From simulation results we find that the major reason for this problem is the loss of hello packets due to interference. Since hello packets are broadcast with an "unreliable MAC" (no RTS/CTS/ACK), when the UDP rate is high and congestion builds up, hello packet mortality is high. This leads to inaccurate neighbor information. If GPSR finds no neighbors in the forward directions, it initiates "perimeter routing" which can lead to loops, and to hop count timeout. In fact, in this experiments the lost packets all had very high hop count except packet losses at

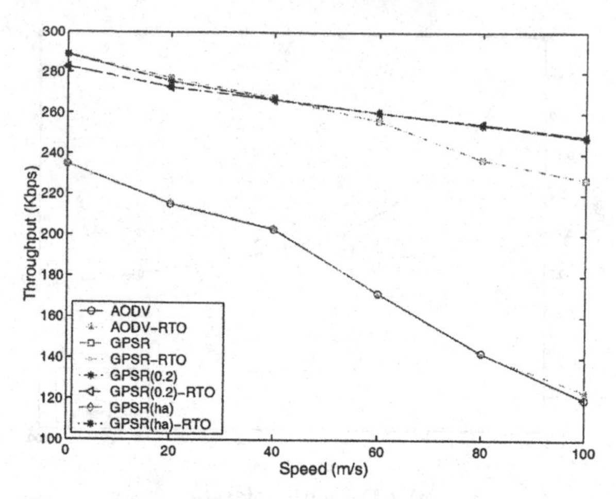

Fig. 5. TCP performance over deterministic motion

the source! Another experimental observation is that, when congestion builds up, most of the packets are dropped at the source node. This information could be useful to adjust (ie. reduce) CBR rate. We will further discuss this property later. To improve the chance that some hello messages are received, we increase the hello exchange rate from 1 hello per second in the initial GPSR to 1 hello per 0.2 second (named as GPSR(0.2)). Fig.4 shows that delivery ratio is significantly improved, especially for high CBR rate. However, high rate hello exchange brings more overhead. In Fig.4(b), the delivery ratio at speed 0m/s in GPSR(0.2) is slightly less than that for GPSR(1.0). From these results, high hello exchange rate is most effective when mobility speed is high.

Suspecting that in general there will be a trade off between routing efficiency and extra network O/H in the hello rate selection, we propose an adaptive hello interval scheme that increases hello rate based on mobility, also taking into account that hello packets will be lost due to interference. Specifically, we select the adaptive hello interval according to the following formula:

$$I = \frac{R}{k \times speed} \tag{1}$$

Where I is the hello interval, R is the transmission range and k is a tunable parameter. The rationale behind the formula is the following. On average two randomly moving neighbors see each other in a window equal to R meters. Thus, the contact interval is R/speed. During the contact interval, a node needs to send several hellos to announce its presence. The factor k should be adjusted to balance the overhead and effectiveness and to account for hello loss. In our simulation, k is set to 16. Additionally, there are two limits for hello interval, an upper limit of 2 second and a lower limit of 0.1 second. Thus, the adaptive hello interval used in the paper is $max(min(I, 2), 0.1)$.

The results for GPSR with adaptive hello exchange rate, named as GPSR(ha), are also shown in Fig.4. Equipped with adaptive hello rate in GPSR, UDP delivery ratio keeps around 100% for low rate UDP, and it is much better than AODV in high rate UDP as well. For high rate UDP, GPSR(ha) is slightly less than GPSR(0.2) for speeds from 20m/s to 60m/s. A more aggressive choice of parameters should be explored. In all, however, the difference ($< 3\%$) is quite small.

After studying UDP performance, we turn to TCP performance in Fig.5. Since TCP consists of two way traffic and a data packet can collide with an ack packet, TCP traffic press much more stress on the routing. From Fig.5, TCP over GPSR is only moderately affected when nodes moves, even at very high speed, due to the GPSR robustness to mobility. The throughput of TCP over GPSR only drops 21% from 0m/s to 100m/s and still achieves high throughput (around 230k at 100m/s), while TCP throughput over AODV drops by 50% and degrades fast for high mobility, just about 120k at 100m/s. Due to the frequent route breakage and more packet losses from two way traffic, TCP never has the chance to perform well and the performance degrades quickly with mobility in AODV. We recall that Fixed-RTO was proposed in TCP as a remedy to path breakage. We note in Fig.5. that Fixed-RTO only has minimal impact on performance over AODV and GPSR (the Fixed-RTO curves are practically overlapped with original TCP curves).

We note that, as a difference from UDP, TCP does not perform too bad with GPSR(1.0). This is due to the fact that TCP does congestion control and thus limits the interference onto hellos. Nevertheless, a reduction from hello interval from 1s to 0.2s brings significant benefits for high mobility as shown in 5, however the performance is worse in low mobility. This calls for adaptation. GPSR with adaptive hello (GPSR-ha) eliminates the overhead problem at low mobility. TCP over GPSR(ha) traces the upper envelope of performance of both GPSR(1.0) in low mobility and GPSR(0.2) for high mobility. Therefore, it satisfies our quest to improve TCP performance under varying mobility.

5.2 Random Movement

In what follows, we study TCP performance in a general case where nodes move randomly. The *random waypoint mobility model* [20] is used in the simulation. Fig.6 illustrates the random moving topology. The sender and receiver are kept at fixed positions, while the remaining 40 nodes are moving randomly in a region of 1000m$\times$1000m. The speed of the nodes ranges from 10m/s to 90m/s.

The performance of UDP over GPSR and TCP with Fixed-RTO in this scenario is pretty similar to that observed in deterministic motion, so we omit their results here. Fig.7 presents TCP results over AODV and GPSR. As expected, TCP over GPSR still outperforms TCP over AODV. However, its performance is by far worse than in the deterministic motion case. We discover that TCP over Geo-routing has a serious out-of-order(OOO) delivery problem in the random movement. In contrast, TCP over AODV suffers no significant OOO problems.

In GPSR, a route is selected on a packet by packet basis and thus can change very rapidly. If a new route is shorter or has lower delivery delay due to lighter load, data packets on the new route could arrive before packets on the old route. OOO packets cause throughput degradation. In fact, TCP receiver responds to OOO data packets with duplicate acks which potentially trigger fast retransmits leading to congestion window reduction and extra inefficiency. This OOO problem was discussed in [21] and some approaches for OOO detection and response were presented. However, the approaches proposed in [21] require the modifications of packet header and cooperations at TCP sender and receiver. In the paper we propose a novel approach, which only involves TCP receiver without modifying the packet header format and TCP sender. TCP receiver determines if a non-in-order packet has come from a different route by simply checking the TTL value in the packet header. If the packet is from a path different from that of the latest in-order packet, there was a route change and the OOO event is detected. The missing packets between this OOO packet and in-order packet could arrive latter. The receiver could wait for some time before issuing a duplicate ack. A challenge here is to estimate the "optimal" waiting window at the receiver. We propose to let the receiver passively estimate RTT and use it to decide the period for the waiting timer. The receiver could use the TCP timestamp option in the packet header to estimate RTT, though such an estimate may be inflated if the sender does not send data packets immediately after receiving an ack [22]. However, the waiting timer is only a coarse timer for predicting when the missing packets will arrive, thus RTT inflation errors can be tolerated.

The receiver computes the waiting time based on this RTT measurement. The following formula is used:

$$\begin{aligned} SRTT^r_{k+1} &= \frac{7}{8} SRTT^r_k + \frac{1}{8} RTT^r_{k+1} \\ RTT^{var}_{k+1} &= \frac{3}{4} RTT^{var}_k + \frac{1}{4} |RTT^r_{k+1} - SRTT^r_{k+1}| \\ RTO^r_{k+1} &= SRTO^r_{k+1} + 4 \times RTT^{var}_{k+1} \end{aligned}$$

Where RTT^r is the RTT estimation at the receiver, $SRTT^r$ is the smoothed RTT. RTT_{var} and RTO^r are RTT variance and waiting timer period at the receiver. This ack waiting timer is started after detecting OOO event, and is canceled after all missing packets arrived.

As shown in Fig.7, the OOO packet handling strategy (GPSR-OOO) enhances TCP performance by about 10%. Incidentally, we also tested OOO delivery in deterministic motion, however we did not find significant OOO delivery effects because all direct paths have the same length. Next, we enhance TCP over GPSR by adjusting hello intervals. Fig.8 presents the TCP performance over GPSR with fast and adaptive hello exchange. Note: we only show results with OOO response. As expected, GPSR(0.2) only provides performance gain for high mobility, while GPSR(ha) integrates the advantages of GPSR in low mobility and GPSR(0.2) in high mobility. TCP over GPSR with adaptive hello interval is considerably better than TCP over AODV. The throughput of TCP over GPSR(ha) only drops from 315kbps at 10m/s to 225kbps at 90m/s (about 28% performance degradation), while AODV drops from 260kbps at 10m/s to 95kbps at 90m/s (about 63% performance degradation).

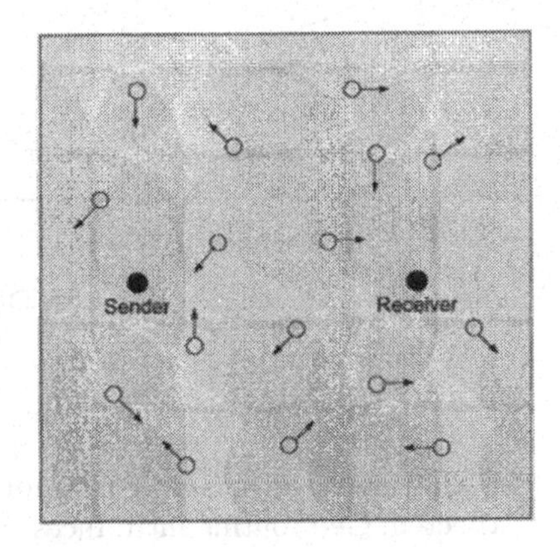

Fig. 6. Random Movement Topology

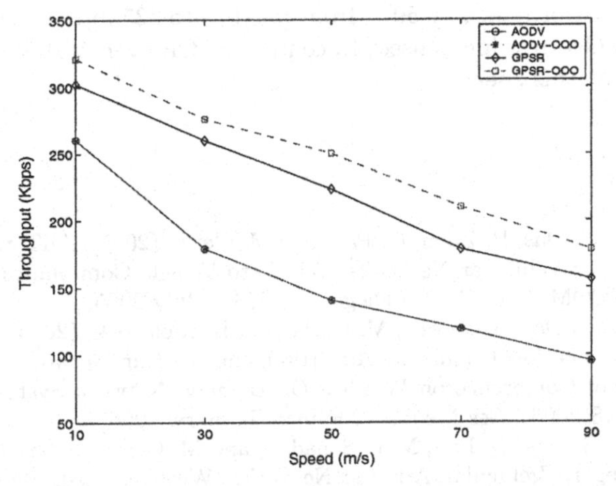

Fig. 7. TCP performance over random motion

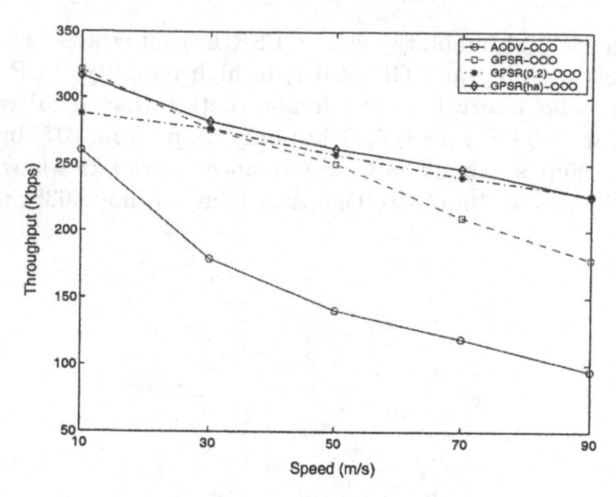

Fig. 8. TCP performance over random motion with OOO response

6 Conclusion

We have studied TCP and UDP performance over Geo-routing in highly mobile ad hoc network. As expected, Geo-routing introduces substantial benefits. Several Geo-routing parameters have been carefully tuned to achieve such benefits. First, we have proposed a hello scheme adaptive to the mobility. Second, we have proposed a novel scheme for handling out-of-order delivery which requires TCP receiver-only modification. These two enhancements can improve TCP performance by 50%, from 150kbps to 225kbps at aircraft speed (90m/s) when Geo-routing is used. In contrast, TCP over AODV delivers less than 100kbps at this speed.

References

1. A. Nandan, S. Das, B. Zhou, G. Pau, and M. Gerla, (2005). AdTorrent: Digital BillBoards for Vehicular Networks. Vehicle-to-Vehicle Communications Workshop (V2VCOMM 2005), San Diego, CA, USA, July 2005.
2. A. Nandan, S. Das, S. Tewari, M. Gerla, and L. Kleinrock, (2006). AdTorrent: Delivering Location Cognizant Advertisements to Car Networks. The Third International Conference on Wireless On Demand Network Systems and Services(WONS 2006), Les Menuires, France, January, 2006
3. A. Nandan, S. Das, G. Pau, M.Y. Sanadidi, and M. Gerla, (2005). Cooperative downloading in Vehicular Ad Hoc Networks. Wireless On-Demand Network Systems and Services (WONS 2005), St Moritz, Switzerland, 2005.
4. U. Lee, E. Magistretti, B. Zhou, M. Gerla, P. Bellavista and A. Corradi, (2006). Efficient Data Harvesting in Mobile Sensor Platforms. IEEE International Workshop on Sensor Networks and Systems for Pervasive Computing (PerSeNS 2006), Pisa, Italy, March, 2006.

5. Mario Gerla, Kaixin Xu, and Allen Moshfegh, (2002). Minuteman: Forward Projection of Unmanned Agents Using the Airborne Internet. IEEE Aerospace Conference 2002, Big Sky, MT, Mar. 2002.
6. Z. Fu, P. Zerfos, H. Luo, S. Lu, L. Zhang, and M. Gerla, (2003). The impact of multihop wireless channel on TCP throughput and loss, IEEE INFOCOM 2003.
7. X. Yu (2004). Improving tcp performance over mobile ad hoc networks by exploiting cross-layer information awareness, MobiCom.
8. A. A. et al., (2000). Performance of tcp over different routing protocols in mobile ad-hoc networks, IEEE VTC.
9. P. Pham and S. Perreau, (2003). Performance analysis of reactive shortest path and multipath routing mechanism with load balance, IEEE INFOCOM.
10. G. Holland and N. H. Vaidya, (1999). Analysis of TCP performance over mobile ad hoc networks, MobiCom.
11. K. Chandran, S. Raghunathan, S. Venkatesan, and R. Prakash, (2001). A feedback-based scheme for improving TCP performance in ad hoc wireless neworks, IEEE Personal Communications Magazine.
12. T. D. Dyer and R. V. Boppana, (2001). A comparison of tcp performance over three routing protocols for mobile ad hoc networks, MobiHoc.
13. B. Karp and H. T. Kung, (2000). GPSR: Greedy perimeter stateless routing for wireless networks, MobiCom.
14. I. S. P. Bose, P. Morin and J. Urrutia, (2001). Routing with guaranteed delivery in ad hoc wireless networks, ACM/Kluwer Wireless Networks.
15. J. Li, J. Jannotti, D. S. J. D. Couto, D. R. Karger, and R. Morris, (2000). A scalable location service for geographic ad hoc routing, MobiCom.
16. D. Niculescu and B. Nath, (2001). Ad hoc positioning system, IEEE GLOBE-COM.
17. S. Capkun, M. Hamdi, and J. P. Hubaux, (2001). Gps-free positioning in mobile ad-hoc networks, Proceedings of HICSS.
18. M. Zorzi and R. R. Rao, (2003). Geographic random forwarding (geraf) for ad hoc and sensor networks: energy and latency performance, IEEE Transaction on Mobile Computing.
19. C. E. Perkins and E. M. Royer, (1999). Ad-hoc on-demand distance vector routing, Proceedings of IEEE WMCSA.
20. C. Bettstetter, H. Hartenstein, and X. Prez-Costa, (2004). Stochastic properties of the random waypoint mobility model, ACM/Kluwer Wireless Networks: Special Issue on Modeling and Analysis of Mobile Networks.
21. Y. Zhang and F. Wang, (2004). Improving TCP performance over mobile ad-hoc networks with out-of-order detection and response, MobiHoc.
22. V. Jacobson, (1992). Tcp extensions for high performance, RFC 1323.

An Efficient QoS Routing Protocol for Mobile Ad-Hoc Networks *

Inwhee Joe

College of Information and Communications
Hanyang University
Seoul, Korea
iwjoe@hanyang.ac.kr

Abstract. To satisfy the user requirements for continuous and real-time multimedia information, the concept of Quality of Service (QoS) has emerged as a main issue in mobile ad-hoc networks. QoS routing is to find a route according to the QoS requirements of the users. In this paper, we propose an efficient QoS routing protocol that is based on AODV over TDMA, one of the typical routing protocols for mobile ad-hoc networks, by making a bandwidth reservation for QoS guarantee. While the existing schemes calculate the maximum available bandwidth for each candidate path, our scheme is to check only if the bandwidth of a given path satisfies the end-to-end QoS requirement. Also, the key idea in the bandwidth reservation is to select carefully time slots without causing any conflicts in the wireless environment, thereby maximizing the bandwidth efficiency. In order to evaluate the performance of the proposed QoS routing protocol, some simulations are carried out in the ad-hoc environment. The simulation results show that the proposed protocol provides sufficiently low and stable delay performance regardless of the offered load.

1 Introduction

In recent years, wireless mobile networks have become increasingly important for users of computing systems. There are currently two types of wireless mobile networks: Infrastructured network and Ad-hoc network. The first type refers to a network with any infrastructure by installing base stations in cellular networks or access points in wireless local area networks. On the other hand, the second type of wireless mobile networks does not rely on any fixed infrastructure. This may happen on conferences, rescue operations, or military actions in enemy terrain, i.e., when mobile users need to communicate to each other in situations and

* This work was supported in part by grant No. IITA-2005-C1090-0501-0022 from the ITRC Support Program of the Ministry of Information and Communication, and in part by grant No. F01-2003-000-20011-0 from the International Cooperative Research Program of the Korea Science and Engineering Foundation.

Please use the following format when citing this chapter:

Joe, I., Park, Y.J., 2006, in International Federation for Information Processing (IFIP), Volume 212, Ad-Hoc Networking, ed. Al Agha, K., (Boston: Springer), pp. 17–28.

places with no infrastructure where rapid deployment of a network is required on a temporary basis.

Mobile ad-hoc networks consist of mobile nodes (each node conceptually consisting of a router, a radio port and one or more host computers). To communicate with mobile nodes that are not within the transmission range, a routing protocol is required for each node. Recently, many routing protocols have been proposed for mobile ad-hoc networks. In general, they can be divided into two main categories: proactive and reactive protocols. In a proactive routing protocol, nodes periodically exchange routing information with other nodes to maintain all the routes on the network beforehand, while in a reactive approach each node attempts to discover a route on demand only when it has data to send. Although there is no single standard routing protocol yet, reactive routing protocols are known to perform better than proactive routing protocols in terms of lower overheads. Typical examples of reactive routing protocols include the dynamic source routing (DSR) protocol and the ad-hoc on-demand distance vector (AODV) routing protocol.

Even if existing routing protocols are designed to cope well with the dynamic change of network topology, they are mainly concerned with best-effort data traffic. The problem of Quality-of-service (QoS) routing to support multimedia traffic over mobile ad-hoc networks is studied here. The goal of QoS routing is to find a route from a source to a destination that satisfies the end-to-end QoS requirements such as bandwidth and delay. Unlike traditional wireless networks, providing QoS is more difficult for mobile ad-hoc networks, because the network topology changes frequently and the end-to-end route is a multi-hop wireless path.

QoS routing in mobile ad-hoc networks has recently started to receive increasing attention in the literature [3, 4, 5]. To find out a route to the destination, QoS routing normally calculates the maximum available bandwidth for each candidate route so that it can check if the bandwidth meets the end-to-end QoS requirement. In fact, the ability to provide QoS is heavily dependent on how the resources like bandwidth are managed at the MAC (Medium Access Control) layer, whether it is TDMA (Time Division Multiple Access) or CDMA (Code Division Multiple Access). In TDMA, calculating the maximum bandwidth for a given multi-hop route is proven to bc NP-complete because of the interference problem [1]. Some use CDMA on top of TDMA to eliminate this problem by assigning a different code to each transmitter [1].

In this paper, we propose a novel QoS routing protocol with bandwidth reservation for mobile ad-hoc networks using TDMA. Our routing protocol is based on AODV [2] to find QoS routes on-demand only as needed. The remainder of this paper is organized as follows. After explaining the concept of bandwidth calculation, we propose our slot section algorithm to maximize the bandwidth efficiency in Section 2. In Section 3 we present a detailed description of the proposed QoS routing protocol. In Section 4 we address performance evaluation results from simulation using our own network simulator. Finally, we conclude the paper by highlighting our contribution.

2 Bandwidth Calculation

In the packet-switched network, QoS is meaningful only for a flow of packets between the source and destination. So, it is assumed that the application is flow-based and requires constant bandwidth as the end-to-end QoS requirement to support multimedia traffic over mobile ad-hoc networks. Since bandwidth guarantee is one of the most critical requirements for multimedia traffic, we only consider bandwidth as the QoS here. In an attempt to satisfy the QoS requirement, the network must ensure that adequate network resources like bandwidth are available for the entire duration of a given flow. Therefore, QoS guarantees can be delivered only with appropriate resource reservation mechanisms. For each flow, QoS routing is the process of finding the route that meets the required bandwidth. In TDMA, the bandwidth is expressed in terms of time slots.

To find a route with sufficient bandwidth, QoS routing normally calculates the maximum available bandwidth for each candidate route, and then make a reservation along the route if the bandwidth is large enough to meet the QoS requirement as a part of the process. In this case, both the hidden terminal and exposed terminal problems should be taken into account so that the interference can be avoided in the wireless environment. If a given route R provides a bandwidth of B time slots, it means that every link along the route has at least B available time slots, and these slots do not interfere with other transmissions. That is, the end-to-end bandwidth of a route is not determined just by the bandwidth of the bottleneck link, because mutual interference among available time slots of links should be considered in the wireless environment.

Each transmission is organized in a frame that contains a fixed number of time slots, N. The entire network is synchronized on a frame and slot basis. The link bandwidth can be defined as the number of free time slots on the link from the sender to the receiver without any conflicts to other transmissions. It is different according to the link direction, because the conflicts are directional. Due to the hidden-terminal and exposed-terminal problems, the link bandwidth is affected only by transmission or reception activities of one-hop neighbor nodes from the sender and the receiver. The available link bandwidth from a sender S to a receiver R can be obtained in terms of free time slots by removing the following unavailable time slots from the total time slots N:

- Time slots that are used already by a sender S or by a receiver R.
- Time slots that are used to receive in one-hop neighbor nodes of a sender S.
- Time slots that are used to send in one-hop neighbor nodes of a receiver R.

For example, when a link bandwidth L is calculated, there are four possible cases around the sender and the receiver, as shown in Fig. 1. If a sender node S and a receiver node R are regarded as one super node, the scope of our interest is one-hop range of the super node, since the link bandwidth is affected only by transmission and reception activities of the one-hop neighbor nodes. On the sender's side, there are two cases whether time slots are used for transmission or reception. First, node A has only reception slots, and these slots cannot contribute to the link bandwidth L because of the hidden-terminal problem. Second, node B has only transmission slots, and these slots can contribute to the link bandwidth L because of the exposed-terminal problem. On the receiver's side, there are also two cases depending on the direction. Node C has only transmission slots, and these slots cannot be counted into the link bandwidth L because of the hidden-terminal problem. Finally, node D has only reception slots, and these slots can be counted into the link bandwidth L, because they don't interfere with the transmission from S to R. In summary, the link bandwidth L can be calculated by counting the number of remaining time slots in the total slots N, after removing the slots that are used by the sender S and receiver R, also used by their neighbor nodes A & C.

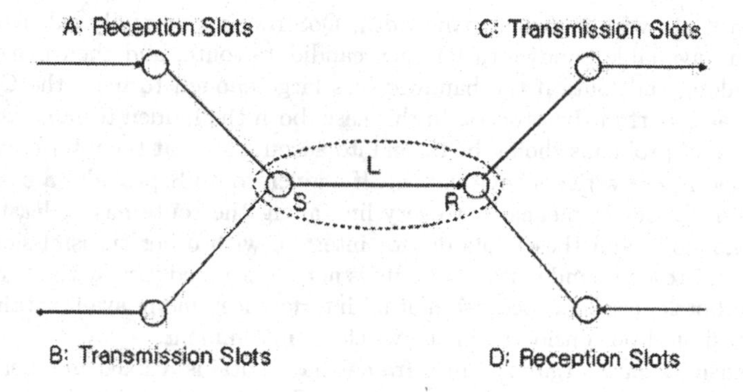

Fig. 1. Link Bandwidth Calculation

The path bandwidth can be defined as the number of free time slots on the route from the source to the destination. If the destination is directly linked to the source, the path bandwidth is equivalent to the link bandwidth in this case. In general, a path consists of several links, and each link bandwidth can be obtained as describe above. However, the path bandwidth is not just determined by the minimum link bandwidth on the route because of the interference problem. Actually, finding the maximum path bandwidth for a given route is proven to be NP-complete in terms of global optimization. That is, it is very hard to find the optimal solution in the sense that the path bandwidth is maximized and at the same time there is no conflict between transmissions along the entire route. Instead of calculating the maximum path bandwidth, we propose only to check if the bandwidth of a given route satisfies the end-to-end QoS requirement.

Once every link bandwidth on the route is calculated in terms of free time slots, then the next step is what slots to choose for the path bandwidth without any conflicts to each other. Due to the hidden-terminal and exposed-terminal problems, the link bandwidth is affected only by one-hop neighbor nodes of the sender and the receiver. It means that for slot selection the path bandwidth should consider all the slots until the two-hop links with the sender and receiver in the center. For example, when slots are chosen for the path bandwidth from node X to Y, both its one-hop and two-hop links should be taken into account, as shown in Fig. 2. In this case, there are two one-hop links from node W to X and from node Y to Z. Also, there are two two-hop links from node S to W and from node Z to D. The difference between the left links and the right links around this link from node X to Y is that the left links already have their slots chosen according to the end-to-end QoS requirement. In particular, Fig.

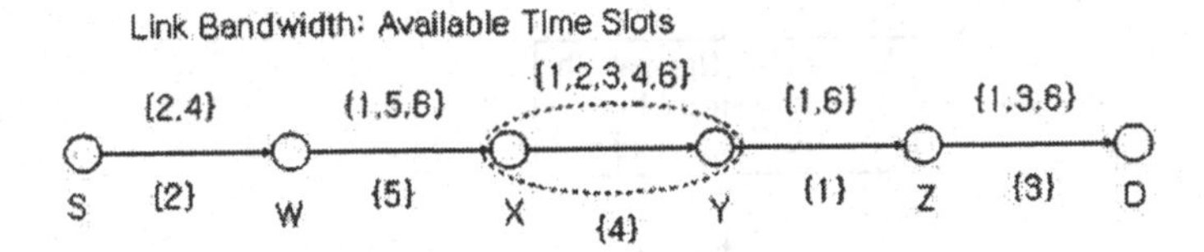

Fig. 2. Slot Selection for Path Bandwidth

2 illustrates how slots are selected along the route as the path bandwidth for a given end-to-end QoS requirement (e.g., 1 time slot) from the source node S to the destination node D. For the first link starting from node S to W, slots are selected from its link bandwidth by avoiding the available slots of the one-hop link from W to X and the two-hop link from X to Y as much as possible. This way, the available path bandwidth is maximized in such that the problem of slot conflicts can be minimized. If there is no slot satisfying this condition, any slots will be chosen randomly (e.g., slot 2) among the available slots on the link. Once the slots are determined for the first link, then this process repeats for the next link from node W to X. However, in this case, there are two one-hop links with respect to the link from W to X: left link from S to W and right link from X to Y. The difference is that the left link has its slots already chosen to the path bandwidth, so only these slots (e.g., slot 2) will be avoided on slot selection instead of the entire link bandwidth (e.g., slots 2 & 4). After removing all the slots of the one-hop and two-hop links, the rest will be selected for this link (e.g., slot 5) as long as there are some left. This process repeats until it reaches the destination node D. If this path can provide enough bandwidth to meet the end-to-end QoS requirement, it is chosen as a QoS route. Our slot selection algorithm can be summarized briefly with a flow chart, as shown in Fig. 3.

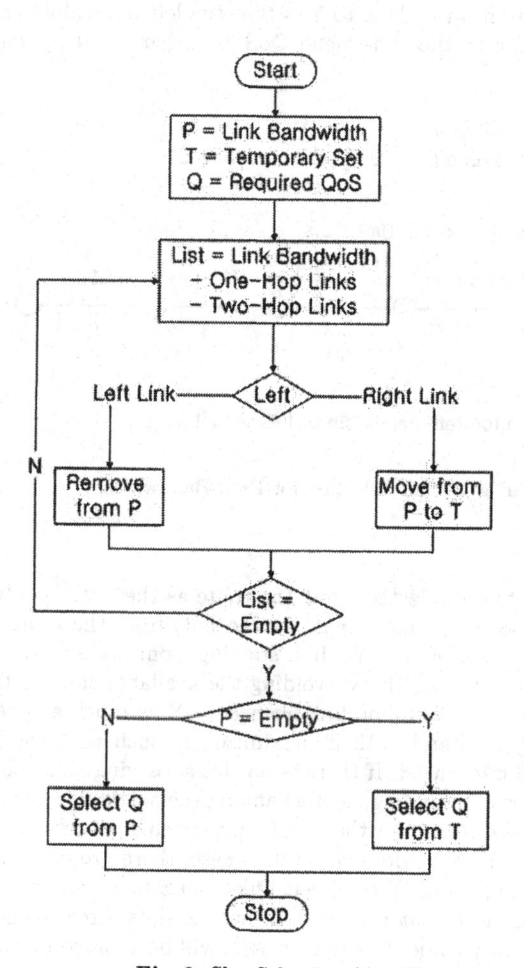

Fig. 3. Slot Selection Algorithm

3 QoS Routing with Bandwidth Reservation

3.1 Hello Message

Each node broadcasts a Hello message on a periodic basis to its one-hop neighbor nodes. The Hello message contains the time slot information extracted from the slot table of each node that maintains which time slots are used for transmission or reception, and which time slots are available. Also, the Hello message contains the time slot information of the one-hop neighbor nodes using the previous Hello messages received from the neighbor nodes. In the Hello message, the sequence number is used to identify which message is more up-to-date. In this way, each node collects the time slot information of all the neighbor nodes in its two-hop range using the periodic Hello messages. As a result, the link bandwidth can be calculated with such information for each link direction, as mentioned in Section 2.

Fig. 4 shows the modified Hello message format. One part of the previous Reserved field in the original Hello message is renamed as the field of Time Frame Length to indicate the total number of time slots for each frame cycle. The Node Count field indicates the total number n of the one-hop neighbor nodes. For each node, the IP address, sequence number, and the time slot information are included in the Hello message. As mentioned earlier, the time slot information represents the current state of each time slot, i.e. which slots are in use for transmission or reception, and which slots are available.

Type	Time Frame Length	Reserved	Node Count (n)
Source IP Address			
Source Sequence Number			
Variable Time Slot Information			
Neighbor node IP Address (1)			
Sequence Number			
Variable Time Slot Information (1)			
...			
Neighbor node IP Address (n)			
Sequence Number			
Variable Time Slot Information (n)			

Fig. 4. Hello Message

3.2 Bandwidth Reservation

To find a route to the destination, the source node initiates the route discovery procedure by broadcasting a route request (RREQ) message to its neighbor nodes like AODV. As the RREQ message proceeds hop by hop until the destination, each intermediate node appends the link bandwidth information to the RREQ message. The link bandwidth is a list of free time slots for each directional link and this information can be obtained using the periodic Hello messages. Once the RREQ message reaches the destination, the destination node extracts all the link bandwidth information between source and destination out of the RREQ message. With this, our slot selection algorithm is applied so that it attempts to choose time slots for each link along the path according to the end-to-end QoS requirement. If the algorithm cannot find the required number of available time slots from each link, the destination node generates no response because this particular route does not meet the end-to-end QoS requirement.

Type	J	R	G	D	U	R	LBW Length	Reserved	Hopcount
RREQ ID									
Destination IP Address									
Destination Sequence Number									
Source IP Address									
Source Sequence Number									
IP Address									
Link Bandwidth Information									
Next IP Address...									
Next Link Bandwidth Information...									

Fig. 5. Route Request Message

Fig. 5 shows the modified RREQ message. In comparison with the original RREQ message, the modified portion is shaded. The R flag indicates whether the QoS guarantee is required or not, depending on the user requirement. The LBW Length field indicates the total number of time slots for each frame cycle. A directional link consists of two nodes, the transmitter node and the receiver node. The first link starts from the source node as a transmitter. Thus, for each link the IP address of the receiver node and the link bandwidth information are added to the last part of the RREQ message, as long as the R flag is set. This process continues on a hop by hop basis until the destination.

Once the required number of free time slots can be chosen for each link along the route from source to destination, it means that this particular route can afford to satisfy the end-to-end QoS requirement. In this case, the destination node creates a route reply (RREP) message and puts the selected time slot information of each link in this message. Since each node receiving the RREQ message caches a route back to the source, the RREP message can be unicast from the destination along the path to the source just like AODV. Whenever the

RREP message is received, each relay node makes a bandwidth reservation using the selected time slot information of the message. In other words, as indicated in the selected time slot information of the RREP message, the corresponding time slots will be reserved for each node to support this particular flow.

Finally, the source node begins to transmit data through the reserved path. Fig. 6 shows the modified RREP message. In comparison with the original RREP message, the modified portion is shaded. The same R flag is used here for QoS requirement. The Selected Slot Number field indicates the number of the time slots selected. The time slot information of each link is expressed in a form of the bit map: Selected Bitmap. This information represents which slots are selected as the path bandwidth for each link along the route from the source to the destination.

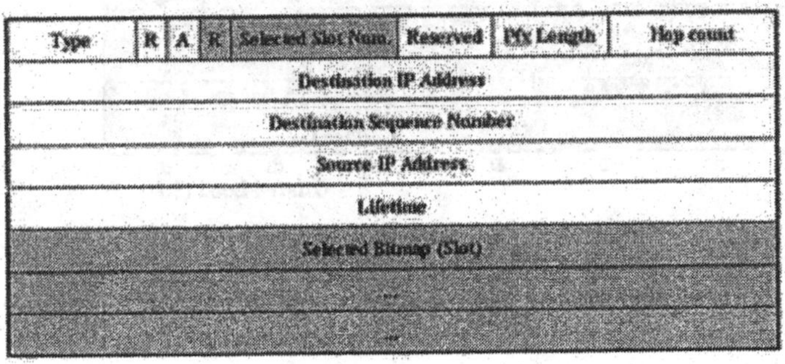

Type	R	A	R	Selected Slot Num.	Reserved	Pfx Length	Hop count
Destination IP Address							
Destination Sequence Number							
Source IP Address							
Lifetime							
Selected Bitmap (Slot)							
...							
...							

Fig. 6. Route Reply Message

4 Simulation

The objective of simulation is to evaluate the performance of our QoS routing protocol with bandwidth reservation for mobile ad-hoc networks. Since the network simulator $ns-2$ does not support TDMA for mobile ad-hoc networks, we developed our own network simulator using C in order to validate the proposed protocol over TDMA. The voice stream is modeled as CBR (Constant Bit Rate) traffic with the coding rate of 8 Kbps, while the video stream is also modeled as CBR traffic with the coding rate of 32 Kbps. If each time slot supports 8 Kbps, 1 time slot is required for the voice traffic and 4 time slots are required for the video traffic as the end-to-end QoS requirements. The simulator places 20 mobile nodes in a random fashion in the area of 100 by 100 meters. The radius of the radio transmission range is assumed to be about 30 meters and the total number of time slots in each frame cycle is set to 20. Given simulation parameters above, we measure the QoS guarantee ratio and the delay performance as a function of the offered load.

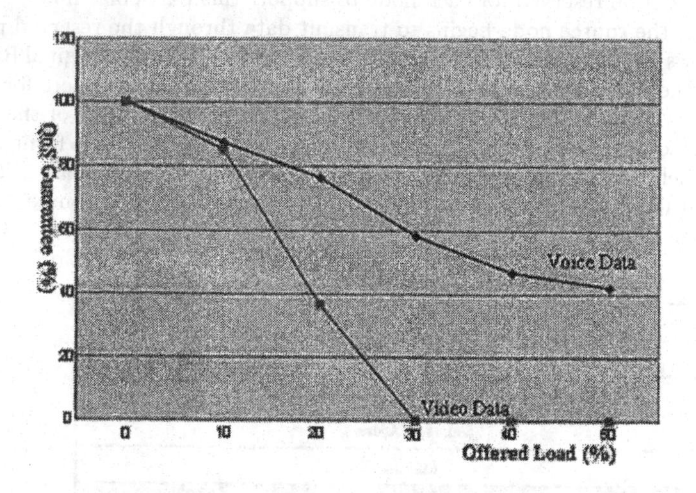

Fig. 7. QoS Guarantee Ratio

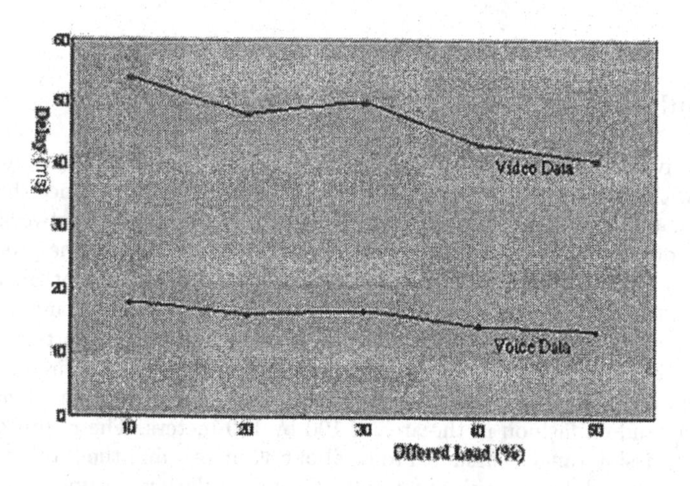

Fig. 8. Delay Performance

Fig. 7 shows the QoS guarantee ratio as a function of the offered load. The QoS guarantee ratio represents the percentage of how much QoS guarantee is successful. As the offered load increases, the QoS guarantee ratio decreases. For the video traffic the curve drops dramatically, while it drops gradually in case of the voice traffic. Since more time slots are required for the video traffic, it explains the behavior of the video curve in terms of the QoS guarantee ratio as compared to the voice case. To support video traffic, four time slots are required for transmission and another four time slots are required for reception at the same time, thereby leading to eight time slots for each relay node. As a result, it is certain that the video curve drops rapidly with the increased offered load, in that the total number of time slots is only 20 for each frame cycle.

On the other hand, Fig. 8 presents the delay performance as a function of the offered load. The delay performance is defined as the end-to-end delay measured at the application layer from the source to the destination. Regardless of the offered load, it is shown that the delay is sufficiently low and stable for both cases. It ensures that our proposed QoS routing protocol works correctly to make a bandwidth reservation with the slot selection algorithm according to the end-to-end QoS requirement. Obviously, the video traffic causes more delay than the voice traffic. If the offered load is 60% or higher, the QoS guarantee is actually hard to deliver, so measuring the delay is not so useful at all. In summary, the simulation results show that the delay performance is very stable and low enough to satisfy the end-to-end QoS requirement regardless of the offered load.

5 Conclusions

In this paper, we have discussed the design and performance of a novel QoS routing protocol with bandwidth reservation for mobile ad-hoc networks. While the existing schemes calculate the maximum available bandwidth for each candidate path, our scheme is to check only if the bandwidth of a given path satisfies the end-to-end QoS requirement. In fact, finding the maximum path bandwidth for a given route is proven to be NP-complete in terms of global optimization. Instead of calculating the maximum path bandwidth, we propose only to check if the path bandwidth meets the end-to-end QoS requirement by applying our slot selection algorithm. The algorithm attempts to choose carefully time slots without causing any conflicts in the wireless environment, thereby maximizing the bandwidth efficiency. If it can find the required number of available time slots for each link along the path, it ensures that the path bandwidth meets the end-to-end QoS requirement.

Also, We have presented simulation results using our own network simulator in order to evaluate the performance of the proposed QoS routing protocol in the ad-hoc environment. From our simulations, we have measured the QoS guarantee ratio and the delay performance as a function of the offered load. The simulation results show that the proposed protocol provides sufficiently low and stable delay performance regardless of the offered load.

References

1. C.R. Lin and J. Liu, "QoS Routing in Ad Hoc Wireless Networks," IEEE Journal on Selected Areas in Communications, Vol. 17, No. 8, pp. 1426-1438, August 1999.
2. C. Perkins, E. Belding-Royer, and S. Das, "Ad Hoc On-Demand Distance Vector (AODV) Routing," IETF RFC 3561, July 2003.
3. W. Liao, Y. Tseng, and K. Shih, "A TDMA-based Bandwidth Reservation Protocol for QoS Routing in a Wireless Mobile Ad Hoc Network," Proceedings of IEEE International Conference on Communications, pp. 3186-3190, April 2002.
4. Q. Xue and A. Ganz, "Ad Hoc QoS On-Demand Routing in Mobile Ad Hoc Network," Journal of Parallel and Distributed Computing, Vol. 63, pp. 154-165, February 2003.
5. C. Zhu and M.S. Corson, "QoS Routing for Mobile Ad Hoc Networks," Proceedings of IEEE INFOCOM, pp. 322-331, June 2002.
6. I. Joe, "Reservation CSMA/CA for QoS Support in Mobile Ad Hoc Networks," Lecture Notes in Computer Science, Vol. 3842, pp. 231-235, January 2006.
7. I. Joe and S.G. Batsell, "MPR-based Hybrid Routing for Mobile Ad Hoc Networks," Proceedings of IEEE Conference on Local Computer Networks, pp. 7-12, November 2002.
8. S. Chakrabarti and A. Mishra, "QoS Issues in Ad Hoc Wireless Networks," IEEE Communications Magazine, Vol. 39, pp. 142-148, 2001.

1

On a QoS Intrusion Tolerant Routing protocol in Ad-hoc Networks

Neïla Krichene, Noureddine Boudriga

CNAS, University of Carthage, Tunisia, k.neila@voila.fr, nab@supcom.rnu.tn

Summary. We propose in this paper a protocol, called *QITAR,* which will secure the ad-hoc routing process while guaranteeing end-to-end QoS requirements in terms of delay or bandwidth constraints. Our approach provides an intrusion tolerant environment and uses and enhances the concept of *Trusted Timely Computing Base* in order to deduce consistent delay information and verify the bandwidth value pretended by untrusted nodes. *QITAR* also proposes a rescue procedure that saves the resources and accelerates the route maintenance in case of node mobility.

Intrusion tolerance, Ad-hoc Routing, QoS.

1.1 Introduction

A Mobile Ad-hoc NETwork is made up by several wireless mobile nodes which are temporary connected by multi-hop links. The nodes can freely move and form a changing topology. Consequently, the nodes should function as hosts and routers in order to communicate. An efficient routing protocol is vital to the deployment of performing MANETs, especially when it is required to provide intrusion tolerance and guarantee a specific level of quality of service (QoS). Most existing routing protocols for MANETs such as *AODV* [1], *DSR* [2] and *DSDV* [3] tried to cope with the variable nature of the network topology by providing a best effort service without considering relevant security issues. However, the dynamic topology makes it hard to keep consistent routing information and detect behavior anomalies. Furthermore, the lack of fixed infrastructure prevents first-line defenses. Meanwhile, the variable capacity, the energy constraints and the open environment increase the vulnerability of nodes and wireless channels; thus resulting in severe security problems.

On the other hand, the emergence of multimedia applications has resulted in a growing need of providing QoS in the MANETs context. The routing protocol should not only find a route but also satisfy the end-to-end QoS requirements, which are often given in terms of delay and bandwidth. As

Please use the following format when citing this chapter:

Krichene, N., Boudriga, N., 2006, in International Federation for Information Processing (IFIP), Volume 212, Ad-Hoc Networking, ed. Al Agha, K., (Boston: Springer), pp. 29–46.

a QoS route is expected to be robust and efficient, the intrusion tolerant property may be viewed as an additional QoS parameter that should be taken into account while searching for a suitable path. Unfortunately, the research activities have been conducted so far, guarantee either intrusion tolerance or QoS since the two properties are considered as conflicting. In fact, intrusion tolerant routing protocols try to secure the route establishment and data transfer at the extent of QoS guarantee while QoS routing protocols ignore security issues since they are resource and time consuming.

To have a complete vision of the routing problem, security requirements and QoS provision should be supported by the same scheme. Our main objective is to design an intrusion tolerant routing protocol for ad-hoc networks while guaranteeing QoS requirements. Our approach is to secure the routing protocol phases while guaranteeing the delay and bandwidth required by the requesting node. The intermediate mobile nodes will cooperate to the routing process; but they will be permanently supervised in order to detect the misbehaving. We will also use the concept of Trusted Timely Computing Base (*TTCB*) defined in [4] and enhance it for need of QoS provision and security. Our contribution in this paper is four-fold. First, we have proposed a new routing protocol called ***QITAR*** that provides accurate QoS while resisting to malicious attacks. Second, we have enhanced the *TTCB* security services so that wormhole attacks and denial of service intrusions are tolerated. Third, we have taken advantage of the *TTCB* reliable time services in order to secure the estimation of the transmission delays. Besides, we have used the estimated delays to verify the accuracy of the bandwidth value pretended by potentially malicious mobile nodes. Finally, we have proposed a rescue procedure that saves the resources and accelerates the route maintenance in case of nodes mobility.

The remainder of this paper is organized as follows. Section 1.2 summarizes the related work in the secure routing and the QoS routing for MANETs. In Section 1.3, we describe our proposed protocol, and in Section 1.4 we detail its design. Section 1.5 develops the proposed secure estimation of the delay and bandwidth. Finally, we discuss in Section 1.6 the security features of our protocol and we show how it is designed to tolerate serious attacks.

1.2 Related Work

Most of the researches in the ad-hoc communication field have addressed separately the routing security and the end-to-end QoS provision. In this section, we consider some existing protocols and discuss some of their shortcomings in order to palliate them while designing our scheme.

1.2.1 Secure routing

Although routing in ad-hoc networks is more vulnerable due to the wireless environment characteristics, many of the encountered security threats are similar to those faced by wired networks. A malicious mobile node may cause a denial of service or attemp a wormhole attack [15]. It also can impersonate other nodes, spread false routing information, or drop all the packets passing through it. The existing secure protocols are either an extension of existing protocols such as *SAODV* [6], a set of mechanisms that can be defined upon any routing protocol such as *SRP* [7], or an independent new routing protocol that addresses some security issues like *ODSBR* [8].

The secure version of *AODV* (*SAODV*) computes digital signatures to authenticate the non-mutable fields of the signaling messages. Furthermore, it computes hash chains to secure the varying values. The resulting information is transmitted with an *AODV* message as an extension that is referred to as *Signature Extension*. *SAODV* is still a work in progress, its authors are currently trying to reduce the processing power requirements due to the use of asymmetric cryptography [6].

A different approach has been proposed by the *SRP* protocol and consists in mitigating the attacks of malicious nodes and guaranteeing the acquisition of correct topological information [7] while integrating mechanisms that protect the network functions against attacks exploiting *SRP* itself. The authors assumed the existence of a *Security Association* between the source and destination. Moreover, malicious nodes are assumed to exhibit arbitrary Byzantine behavior. *SRP* is able to operate without the existence of an on-line certification authority [7]. However, *SRP* does not guarantee the authenticity and integrity of the vital route error messages; thus enabling an attacker to harm the route it belongs to.

To resist to byzantine failures caused by individual or colluding nodes [8], *ODSBR* trusts only the source and the destination nodes and authenticates any intermediate mobile node (*MN*), while it expects the *MNs* to exhibit a byzantine behavior alone or in collusion with other nodes. Protocol *ODSBR* proposes an interesting procedure of detecting faulty links which are avoided in the process of route discovery. It is made up of three successive phases: 1) the *Route Discovery*; 2) the *Byzantine Fault Detection*, and 3) the *Link Weight Management* and employs on-demand shared keys to secure communications.

In this paper we propose an intrusion tolerant routing protocol that resists to common and serious attacks while securely estimating and providing the required QoS.

1.2.2 QoS Routing

Wireless ad-hoc networks have a fast-changing topology which influences the load conditions and the connectivity of the nodes. This dynamic nature makes it difficult to adapt nodes to changing conditions and monitor connection states and reservations. For all these reasons, supporting real-time and advanced applications with constraining QoS requirements in MANETs is considered as a challenging issue. Moreover, most of the existing protocols such as QoS for *AODV* [9] and *SWAN* [10] face important security threats.

The authors of the protocol *AODV* have specified extensions which can be used to guarantee a maximum delay and a minimum bandwidth along a route [9] but they did not protect the route against attacks. In fact, a mobile node independently computes its own delay and available bandwidth; hence it may make believe erroneous values of the information it sends in order to cause a denial of service or exhibit a selfish behavior. Moreover, any intermediate node can violate the integrity of the control packets. Finally, each node knows only its neighbors so it can not verify the behavior of the other members of the route it belongs to.

To address this issues, a maximum delay and a minimum bandwidth thresholds can be stated; thus obliging attackers to provide a minimum level of QoS. Furthermore, a cryptographic scheme must be utilized to provide integrity. Finally, a source node which does not receive the data packets acknowledgments should be able to ask its immediate neighbor for its signed delay value, the neighbor should ask its successor for the same data. This procedure will allow the source comparing the pretended QoS values to the QoS requirements it needs and detecting malicious nodes.

SWAN is a stateless network model which uses distributed rate control and feed-back control mechanisms in order to provide soft real-time services and service differentiation by regulating the admitted traffic in case of topology and QoS changes [10]. *SWAN* uses "probing" to obtain the minimal bandwidth available on a path. The admission control decision is only taken at source nodes. To regulate real-time sessions, each node continuously (and independently) measures the utilization of its traffic and starts marking the *Explicit Congestion Notification (ECN)* bits in the *IP* header of the real time packets whenever it detects serious violations. The destination monitors the *ECN* bits and notifies the source which may re-establish a new real-time session or terminate the pending one, if the QoS requirements can no longer be met. As other QoS routing protocols, *SWAN* did not address security issues. In fact, when a node wants to determine the delay on the link between it and its neighbor, it may accept false information and back off its rate causing best effort traffic starvation. Moreover, some attacking nodes will not correctly probe the network before admitting new real-time sessions; thus inducing a denial of service. Finally, attackers may corrupt the exchanged control packets or impersonate nodes.

As some malicious nodes may detect long delays but refuse to regulate their best effort traffic, a minimum threshold value $r_{\mathrm{BE}_{min}}$ should be specified so that the well-behaving neighbors can back off their best effort traffic rate until they reach the specified threshold. Moreover, a black-list containing the source of congestioned traffic should be defined at every intermediate node so that attackers can be isolated for awhile. In addition, a cryptographic scheme should be adopted in order to guarantee the authenticity and integrity of the exchanged control and data. Finally, a maximum threshold of session-re-establishments should be set at each source so that malicious nodes, which arbitrarily mark *Congestion Experienced* packets, cannot cause a denial of service. Our work in the following is the design of a routing protocol that provides the aforementioned requirements, while considering the security as an additional QoS parameter that should be guaranteed.

1.3 The QITAR protocol: a QoS intrusion tolerant routing protocol

Our proposal will combine intrusion tolerance and QoS provision in one protocol called ***QITAR*** (*Qos and Intrusion Tolerant Ad-hoc Routing*). As mentioned earlier, ***QITAR*** uses a *Trusted Timely Computing Base* [4] modified version in order to detect the malicious behaviors and accurately meet the QoS requirements.

1.3.1 TTCB concept

The *TTCB* can be defined as a secure real-time distributed component which provides a set of trusted services related to time and security such as the trusted block agreement, trusted duration measurement, and trusted absolute timestamping [4]. The architecture of a system with a *TTCB* is suggested in Figure 1.1.

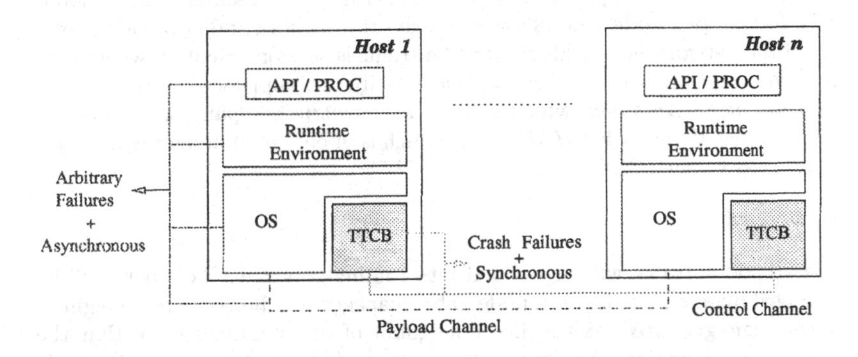

Fig. 1.1. Interconnection of the *TTCB* modules within a payload network

Each host is assumed to have a local module called the *local TTCB*. These modules are also assumed to be interconnected by a completely secure *Control Channel* and form what is called the *Distributed Trusted Component* (*DTC*). A *TTCB* assists the applications running between participants in the concerned hosts which are interconnected by a vulnerable *Payload Channel* forming a payload system subject to arbitrary byzantine failures.

The fail-controlled with distributed trusted components intrusion-tolerance strategy which has been proposed by the *MAFTIA* team states that some global actions can be trusted despite a generally malicious communication [14]. The *TTCB* allows the payload system to take advantage of its possible synchronism by assisting the application to determine useful facts about time (such as the execution time of an operation, its duration, etc). However, this is trusted to the following extent: It is assumed to be not feasible to subvert a *TTCB*; but it may be possible to interfere with its interaction with software components.

We have chosen to rely on tamperproof *TTCB* modules in the design of our protocol because a timed behavior can be supported globally in an intrusion-resilient way. This is able to help limiting the potential damage of malicious behavior while having accurate information about the available QoS.

1.3.2 The QITAR protocol description

QITAR Assumptions

We assume available an ad-hoc network with medium density and bi-directional wireless links. We also adopt a reactive approach. The number of *TTCB* modules is set according to the hostility of the environment and the node density. Besides, we assume that only some mobile nodes can host such secure real-time components. We also decide to rely on these components to provide intrusion tolerance and secure QoS estimation. Furthermore, we assume that a mobile *TTCB*-equipped node is not allowed to leave the network and is already known by all the network nodes. Moreover, the traffic is session-oriented, where each unidirectional session is called a *flow*. Finally, we suppose the existence of a *Certification Authority* which delivers asymmetric key pairs as assumed in [18] and [19] along with *DHCP* server which is in charge of assigning a unique IP address to each *MN*.

Network model

The ad-hoc network will be divided into routing-zones, each of them will be managed by a *TTCB*-hosting node. This manager will be the direct neighbor of the managed *MNs* and a direct neighbor of other managers so that the routing-zones overlap. We denote the source node by S, the destination node by D, the *TTCB* module of the node managing the source by S_TTCB, the destination' *TTCB* manager by D_TTCB and the intermediate *TTCBs* by I_TTCB as illustrated below in Figure 1.2. Each *TTCB* communicates locally with its agents (denoted by the letter A) in the same figure. Five phases can be considered: the neighborhood discovery phase; the mobile nodes registration phase; the route establishment phase; the maintenance phase; and the data transfer phase.

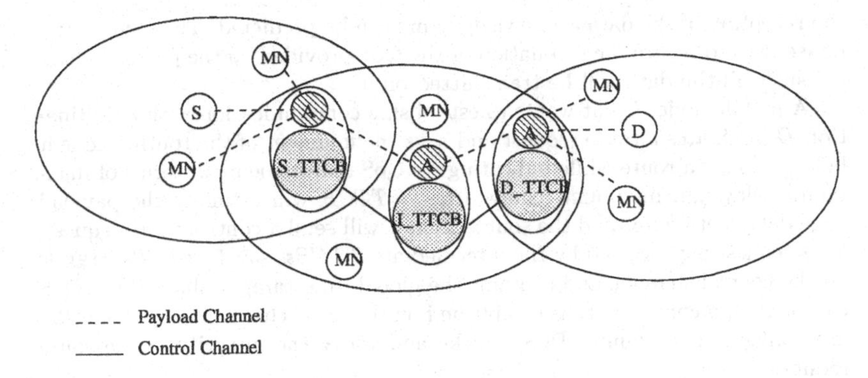

Fig. 1.2. Notations

TTCB*s' neighborhood discovery phase*

The managers have to enter in agreement in order to securely forward the signaling messages hop by hop on the control channel. Consequently, they must always have an accurate list of their *TTCB* neighbors. *TTCB* modules should periodically enter in agreement in order to update their neighborhood information. The period duration can be stated by the network manager. However, malicious agents may try to cause a denial of service by changing the agreement identifiers or refusing to propose a value for the agreement on time. Thanks to the *TTCB* properties, the other neighbors will decide their values as if the attacked manager could not hear them, even though they cannot have a complete vision of the network topology before the next period.

Registration phase

Each mobile node has to register to a manager in order to become reachable and emit route requests. To secure the pending communication and the further ones, each *MN* should share a key with its *S_TTCB*. We assume that the registration phase is periodically executed in order to renew the symmetric key and change the manager in case of mobility. The registration procedure includes some mechanisms in order to tolerate the potential denial of service attacks.

Route establishment phase

The route establishment phase is divided into two sub-phases. The first securely establishes a path on the control channel in order to counter the wormhole attack and estimates the control information transmission delays so that the reception of the data acknowledgments can be predicted. The second sub-phase tries to secure the estimation of the QoS provided on the payload channel since all the data will be transmitted on it.

A mobile node S that wants to establish a communication with a destination D originates a route request and asks the manager of the routing-zone it belongs to for a route while indicating its QoS requirements in terms of maximum delay and minimum bandwidth. S_TTCB will estimate the payload edge delay between it and the source then it will send a control route request. This request is processed by the intermediate $TTCBs$, say I_TTCBs, travels on the control channel, and contains the global timestamps values. If the QoS can be met, a control path is established on the same channel. The I_TTCBs are configured to counter DoS attacks and verify the integrity of the route request.

To have an accurate value of the effectively providable QoS while tolerating intrusions, we need to estimate it on the payload path corresponding to the pre-established control route. For this, S_TTCB creates a new agent then asks it to begin estimating the delay on the payload channel providing it with the list of the intermediate $TTCBs$ and the timestamp of the second sub-phase's beginning time. A second copy of the same payload route request will travel on the control channel so that the I_TTCBs can verify whether the packet is authentic and whether it has been sent by the predecessor on the pre-established route. When this request reaches D_TTCB, one can be sure that the required QoS can be met on the entire payload path. If the checked estimated bandwidth is correct, it will be reserved immediately, e.g during the request phase, otherwise, the agents must re-estimate the QoS and the $TTCBs$ must verify it during the reply phase; thus causing an important and unnecessary overhead. Because not all the nodes of the established route on the control channel are surely able to provide the required QoS, the network must release the reserved resources and update the throughput information as soon as possible, if the route is not used.

Maintenance phase

The managers' mobility breaks down the established routes so that the aforementioned phases are re-executed, without being sure that suitable paths can be found at the end. For this, we propose a rescue tentative which relies on the direct common neighbors of the affected managers in order to replace only the two broken links; thus reducing the overhead.

Data transfer phase

The data transfer phase takes place once a route on the payload channel respecting the QoS requirements has been established. Multiple routes can be found and may be useful when one or more I_TTCB leaves an active route. However, resources may still be reserved unnecessarily. Therefore, source S should send its data on only one route while the other path(s) should be released shortly after. All the data must be acknowledged and securely transmitted.

1.4 QITAR design

To discover its neighborhood, each *TTCB* should periodically send a hello message to all existing *TTCBs* since all the modules are globally synchronized. Only the *TTCB*s which can "*hear*" the hello are able to decide a value. When a new *MN* enters the ad-hoc network, it should generate a registration request. Each *TTCB* hearing the request should send back a signed and encrypted response containing a shared key value that can be used to authenticate the initiator and encrypt the further exchanged messages. The concerned *MN* replies by a confirmation message in order to be registered. However, malicious mobile nodes and attacking agents may try a denial of service attack by generating many registration requests with unknown addresses, initiating many registration requests within a short period of time, or altering the needed control packets. To tolerate such intrusions, each *MN* must be authenticated. Moreover, each manager must be configured to process a limited number of registrations and frequently renew its agents.

A *MN* wishing to communicate with a destination should generate a route request containing its QoS requirements. *S_ TTCB* receiving it starts by estimating the edge payload delay between it and the source node as detailed in section 1.5. If the delay is inferior to the specified one, *S_ TTCB* appends its identity and the time of transmission to a control route request. Then it broadcasts it to its *TTCB* neighbors through the control channel. The *I_ TTCBs* process the request by adding their identifiers and the reception's timestamp and create a new table entry for this flow if the delay requirements can be fulfilled. A control route request initiated by a source and reaching the same destination must be transmitted during a certain threshold interval only once. On the receipt of request, *D_ TTCB* estimates the delay on the final direct payload link and forwards the control route reply on the reverse path if the QoS can be met.

If an *I_ TTCB* does not receive the control route reply within a threshold period of time, the flow's table entry must be deleted; otherwise, it is confirmed. On receiving the replay, *S_ TTCB* can exactly determine each intermediate manager on the path and the corresponding delays on each control link. However, a malicious mobile node may try denial of service attacks. Therefore, each *TTCB* must be configured to reject the redundant messages. In addition, a malicious agent may not immediately forward the request or the reply messages in order to make the delay look higher than it really is. Consequently, *S_ TTCB* and *D_ TTCB* modules should frequently renew their agents and restart the edge delay estimation procedure if they do not receive the correspondent messages after a timeout.

To guarantee more robustness during the delays estimation on the payload pre-established path, we propose that the agent, say *Agent(n)*, at the nth *I_ TTCB*, denoted by *I_ TTCB(n)*, gives the payload route request to its local *I_ TTCB*, which adds the timestamp of reception, signs the control packet, gives it back to *Agent(n), and* forwards a non-signed copy on the control channel to *I_ TTCB(n+1)* if the QoS can be met. When receiving the signed request, *Agent(n)* sends it on the payload channel to *Agent (n+1)*. Since the control channel is faster than the payload channel, the copy sent on the control channel may arrive first so that *I_ TTCB(n+1)* may have to wait for the payload copy and compare the two received packets. If the copies are identical, *I_ TTCB(n+1)* asks for the available bandwidth and checks it. Then, it provides its *Agent(n+1)* with a new encrypted request message if the QoS can be met. If the pretended bandwidth value is not correct, *I_ TTCB(n+1)* should kill its agent and ask for a new bandwidth value. Moreover, if the two copies of the same route request are not identical, *I_ TTCB(n+1)* kills its agent and asks *I_ TTCB(n)* to manage a new agent by sending a kill request on the control channel. *I_ TTCB(n)* provides the newly created agent with a signed kill reply then forwards a non signed copy to *I_ TTCB(n+1)* which has to wait for the second signed copy. However, this procedure cannot be executed more than a fixed number of times. When the payload request message reaches *D_ TTCB*, this latter should estimate the QoS on the final edge link. If the QoS is met on the entire payload path, *D_ TTCB* should send back a reply message in order to inform *S_ TTCB* that the route is ready for data transmission.

The reservation management is performed as follows: *I_ TTCB(n)* assigns a token bucket to each flow if the required bandwidth is inferior to the available one. If the QoS cannot be met at the manager *(n+i)*, *I_ TTCB(n+i)* should send a release request to the intermediate *TTCB* neighbor on the reverse path in order to release the previously reserved resources.

To improve the performance of the maintenance phase, we propose that before quitting a route, *I_ TTCB(n)* asks *I_ TTCB(n-1)* and *I_ TTCB(n+1)* for the list of their *TTCB* neighbors in order to search for a common one. A common manager can initiate a QoS estimation on the payload channel and send a rescue reply message to inform *I_ TTCB(n-1)* and *I_ TTCB(n+1)* about the path modification if the requirements can be met. If there is not any common manager or if the common neighbors can not provide the required QoS, *I_ TTCB(n)* should send an error notification on the control channel in order to release the reserved resources on both direction. Every *TTCB* should frequently renew its agents and the rescue procedure will be retried for a configured number of times for further security.

The data transfer phase begins when *S_ TTCB* sends a data request message to the source node informing it that a suitable route has been found. A source node can receive many route replies since it can be managed by several *TTCBs*. The resulting multiple routes are useful when *I_ TTCBs* are likely to leave established active routes. However, managing multiple routes for the same flow keeps resources reserved unnecessarily in the other paths. To address this issue, S should send its data only on one route and D should inform its D_TTCBs about any duplication using a signed release request. After a threshold period of time, if there are no received data packets, D_TTCB is allowed to release the route. However, S and D may be malicious and cause denial of service attacks by unnecessary requesting routes or by pretending duplications. Consequently, if there are no data received after a timeout, the concerned S_TTCB should send a release message on the control channel and stop processing other route requests issued from the same source during a threshold delay. In addition, S_TTCB must forward the received request release signed by D to S. S must collect all these requests, and if all the established routes have been released on demand, it will send back the control packets to all its managers so that they can deduce that the destination node is malicious.

To implement the previously described phases in a secure manner, our protocol uses several signaling messages mainly transmitted on the control channel. A non exhaustive list of messages is depicted as follows:

- A ***NeighReq*** request is periodically sent in order to determine the $TTCB$ neighborhood.

- The mobile node registration needs the exchange of a ***RegReq*** request, a shared key ***SK*** message, and its confirmation reply ***SKConf***.

- A mobile node will initiate the route establishment phase by indicating its QoS requirements in a ***RReq*** request.

- The beginning of the edge delay estimation is marked by a ***DelayReq*** and the correspondent reply reception ***DelayRep*** will permit the delay calculation.

- A ***CRReq*** will travel on the control channel in order to establish a control path while the arrival of the correspondent ***CRRep*** confirms that route.

- The QoS estimation on the payload channel begins by the transmission of a ***PRReq*** request and ends by the reception of the correspondent ***PRRep***.

- Two messages, ***KReq*** and ***KRep,*** may be used for killing the malicious agents.

- The ***Release*** message orders the release of a route.

- The maintenance phase employs the ***ResNeighReq***, ***ResNeighRep***, ***ResReq*** and ***ResRep*** messages in order to ask for rescuing neighbors and check whether the required QoS can be met.

- A ***Bye*** message is sent by the leaving manager and an ***ErrorNot*** is forwarded to annunciate the breakage of the established route and order the release of the reserved resources.

- A ***DataReq*** invites the *MN* to transmit its data while a ***NAck*** indicates that there is no suitable route found.

1.5 Secure bandwidth and delay estimation

Delay estimation

We provide in this section a secured procedure for the estimation of delays using the *TTCB* time-related services. Control channel delays will be used to determine the reception time of data acknowledgment and detect malicious agents.

To estimate the communication delay on the edge payload link, a managed *MN* should first initiate a route request. The manager's agent which receives the control packet informs *S_ TTCB* which triggers the duration measurement service and order a delay request message. The local agent must then relay the message to the source node then wait for a reply in order to relay it back to *S_ TTCB*. Once the correspondent reply is received, *S_ TTCB* ends the service and provides an accurate result reflecting the edge delay. This procedure is summarized by Figure 1.3. For the sake of clarity, we assume that the delay of local communication duration between the agent and its *TTCB* can be neglected.

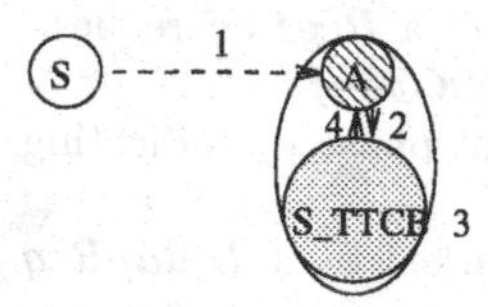

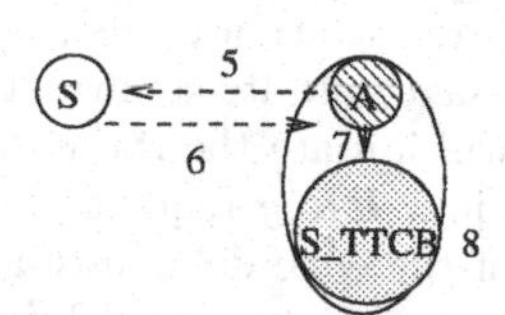

1- MN sends a RReq
2-Agent relays the RReq to S_TTCB
3-S_TTCB triggers the duration measurement service
4-S_TTCB orders a DelayReq

5-Agent relays the DelayReq
6-MN sends a DelayRep
7-Agent relays the DelayRep
8- S_TTCB stops the duration measurement service and deduces the result (the edge delay value).

Fig. 1.3. Edge delay estimation

To estimate the delay on the control channel, *S_ TTCB* should broadcast to its *TTCBs* direct neighbors a control route request containing the pre-estimated edge delay $D_{S \to STTCB}$ and the current timestamp. When receiving the request, each *TTCB* reads the global timestamp value then subtracts the timestamp indicated by *S_ TTCB* from it in order to deduce $d_{STTCB \to TTCB}$(where $d_{X \to Y}$designates the delay between X and Y on the control channel). If the sum of both delays is inferior to the maximum delay allowed (e.g., if $D_{S \to STTCB} + d_{STTCB \to TTCB} < max - delay - allowed$), *I_ TTCB* broadcasts the request further to all its *TTCBs* neighbors, and so on. When *D_ TTCB* receives the control packet, it sums up all the delays on the previous control links and computes a delay estimation. If the cumulated delay is smaller than the delay allowed, say:

$$D_{S \to STTCB} + \sum_{j=STTCB}^{ITTCB(f)} d_{j \to j+1} + D_{DTTCB \to D} < max - delay - allowed \quad (1.1)$$

D_ TTCB will send back a control reply to inform that a control path has been established.

The delay estimation on the payload channel is done as follows: *S_ TTCB* signs a payload request then gives it to its local agent, which is in charge of sending it to the next agent on the pre-established path. When *I_ TTCB(n)* receives that request from its agent, it begins by reading the global timestamp value and subtracting the timestamp value indicated by *I_ TTCB(n-1)* from it. The deduction of delay $D_{n-1 \to n}$ on payload link $n - 1 \to n$ is described by Figure 1.4.

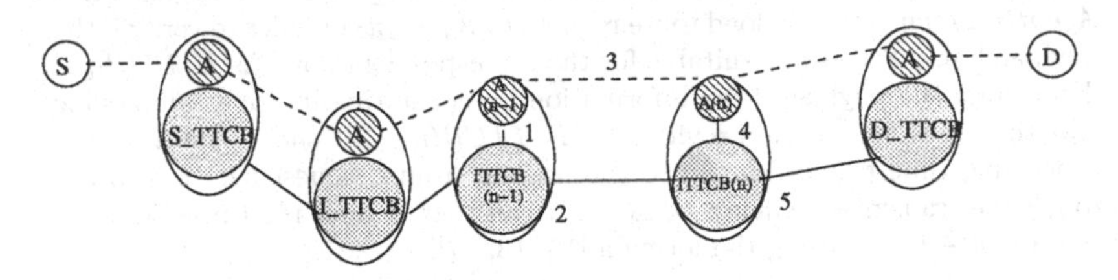

1- Agent (n–1) gives the payload route request to TTCB(n–1)

2- TTCB(n–1)verifies if the delay requirements can be met. If it is the case, it adds its identifier and its timestamp value then gives a signed updated copy back to its agent and forwards a non signed one to TTCB(n)

3- Agent (n–1) forwards the route request to Agent (n)

4- Agent (n) gives the sigend copy of the route request to TTCB (n)

5- TTCB(n) consults the global timestamp value and subtracts the timestamp value indicated by TTCB(n–1) in order to deduce the payload delay on the link n–1 --> n.

Fig. 1.4. Delay estimation on the payload channel

Finally, *I_ TTCB(n)* sums up the delays on the previous links forming the path (i.e., computes $D_{S \to STTCB} + \sum_{j=1}^{n-2} D_{j \to j+1}$, where $TTCB(1) = S\_TTCB$) and adds its own delay. The delay on the payload channel is then given by:

$$D_p = D_{S \to STTCB} + \sum_{j=1}^{n-2} D_{j \to j+1} + D_{n-1 \to n} \quad (1.2)$$

If D_p is inferior to the allowed maximum delay, *I_ TTCB(n)* adds its identifier and its timestamp value to the request then gives a signed copy to its local agent and forwards a control copy further. The same procedure is repeated and the payload request will reach *D_ TTCB* only if the QoS can be met on the payload path. It is worth noticing that the computed results include the transmission and processing delays.

Bandwidth estimation

In ad-hoc networks, the resource estimation is often based on the statistical information provided by the *MAC* layer. In fact, the *MNs* monitor the channel status to determine the busy and idle periods of the shared wireless media then deduce the available bandwidth. This means that the available bandwidth on the payload channel is computed by insecure agents which may provide false estimation. To secure the bandwidth estimation, the provided values need to be verified using the delay information given by the *TTCBs*. Our secured bandwidth estimation on the payload channel at *I_ TTCB(n)* begins when *Agent(n-1)* sends the payload route request to *Agent(n)* in order to verify if the payload link $n-1 \rightarrow n$ is suitable for the correspondent flow. As *I_ TTCB(n)* determines the payload delay information by consulting its timestamp value and the timestamp value provided by *I_ TTCB(n-1)*, it should subtract the processing time proportionally to the payload route request length in order to get the transmission delay $D_{n-1 \rightarrow n}$, it can then deduce the throughput on the link $n-1 \rightarrow n$ using the formula [16, 13, 17]:

$$Throughput_{on\, the\, link} = \frac{Packet\, Size}{D_{n-1 \rightarrow n}} \tag{1.3}$$

Moreover, to detect selfish nodes, we assume that the availability of the wireless channel can not be less than a threshold value reflecting the minimal QoS level that has to be offered by the network. As *Agent(n)* provides its local *I_ TTCB(n)* with a computed bandwidth information, *I_ TTCB(n)* will be able to verify the accuracy of the presented value by evaluating the channel availability ratio using the formula :

$$BW_{Available} = (1-u) * Throughput_{on\, the\, link} \tag{1.4}$$

[16, 13, 17] where $1-u = \frac{Idle\, times\, in\, window}{window\, duration}$ is the link availability and $idle\, times\, in\, window$ represent the fraction of time within which the agent is sensing the channel as being idle (e.g., the channel is not idle if the agent is transmitting or receiving packets or if some other nodes within its neighborhood are transmitting data or RTS/CTS packets).

In fact, let us assume that the estimated throughput equals y and that *Agent(n)* pretends an available bandwidth value equaling $x\, Mb/s$. Therefore,

$$BW_{Available} = (1-u) * Throughput_{on\,link\,n-1 \to n} = (1-u) * y = x\,MB/s$$

Thus, $(1-u) = x/y$. If $1-u \leq 1$ and $1-u \geq minimal\,threshold\,value$, we can assume that the agent is neither attempting a denial of service attack nor trying to avoid routing packets; thus, the probability that it has pretended a correct bandwidth value is high.

To calculate the available bandwidth, *Agent(n)* should first calculate the channel utilization ratio R. Suppose the last channel utilization ratio is $R_{t-1}$and the channel utilization ratio measured in the current sampling time window is $R = \frac{channel-busy-period}{window\,duration}$. Then, the current channel utilization ratio is given as $R_t = \alpha R_{t-1} + (1-\alpha)R$ where α is a smoothing constant $\alpha \in [0,1]$. The agent can deduce its available bandwidth at time t using the formula

$$BW_t = W(1 - R_t) \tag{1.5}$$

where W is the raw channel bandwidth (*e.g.*, $2\,Mb/s$ for a standard 802.11 radio) [12].

1.6 QITAR security features

To enhance the security of the routing, the ***QITAR*** protocol tried to prevent the denial of service attacks. In fact, malicious mobile nodes may collude or independently overflow the managers by multiple requests, unnecessarily ask for the routing service or replay the same messages. Moreover, the malicious agents may corrupt the control packets or refuse to forward them to the local *TTCB* modules. The impersonation attack may also be a form of denial of service. In fact, if the *MN*'s identity has been spoofed, the *MN* can no longer register to the mangers. In addition, a modified request cannot reflect the required QoS and the victim node will not be served. To address these issues, we have modified the *TTCB* kernel developed in *MAFTIA* project [14] in order to configure threshold values related to the number of processed requests, and the number of overall processed messages. Finally a procedure to stop providing routing services is added in the case of malicious source and destination. A threshold value related to the number of re-attempts is also added.

Moreover, an asymmetric cryptography scheme is used in order to authenticate each new-arriving mobile node, it will then be replaced by a symmetric one when the *MN* shares a key with its managing *TTCB*; thus reducing the processing efforts, accelerating the communications and guaranteeing the authenticity of the sender and both the integrity and confidentiality of the exchanged messages on the payload edge link. This shared key is periodically renewed in order to guarantee more robustness and cope with the possible mobility of the managing-nodes.

A man in the middle may sniff many registration requests coming from *MN*s that belong to different routing zones then redirect them to a distant

TTCB-hosting node that is unable to manage them. The victim manager will waste its resources in processing the request and sending back the shared key message. The hacker then relays the control message and its confirmation and the manager finally registers an unreachable *MN*. To counter this attack, the *MN* authentication can use the combination of MAC and IP addresses.

A major advantage of using the *TTCB* kernels is the protection against the wormhole attacks. In fact, after the secure delay estimation on the reliable control channel, a malicious agent on the path between the source and the destination will not be able to tunnel the route request message to another one during the delay estimation on the payload channel. In fact, the intermediate *I_ TTCBs* already know all the nodes forming the route. Moreover, they can easily verify that the control message has been forwarded by the previous *I_ TTCB* thanks to the **PRReq** copy traveling on the control channel. Let us demonstrate this assertion by the example below:

- **First case:** *Agent(n)* and *Agent(m)* are two colluding ends of a wormhole tunnel and are both malicious; however, *Agent(m)* does not belong to the route. *Agent(m)* will forward the **PRReq** packet to a well-behaving *Agent(l)* belonging to the route. *I_ TTCB(l)* will discover that the received **PRReq** was not forwarded by its predecessor on the route because the message is not signed by the predecessor. Consequently, it ignores it.
- **Second case:** *Agent(n)* and *Agent(m)* are two colluding ends of a wormhole tunnel. They are both malicious and belong to the route. All the *I_ TTCBs* including between *I_ TTCB(n+1)* and *I_ TTCB(m-1)* will not receive the payload request copy at time. Moreover, *I_ TTCB(m)* will receive a payload copy that is not signed by its predecessor on the route. As a result, the malicious agents will be killed and the delay can then be correctly estimated.

Finally, because it is assumed that a *TTCB* can not be compromised, it is possible for a group of *TTCBs* to support a reliable protocol with $f + 2$ replicas, requiring an attacker to compromise $f + 1$managers in order to cause an intrusion (the traditional approach requires $3f + 1$ replicas to tolerate f failures) [14]. Since we assumed that the mobile *TTCB*-equipped nodes are not authorized to leave the network and that they are already known by all members, it is possible to determine the number of such managing nodes depending of the hostility degree of the environment.

We believe that our protocol is more efficient than the others because it has addressed especially dangerous attacks such as the denial of service and the wormhole while trying to provide high QoS guarantees.

1.7 Conclusion

The focus of this paper is on providing a *TTCB*-based routing protocol which guarantees QoS constraints such as delays and bandwidth to independent flows, while tolerating some common attacks. Our protocol implements cryptographic operations in order to guarantee the integrity and the confidentiality of the exchanged data. In addition, it secures the QoS estimation by verifying the pretended bandwidth values using the timestamp data provided by the *TTCBs*. We have provided a modified version of the *TTCB* kernel developed by MAFTIA to support new functionalities such as the determination of the *I_TTCBs* neighbors and the registration of the managed mobile nodes.

References

1. C. Perkins, E. M. Royer and S. R. Das, "Ad hoc On-demand Distance Vector routing", In IETF Internet Draft, draft-ietf-manet-AODV-12.txt, November 2002.
2. D.B Johnson, D.A Maltz and J. Broch, "DSR: The dynamic Source Routing Protocol for Multi-hop wireless Ad Hoc Networks", in Ad Hoc Networking, ch. 5, pp. 139-172, Addison-Wesley, 2001.
3. C.E. Perkins and P. Bhagwat, "Highly Dynamic Destination-Sequenced Distance Vector Routing (DSDV) for Mobile Computers", in ACM SIGCOMM'94, October 1994.
4. N. Ferreira and P. Verrissimo, "Complete Specification of APIs and Protocols for the MAFTIA Middleware", MAFTIA deliverable D9, 2002.
5. S. Bouam and J. Ben Othman, "Securing Data Transmission and Retransmissions Management in Ad Hoc Networks", Proceedings of the International Conference on Wireless Networks, ICWN '04, June 2004.
6. M. G. Zapata and N. Asokan, "Securing Ad Hoc Routing Protocols", in WiSe'02, September 2002 .
7. P. Papadimitratos and Z. J. Haas, "Secure Routing for Mobile Ad Hoc Networks", In proceedings of the CNDS conference, San Antonio, TX, 2002.
8. B. Awerbuch, R. Curtmola, D. Holmer, C. Nita-Rotaru and H. Rubens, "ODSBR: An On-Demand Secure Byzantine Routing Protocol", Technical report, October 2003.
9. C. E. Perkins, E. M. Royer and S. R. Das, "Quality of Service for Ad hoc On-demand Distance Vector Routing", IETF Internet Draft, work in progress, July 2000.
10. G.S. Ahn, A.T. Campbell, A.Veres and L.H. Sun, "SWAN: Service Differentiation in Stateless Wireless Ad Hoc Networks", Proceedings of IEEE INFOCOM 2002, June 2002.
11. D.Powell and R. Stroud, "Conceptual Model and Architecture of MAFTIA", MAFTIA deliverable D21, 2003.
12. K. Xu, K. Tang, R. Bagrodia, M. Gerla, M. Bereschinsky, "Adaptive Bandwidth Management and QoS Provisioning in Large Scale Ad Hoc Networks", IEEE MILCOM'03, Boston, Massachusetts, October 2003
13. S. Lohier, S. M. Senouci, Y. M. Ghamri. Doudane and G. Pujolle, "A reactive QoS Routing Protocol for Ad Hoc Networks", European Symposium on Ambient Intelligence (EUSAI2003), Eindhoven, Netherlands, November 2003, Lecture Notes in Computer Science, Springer Verlag.
14. D. Powell and R. Stroud, "Conceptual Model and Architecture of MAFTIA", MAFTIA deliverable D21, 2003.

15. Y. C. Hu, A. Perrig and D. B. Johnson, "Packet Leashes : A Defense against Wormhole Attacks in Wireless Ad Hoc Networks", Technical report TR01-384, Revised September 2002.
16. M. Kazantzidis and M. Gerla , "End-to-end versus Explicit Feedback Measurement in 802.11 Networks", In Seventh IEEE Symposium on Computers and Communications, 2002.
17. H. Badis, A. Munaretto, K. Al Agha and G. Pujolle, "QoS for Ad hoc Networking Based on Multiple Metrics : Bandwidth and Delay", IFIP/IEEE MWCN 2003, Singapore, October 27-29, 2003.
18. W. Yu, Y. Sun and K. J. R. Liu, "HADOF : Defense Against Routing Disruptions in Mobile Ad Hoc Networks", in Proc. IEEE INFOCOM'04, Hong Kong 2004.
19. B. Awerbuch, D. Holmer and H. Rubens, "Provably Secure Competitive Routing against Proactive Byzantine Adversaries via Reinforcement Learning", John Hopkings Univ, Tech. Rep, May 2003.

Randomized Permutation Routing in Multi-hop Ad Hoc Networks with Unknown Destinations

Djibo Karimou and Jean Frédéric Myoupo
LaRIA, CNRS, FRE 2733,
Université de Picardie Jules-Verne
33, rue Saint Leu, 80039 Amiens, France
E-mail:{karimou, myoupo}@laria.u-picardie.fr

Abstract. A large variety of permutation routing protocols in a single-hop Network are known to day. Since they are single hop, there is always a wireless path connecting two nodes. One way to solve this problem in a multiple hop environment is to partition nodes into clusters, where a node in each cluster called clusterhead is responsible for the routing service. In this paper, we propose a clustering mechanism to perform permutation routing in multi-hop ad hoc Networks having p stations and in which n data items are saved. We first develop a clustering algorithm to partition stations into clusters. Secondly, we run a locally permutation routing to broadcast items to their local destinations in each group. Finally we use a multicast procedure to transmit outgoing items to their final cluster destination. We show that the approach of this paper can solve the permutation problem in a multi hop ad hoc network in $(\frac{6}{q} + 13)n + O(q^{\frac{4}{3}} \log^{\frac{10}{3}} q) + D_b - 1$ broadcast rounds in the worst case with the probability at least $1 - \frac{1}{p}$ whenever $q \le \frac{p}{3 \log p}$. Where D_b is the blocking diameter, q is the number of clusters of the network. In our knowledge, it is the first algorithm for permutation routing in multi-hop ad hoc networks.

1 Introduction

In an environment where there is no communication infrastructure, wireless mobile users may still be able to communicate through the formation of an ad hoc network. Mobile ad-hoc networks are formed by a collection of mobile wireless nodes (stations) which can communicate with each other and dynamically self organize without any static network interaction. Each mobile host has the capability to communicate directly with another mobile host in its vicinity via a channel of transmission. It can also send packets destined for other nodes.

Please use the following format when citing this chapter:

Karimou, D., Myoupo, J.F., 2006, in International Federation for Information Processing (IFIP), Volume 212, Ad-Hoc Networking, ed. Al Agha, K., (Boston: Springer), pp. 47–59.

Communication links are formed and disappear as nodes come into and go out of each other communication range. Such networks have many practical applications, including home networking, search-and-rescue, and military operations. There are two types of ad hoc networks: Single hop ad hoc network in which each station can transmit or communicate directly with each other station. All the stations use the same channel to communicate, and the message broadcasted by one of the stations on the common channel is simultaneously received by all other stations. In the multi-hop ad hoc networks intermediate nodes are used to route message from the source to the destination. In this paper only to multi-hop ad hoc networks are considered.

Permutation Problem: Consider a MANET (n, p) of p stations with n items pretitled on it. Each item has a unique destination which is one of the p stations. Each item has a unique destination which is one of the p stations. Each station has a local memory of size p/n in which n/p items are stored.

It is important to note that in general, some of the n/p items stored in the station, say i, have not i as destination station. And even, it can happen that none of these n/p items belongs to it. In the other hand, the situation in which initially all items in i belong to i can also occur. The permutation routing problem is to route the items in such a way that for all i, $1 \leq i \leq p$, station i contains all its own items.

A large variety of permutation routing protocols in a single-hop Network are known to day. These permutation routing protocols assume that the network are a single Hop Ad-Hoc Network, hence there is always a path connected by wireless links between a source and the destination. However, these varieties of methods are not adapted in the case of multi-hop Ad Hoc Networks. One way to solve this problem is to partition nodes into clusters where principal node in each cluster, called clusterhead, is responsible for routing items. In this paper, we suggest a combination of methods which guarantee a permutation routing protocol in multi-hop ad hoc network.

1.1 Known Results

The number of studies specifically targeted to permutation routing in single hop mobile ad hoc networks has grown significantly:

It is shown in [9] that the permutation routing of n items pretitled on mobile ad hoc network of p stations (p known) and k channels (MANET(n, p, k) for short) with $k < p$, can be carried out in $2n/p + k-1$ broadcast rounds if $k \leq \sqrt{p}$ and if each station has a $O(n/k)$-memory locations. If $k \leq \sqrt{(p/2)}$ and if each station has a $O(n/p)$-memory locations, the permutations of these n pretitled items can be done also in $2n/p + k-1$ broadcast rounds. In [8], we solve the problem showing how the restriction can be left. More precisely, we show that the permutation routing problem can be solved on it in $O(p/ln2) + (2/k + 1)n + k-1$ broadcast rounds in the worst case. It can be solved in $O(p/ln2) + (2/k)n + k + 1$ broadcast rounds in the better case, without any restriction on k. In [4], we solve the problem with n unknown.

Recently, Datta in [2] presented a fault tolerant permutation routing protocol of n items pretitled on mobile Ad-hoc network of p stations and k channels MANET(n, p, k) for short. He solved the fault-tolerant permutation routing problem in $2n/k + (p/k)^2 + 3p/k + 2k^2 - 1$ slots and each station needs to be awake for at most $(4nf_i)/p + 2n/p + 3p/k + k^2 + p/2k + p/k + 4k$ slots, where f_i is the number of faulty stations in a group of p stations. He also assumed *that* $k \leq \sqrt{(p/2)}$ and in the presence of faulty stations some data items are lost. We came out with our work in [5] presenting a fault tolerant protocol which avoids the lost of items. The authors in [10] came out with the first energy-efficient permutation routing. A more efficient energy-efficient permutation routing protocol appeared in [3].

Finally, in [2, 9, 10] it is assumed that a station knows the destination stations of each data item it holds. And that even after the partition in groups, a station knows the destination group of each item of its local memory.

1.2 Our Results

We consider a MANET(n, p) with n items, p stations. A station does not know the destination stations of data items it holds. We develop a protocol which first partitions the stations in clusters. Next we show that the permutation routing problem in multi-hop ad hoc network can be solved on it in $(\frac{6}{q} + 13)n + O(q^{\frac{4}{3}} \log^{\frac{10}{3}} q) + D_b - 1$ broadcast rounds in the worst case with the probability at least $1 - \frac{1}{p}$ whenever $q \leq \frac{p}{3 \log p}$. Where q is the number of clusters of the network. To the best of our knowledge, this is the first permutation routing algorithm in a multi-hop ad hoc network.

The rest of this work is organized as follows: Some definitions and the environment considered in this work are presented in section 2. In section 3 we introduce some probability tools which are essential for the rest of the paper. The phases of permutation routing are presented in section 5. A conclusion ends the paper.

2 Preliminaries

An Ad Hoc Network is a set of n radio transceivers or stations which can transmit and/or receive messages from each other. The time is assumed to be slotted and all stations have a local clock that keeps synchronous time. In any time slot, a station can tune into one channel and/or broadcast on at most one channel. A broadcast operation involves a data packet whose length is such that the broadcast operation can be completed within one time slot. So, in the MANET with Collision detection (CD for short), the status of an n-station MANET channel is:

-NULL: if no station broadcasts on the channel in the current slot,

-SINGLE: if exactly one station broadcasts on the channel and

-COLLISION: if two or more stations broadcast on the channel in the current time slot.

Also, all the communications are performed at time slots boundaries i.e. the duration operation is assumed to be sufficiently short.

(i) . All communication is over wireless links. A wireless link can be established between a pair of nodes only if they were within wireless range of each other. Two nodes that have a wireless link, will be said to be 1 wireless hop away from each other. There are also called neighbours.

(ii) . Each station belonging to a cluster is a resident of cluster. Hence, this station may in a given time unit, broadcast a message to its neighbours.

Definition 1

Let us consider *p* stations *1, 2,..., p* which communicate in a multi-hop ad hoc Network MANET (n, p). We suppose that we have n items in the system. Then each station of a MANET (n, p) is assumed to have a local memory of size at least $O(n)$.

2.1 Problem Description

We suppose that the n items denoted $a_1, a_2, ..., a_n$ are pretitled on a MANET(n, p) such that for every i, $1 \leq i \leq p$, station i stores the n/p items $a_{(i-1).\,n/p+1}, a_{(i-1).\,n/p+2}, \ldots, a_{(i).n/p}$. Each item has a unique destination station. It is important to note that hereafter a station does not know the destination of items it holds. It is assumed that the items are encoded in such a way that only the destination stations can recognize its own data items. A station which has received and cracked an encoded data item is capable to recognize that it is its item. If it is not its own item, then it is impossible for it to know the destination station to whom belongs the item. For every v, $1 \leq v \leq p$, let h_v be the set of items whose destination is station v.

The permutation routing problem with unknown destinations is to route items in such a way that for all v, $1 \leq v \leq p$, station v contains all items in h_v . Consequently, each h_v must contain exactly $\frac{n}{p}$ items (see figure 1 for an example).

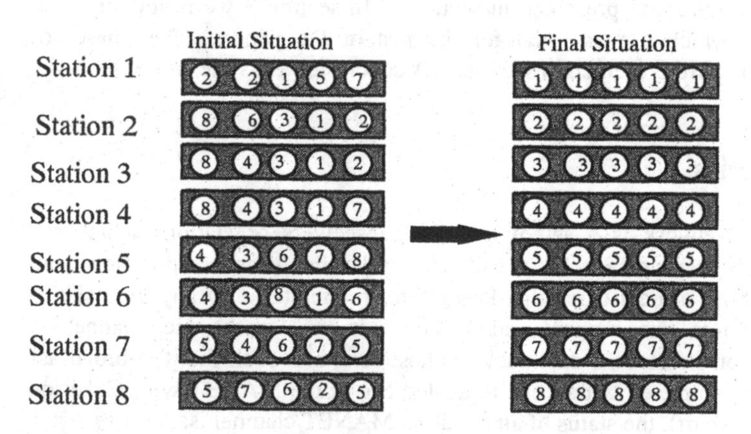

Figure 1: Permutation routing

It is important to note that hereafter a station does not know the destinations of items it holds. It is assumed that the items are encoded in such a way that only the destination stations can recognize its own data items. A station which has received and cracked an encoded data item is capable to recognize that it is its item. If it is not its own item, then it is impossible for it to know the destination station to which owns the item.

3 Some probability tools

Throughout this paper Pr[E] will denote the probability of event E. For a random variable X, E[X] denotes the expected value of X. Let X be a random variable denoting the number of successes in p independent *Bernouilli* trials with parameters *v* and *1-v*. It is well known that X has a *binomial distribution* and that for every r, $(0 \leq r \leq p)$,

$$\Pr[X = r] = \binom{p}{r} v^r (1-v)^{p-r} \quad (1)$$

The expected value of X is then given by

$$E[X] = \sum_{r=0}^{p} r.\Pr[X = r] = pv \quad (2)$$

To analyse the tail of the binomial distribution, the following estimates, commonly referred to as *Chernoff bounds* [7], are considered:

$$\Pr[X \leq (1-\varepsilon)E[X]] \leq e^{-\frac{\varepsilon^2}{2}E[X]}, 0 \leq \varepsilon \leq 1 \quad (3)$$

$$\Pr[X \geq (1+\varepsilon)E[X]] \leq e^{-\frac{\varepsilon^2}{3}E[X]}, 0 \leq \varepsilon \leq 1 \quad (4)$$

4 Permutation routing protocol

Our Approach to provide permutation routing in multi-hop Ad Hoc network consists of the following four steps:

1. Partitioning stations into clusters. This method of clustering is based on [1].
2. Local cluster broadcasting: In each cluster, we apply a method of local permutation routing within each cluster. Data items which belong to a resident of a cluster are locally broadcasted to their destinations.
3. Extra-cluster broadcasting: it allows broadcastings of items which were recorded not belong to local stations, (say outgoing items) to their final cluster destinations.
4. Ordering the cluster for broadcasting: after this phase each clusterhead knows when it is going to carry out broadcastings.
5. Local cluster re-broadcasting. Again, we run a local broadcast in each cluster to transmit the new arrived items to their final destinations.

step 1: Clustering procedure

The main task of this section is to partition multi-hop network into clusters, so that local broadcastings can be accomplished in parallel in clusters. The goal of the clustering algorithm is to partition network into several clusters. Assume that we have undirected graph G(V, E) representing a communication network where V is the set of nodes (mobiles) $V = \{v_1, v_2, ...v_p\}$, $\{|V|\}$, and E is the set of edges representing communication links. We consider that each node v_i has a positive weight (w_i). For two nodes v_i, v_j, $w_i \neq w_j$. for $i \neq j$. Also, we assume that for two nodes vi, v_j, edges $e_{ij} = e_{ji}$, since the graph is symmetric. The clusters are denoted by C_i for $1 \leq i \leq q$ and cluster heads CH_i for $1 \leq i \leq q$. The clustering divides V into a collection of k subsets $V_1, V_2, ...V_k$ where $V = U_{i=1} V_i$; such that each subsets V_i induces a connected sub-graph of G.

In some case, sub-graphs can overlaps or not, and each subset is considered as a cluster. This approach is based on [1] in which Basagni proposed to use node's weights instead of lowest ID or nodes degrees in cluster head decisions.

We make the following assumptions underlying the construction of the clusters.

- Every node knows its degree, its weight, the degrees and the weights of its neighbours
- At the end of the clustering each cluster head knows the weight of the others cluster heads.

This clustering involves two phases:

Phase 1: Choice of cluster head. Each cluster is formed with a cluster head and some neighbour nodes called ordinary nodes. The choice of the cluster head is based on the degree associated to each node. In the case of equality, the bigger the weight of the node is, the better that node is for the role of cluster head. Then nodes with highest degrees initiate the clustering process by flooding [11] request to be cluster head to all its neighbours nodes. Hence, all nodes which degree is bigger than those of all its neighbours broadcasts its decision to be a cluster head. If a node knows one of its neighbours with highest degree than itself, it resigns and adopts that node as a cluster head. A node v_i becomes a cluster head if at least one of the following propriety is satisfied:

- v_i has the highest degree among all nodes within 1 wireless hop from him, or
- v_i has not the highest degree among its neighbours but all its 1 wireless hop nodes belong to other clusters.

Phase 2: Choice of ordinary nodes. For a node which degree is smaller than the ones of its neighbours, two cases can happen:

- if this node has one neighbour who is a cluster head, in this case, it moves directly to belong to the cluster formed by this neighbour.
- if its neighbour with highest degree belongs to another cluster then two cases are possible: if there is another cluster head among its neighbours, it moves or becomes a member of this cluster, else it creates a new cluster.

We assume that at the end, our approach yields k clusters.

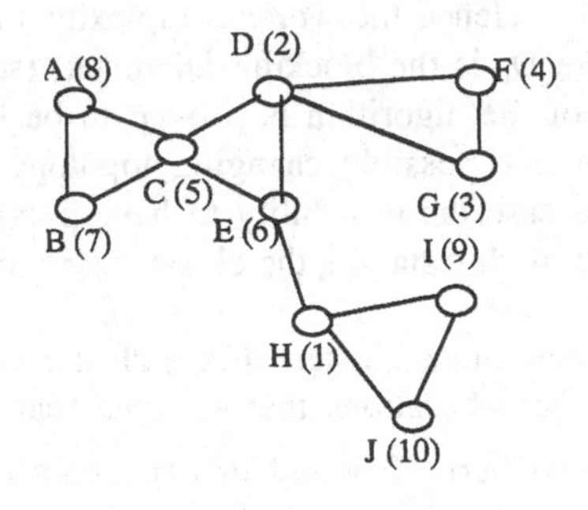

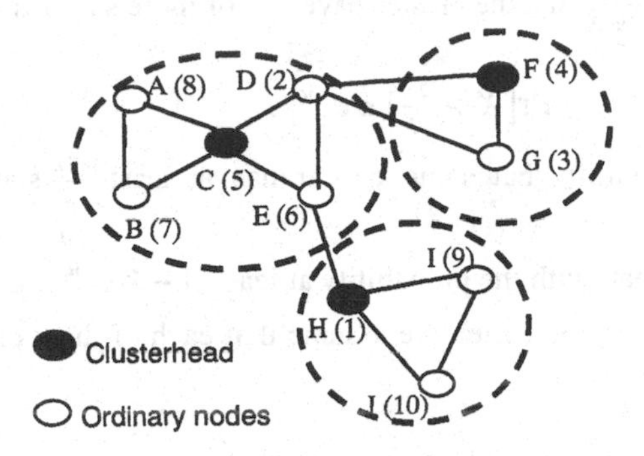

Figure 3 : clustering algorithm

For example, the clustering algorithm in figure 2 produces clusters as indicated in figure 3. The algorithm creates a non-overlapping clusters in which each node selects one of its several neighbouring cluster head. At the end of the clustering the following proprieties are satisfied:

- Entire network is divided into clusters. Each node belongs to exactly one cluster and a node is either a cluster head or ordinary node which is directly connected to one of the cluster head among its neighbours with highest degree.
- All clusters have a radius of size two. A node either becomes a clusterhead, or is at most 1 wireless hop away from its clusterhead.
- Also at the end of clustering, the number of nodes (p_i) in each cluster is known by the cluster head. Nodes at the periphery of a cluster called gateway nodes are known from the two cluster heads. Gateway nodes are the nodes at the border of a cluster and typically communicate with gateway nodes of the other clusters. They fetch into their cluster items broadcasted by cluster heads of the other clusters. And also, they are the nodes that have the responsibility of routing items which were recorded not belonging to any local node to the other clusters.
- Every ordinary node has at least a cluster head as a neighbour and belongs to a cluster formed by its neighbours with highest degree.
- No two cluster heads can be neighbours and also ordinary nodes are 1-hop to a cluster head.

Our algorithm is based on the method of Basagni [1], certainly with a slight (we take the degree into account) modification but, which does not influence the complexity of the algorithm. Hence the worst complexity of the algorithm is D_b-1 steps with $D_b \leq$ p-1 (where D_b is the blocking Diameter. (see [1] for more detail). Although the complexity of the algorithm is proved to be bounded by a network parameter that depends on the possibly changing topology of the mobile ad hoc network, rather p, in some case the possibility to have p can occur. Hence, with a multi-hop Ad Hoc network, with p station, the clustering procedure needs in average p broadcast rounds.

We now assume that there are q clusters. Fix a cluster and let X be the random variable denoting the number of stations that selected that cluster. Thus we have $E[X] = \frac{p}{q}$. By using the Chernoff bound in (4) with $\varepsilon = 1$, we can bound the probability $\Pr[X \geq \frac{2p}{q}]$ that the cluster have $\frac{2p}{q}$ or more stations as follows:

$$\Pr[X \geq \tfrac{2p}{q}] \leq e^{\frac{-2p}{3q}}.$$

Thus, the probability that some cluster has at least $\frac{2p}{q}$ stations is less than $k.e^{\frac{-2p}{3q}}$. It follows that, with the probability at least $1 - k.e^{\frac{-2p}{3q}}$, all the clusters have fewer than $\frac{2p}{q}$ stations. Hereafter, we assume that each of the k clusters contains in maximum $\frac{2p}{q}$ stations.

Step 2. Local Cluster Broadcastings

We assume that the multi-hop ad hoc networks is partitioned into k clusters, C_1, C_2 ...C_k. Cluster heads are known, and also gateway nodes are known in each cluster. We consider that cluster head (CH_i is vested with the responsibility to perform local broadcast in cluster C_i. All local stations are at 1 wireless hop of their clusterheads. Each node has a local memory of size *O(n)*.

Assumption 4.1
Hereafter we assume that we are always in the worst case, i.e. non data item in a cluster C_i belongs to a station in C_i.

After this clarification, it is important to note that here broadcastings are local in each cluster. Every data item broadcasted is accompanied with a bit 0 to mean that the broadcast is local. Therefore cluster gateway may not broadcast data items out of the cluster. We only focus on the routing that takes place in cluster C_1, the local broadcasts on all other groups are similar. The cluster head knows the weight of its residents. With the help of these weights, the cluster head knows the turn of broadcasting of each resident, from the smaller weight to the bigger. The cluster invited each of its residents to broadcast to him all the data items which are not their own data items. Hence, each node broadcasts in its turn according to its weights. It begins with the nodes with the highest weight, followed by the next with the highest weight, and so on (figure 4).

phase i: First, one after another, from station with highest weight to station with least weight, in this order, stations broadcast items which do not belong to them, to their cluster heads, one by one. The cluster head CH_1 copies these items to its local

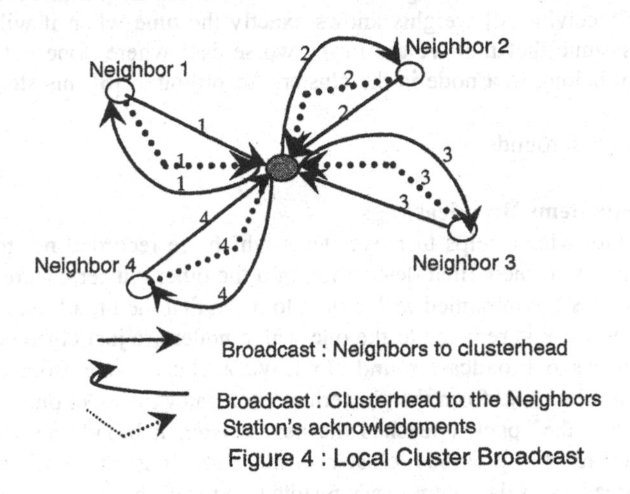

Figure 4 : Local Cluster Broadcast

memory and keeps those which are its own items. This sub-phase needs $\frac{2p}{q} \times \frac{n}{p} = \frac{2n}{q}$ broadcast rounds in the worst case in cluster C_i)

phase ii: The cluster head broadcasts all data items (except those which are its own) it receives to its neighbours simultaneously, one by one by multiplexing. Assume that the cluster head CH_i is carrying out the local broadcasting to a station v, two cases can occur:

- if a item belongs to v, then v copies this items to its local memory. In the next slot v broadcasts a positive acknowledgment to CH_1 to inform that it is its item.
- if a item does not belongs to v, then no positive acknowledgment will be send. After a timeout it is recorded not belonging to any resident of the cluster C_1, it is a outgoing item. It is then saved by the cluster head as outgoing item.

So, at the end of the step, all the items which were recorded not belong to any node in C_1 are identified and stored by the cluster head CH_1 as outgoing items. Since, each station in C_1 has $\frac{n}{p}$ items, this step needs $2\frac{n}{p} \times \frac{2p}{q} = \frac{4n}{q}$ broadcast rounds (it is clear that the number of nodes in cluster C_1 is $\frac{2p}{q}$). Therefore $\frac{4n}{q}$ rounds are necessary in the worst case to carry out this step, *1. i≤q.* Note that the worst case is the one in which no node detains any of its own data items.

Then $\frac{6n}{q}$ broadcast rounds are necessary to carry out step 2.

Step 3: Ordering the clusters for broadcastings: gossiping
It is important to know the order in which the clusters are going to broadcast. The clusters broadcast simultaneously theirs weights to each other. Since all weights are different, a cluster after receiving all weights knows exactly the time when it will start broadcasting. We assume that that we are in the worse case where none data item in a cluster does not belong to a node in the cluster. According to [6] this step needs $O(q^{\frac{4}{3}} \log^{\frac{10}{3}} q)$ broadcast rounds.

Step 4: Out-going data items Broadcastings
This step is a procedure which helps to move items which are recorded not to belonging to any local station to their final destination into the other clusters. Here, every data item broadcasted is accompanied with a bit 1 to mean that the broadcast is extra cluster. In fact the network is reduced to the one which nodes are just clusters. Therefore a data item needs 6 broadcast rounds to leave a cluster: one from a gateway node to the clusterhead, one from the clusterhead to a gateway node, one to leave the cluster, and when the packet reaches the next cluster, it broadcasts an acknowledgement packet to the previous cluster which has sent the packet. Consequently a cluster broadcast a data item every 6 slots (we recall that the time is slotted). On the level of each cluster C_i, supervised by its clusterhead CH_i, CH_i sends one by one each items which were recorded not to belonging to any station in C_i (outgoings items) to the other clusters C_j ($i \neq j$). It should be noted that the gateway nodes serve only as routers to relay items towards the clusterheads nodes to which they are connected.

Again, we only focus on the multicast from C_1. The clusterhead in C_1 broadcasts first, followed by those in C_2, next C_3 until C_k (ordered by their weights). The clusterhead of C_1 (CH_i) sends one by one, every 6 slots, each outgoing item to all the destinations, among C_2, C_3 ....C_k, to which it is connected, via its gateway nodes. Each clusterhead copies received items in its local memory, i.e. the n data items. After C_1 has broadcasted all its outgoing items, it broadcasts an information to the next cluster, say C_2 to mean that it is its turn to carry out multicast broadcasting.

Now to evaluate upper bound of the running time of this step, note that k is the diameter of the network formed by clusters (here each cluster is considered as a simple node). A cluster needs $6(\frac{2p}{q} \times \frac{n}{p}) = \frac{12n}{q}$ broadcast rounds are used by the nodes in cluster C_i to forward their outgoing items. In total this step takes $q(\frac{12n}{q}) = 12n$ where k is the number of clusters. As we always assume that we are in the worst case, this step brings into C_i all data items which destination stations are in a cluster C_i.

Step 5 : Local cluster re-broadcastings

This step is similar to step2. Each cluster head broadcasts the data items that were stored during step4 to all its neighbours (ordinary nodes). The procedure is carried out in parallel in clusters. One by one, the data items are simultaneously broadcasted, by multiplexing, from the cluster heads to its neighbours. At the end of this step, ach ordinary node recovers all its own items. The reader should not have difficulty to confirm that this procedure in cluster C_i, needs n broadcast rounds in the worst case.

Theorem 4. 1
Let p mobile stations in a Multi-hop Ad-Hoc network (n, p), with p stations and n items pretitled on it. The permutation routing problem can be solved in $(\frac{6}{q}+13)n+O(q^{\frac{4}{3}}\log^{\frac{10}{3}} q)+D_b-1$ *broadcast rounds in the worst case with the probability at least* $1-q.e^{\frac{-2p}{3k}}$. *Where k is the number of clusters,* D_b *is the blocking diameter.*

Proof:
i) Step 1 of the algorithm need D_b - 1 steps with $D_b \leq p-1$

ii.) In step 2, $\frac{6n}{q}$ broadcast rounds are necessary for its execution in the worst case

iii.) Step 3 needs $O(q^{\frac{4}{3}}\log^{\frac{10}{3}} q)$ broadcast rounds

iv.) Step 4 runs in *12n* broadcast rounds.

v.) Step 5 runs in n broadcast rounds.

Therefore the number of broadcast rounds need by the protocol results of the summation of the running time of the five steps. Therefore, our protocol runs in $(\frac{6}{q}+13)n+O(q^{\frac{4}{3}}\log^{\frac{10}{3}} q)+D_b-1$ broadcast rounds. Where is D_b is the blocking Diameter ($D_b \leq p-1$).

Remark4.1. If we assume that $q \leq \frac{p}{3\log p}$, then one has $qe^{\frac{-2p}{3q}} \leq \frac{p}{3\log p}.e^{-2\log p} < \frac{1}{p}$. Consequently, we have the following:

Corollary 4. 1. *Let p mobile stations in a Multi-hop Ad-Hoc network (n, p),with p stations and n items pretitled on it. The permutation routing problem can be solved* *in* $(\frac{6}{q}+13)n+O(q^{\frac{4}{3}}\log^{\frac{10}{3}}q)+D_b-1$ *broadcast rounds in the worst case with the probability at least* $1-\frac{1}{p}$ *whenever* $q\leq\frac{p}{3\log p}$.

4 Conclusion

In this paper, we have considered a Multihop ad hoc network with n items, p stations, with p unknown. First, we present a clustering approach to partition stations into k groups. Finally, we show that the permutation routing problem can be solved in $(\frac{6}{q}+13)n+O(q^{\frac{4}{3}}\log^{\frac{10}{3}}q)+D_b-1$ broadcast rounds in the worst case *with the probability at least* $1-\frac{1}{p}$ whenever $q\leq\frac{p}{3\log p}$. To the best of our knowledge, this is the first algorithm on the permutation routing in a multi-hop ad hoc networks. A slight modification of our protocol as follows can help to manage simultaneous broadcastings to the clusterhead: a gateway station can broadcast to the clusterhead only if he is invited to do so by the clusterhead. Our approach assumes that the q most weighted stations are first thrown in the area. Then each of the p-q remained stations chooses at random to be a neighbour of one of the q clusterheads.

However some open problems remains. The derivation from the idea of this paper of a fault tolerant algorithm, which guarantees the delivery of data items to non faulty nodes, is to be investigated. Also, the construction of an energy-efficient permutation routing protocol for multi-hop ad hoc network is a challenge.

References

[1] S. Basagni. Distributed clustering for multihop wireless networks. *In A. Annamalai and C. Tellambura, Proceedings of the IEEE International Symposium on Wireless Communications (ISWC'99)*, pp. 41-42, June 3-4 1999.

[2] A. Datta. Fault-tolerant and Energy-efficient Permutation Routing Protocol for Wireless Networks. 17th *IEEE Intern. Parallel and Distributed Processing Symposium (IPDPS'03)*, Nice, France, 2003.

[3] Amitava Datta, Albert Y. Zomaya: An Energy-Efficient Permutation Routing Protocol for Single-Hop Radio Networks. *IEEE Trans. Parallel Distrib. Syst. 15*(4): 331-338 (2004)

[4] D. Karimou, J. F. Myoupo. An Application of an Initialization Protocol to Permutation Routing in a Single-hop Mobile Ad-Hoc Networks. *The journal of Supercomputing* vol. 31, p. 215-226, 2005.

[5] D. Karimou and J.F. Myoupo. A Fault Tolerant Permutation Routing Algorithm in Mobile Ad Hoc Networks. *International Conference on Networks (ICN'05)*, Part II, LNCS 3421, pp.107-115, *2005*.

[6] L. Gasieniec, T. Radzik and Q. Xin. Faster deterministic gossiping in ad hoc radio networks. *Proc. 9th Scandinavian Workshop on Algorithm Theory, SWAT 2004*, Humlebaek, Danmark, *LNCS 3111*, pp. 397-407.

[7] R. Motwani and P. Raghavan. *Randomized Algorithms*. Cambridge University Press, 1995.

[8] J. F. Myoupo. Concurrent Broadcasts-Based Permutation Routing algorithms in Radio Networks. *IEEE Symposium on Computers and Communications, (ISCC'03)*, Antalya, Turkey, 2003.

[9] K. Nakano, S. Olariu and J.L. Schwing. Broadcast-Efficient protocols for Mobile Radio Networks. *IEEE Trans. Parallel Distr. Syst.* vol.10, pp.12, 1276-1289, 1999.

[10] Koji Nakano, Stephan Olariu, Albert Y. Zomaya: Energy-Efficient Permutation Routing in Radio Networks. *IEEE Trans. Parallel Distrib. Syst. 12*(6): 544-557 (2001)

[11] Y.C. Tseng, S-Y Ni, Y-S Chen and J.-P Sheu. The Broadcast Storm Problem in a Mobile Ad Hoc Network. *ACM Wireless Networks* 8, 153-167, 2002

Beaconless Position Based Routing with Guaranteed Delivery for Wireless Ad-Hoc and Sensor Networks

Mohit Chawla[1], Nishith Goel[2], Kalai Kalaichelvan[3], Amiya Nayak[4], and Ivan Stojmenovic[4]

1 IIT Guwahati, B.Tech, Computer Science & Engineering, Guwahati, Assam, India mchawal@iitg.ernet.in

2 Cistel Technology Inc., Ottawa, ON K2E 7V7, Canada ngoel@cistel.com

3 EION Technology Inc., Ottawa, Ontario K1Y 2X5, Canada kalai@eion.com

4 SITE, University of Ottawa, 800 King Edward, Ottawa Ontario K1N 6N5, Canada {anayak,ivan}@site.uottawa.ca,

Abstract. Existing position-based routing algorithms, where packets are forwarded in the geographic direction of the destination, normally require that the forwarding node knows the positions of all neighbors in its transmission range. This information on direct neighbors is gained by observing beacon messages that each node sends out periodically. Several beaconless greedy routing schemes have been proposed recently. However, none of the existing beaconless schemes guarantee the delivery of packets. Moreover, they incur communication overhead by sending excessive control messages or by broadcasting data packets. In this paper, we describe how existing localized position based routing schemes that guarantee delivery can be made beaconless, while preserving the same routes. In our *guaranteed delivery beaconless routing scheme,* the next hop is selected through the use of control RTS/CTS messages and biased timeouts. In greedy mode, neighbor closest to destination responds first. In recovery mode, nodes closer to the source will select shorter timeouts, so that other neighbors, overhearing CTS packets, can eliminate their own CTS packets if they realize that their link to the source is not part of Gabriel graph. Nodes also cancel their packets after receiving data message sent by source to the selected neighbor. We analyze the behavior of our scheme on our simulation environment assuming ideal MAC, following GOAFR+ and GFG routing schemes. Our results demonstrate low communication overhead in addition to guaranteed delivery.

Please use the following format when citing this chapter:

Chawla, M., Goel, N., Kalaichelvan, K., Nayak, A., Stojmenovic, I., 2006, in International Federation for Information Processing (IFIP), Volume 212, Ad-Hoc Networking, ed. Al Agha, K., (Boston: Springer), pp. 61–70.

1 Introduction

Position-based routing was originally developed for packet radio networks in the 1980s [6]. It received renewed interest during the last few years as a method for routing in mobile wireless ad hoc and sensor networks [1, 2, 4]. The general idea of is to select the next hop based on position information such that the packet is forwarded in the geographical direction of the destination. Position-based routing can be divided into two main components: the location service and position-based forwarding. The *location service* [5, 13] is used for mapping the unique identifier (for example an IP address) of a node to its geographical position. In mobile ad hoc networks, providing accurate location service for position based routing, with low communication overhead, appears to be more difficult task than routing itself [13]. In case of sensor networks, however, destination is a sink or base station whose position is made available to source sensors by flooding. *Position-based forwarding* is performed by a node to select one of its neighbors as the next hop the packet should be forwarded to. Usually, the following information is required for the forwarding decision: the node's own geographical position, the position of all neighbors within transmission range and the position of the destination. Based on this information, the forwarding node selects one of its neighbors as the next hop such that the packet makes progress toward the geographical position of the destination. It is possible that there is no neighbor with positive progress towards the destination while a valid route exists. In this case, a recovery strategy [4] may be used to find a path to the destination. The most important characteristic of position-based routing is that forwarding decisions are based on local knowledge [5, 13]. It is not necessary to create and maintain a global route from the sender to the destination [11]. Therefore, position-based routing is commonly regarded as highly scalable and very robust against frequent topological changes.

In most existing strategies for position-based unicast forwarding [8], the position of a node is made available to its direct neighbors by periodically transmitting beacons. Each node stores the information it receives about its neighbors in a table and thus maintains more or less accurate position information of all direct neighbors. The transmission of beacons and the storage of neighbor information consume resources. Due to mobility, collected neighbor information can quickly get outdated which in turn can lead to packet drops. Sending and receiving beacon messages consumes energy and disturbs sleeping cycles, which is not desirable for devices with strict limitations in energy consumption [9].

In this paper, we consider position-based forwarding without the help of beacons and without the maintenance of information about the immediate neighbors of a node. Instead, all suitable neighbors of the forwarding node participate in the next hop selection process and the forwarding decision is based on the actual topology at the time a packet is forwarded. The existing beaconless routing protocols [3, 7, 9, 14] do not guarantee the delivery of the packet and also either broadcast the data packet [9] or have too many messages involved or duplicate messages [7]. We describe here a beaconless position based routing protocol which guarantees delivery in connected networks, assuming an ideal MAC layer, without collisions, and unit disk graph model without obstacles. The proposed *Guaranteed Delivery Beaconless Forwarding* (GDBF) protocol involves selecting the appropriate next hop by means of RTS (Ready To Send) and CTS (Clear To

Send) packets. In greedy mode, similarly as in [14], only the forwarding neighbor sends CTS back to the node having the data packet. GDBF is a generic framework that can be applied to location based schemes. It guarantees delivery, when the underlying protocol is a guaranteed delivery protocol. The main contribution of this article is in protocol operation in recovery mode. GDBF reduces the number of messages (CTS's) sent by the neighbors of current node in recovery mode by using a special suppression scheme. We show that only neighbors of current node in Gabriel graph (of the set of all nodes) respond in our scheme, so that current node is enabled proper choice of forwarding node and preserving routes as if 1-hop knowledge was available.

We assume that nodes are placed in the Euclidean plane. In order to represent ad-hoc networks we adopt the widely used model, where every node has the same transmission range, without loss of generality normalized to 1. The resulting graph, having an edge between two nodes u and v if and only if the Euclidean distance $| uv | \leq 1$, is the unit disk graph (UDG).

We begin the paper by outlining the details of the algorithm that we simulate, namely GFG [4], in Section 2, which also describes some of the existing beaconless greedy routing schemes. Following this, GDBF has been fully explained in Section 3. We analyze GDBF on our simulation environment assuming the ideal MAC, with GFG and GOAFR+ as the underlying protocols, in Section 4. In Section 5 we conclude the paper and present some of the insightful issues that can be the subject of future research.

2 Related Work

2.1 Beaconless Greedy Routing

Heissenbuttel and Braun [9] proposed the *beacon-less routing (BLR)* algorithm. The *contention-based forwarding (CBF)* by Fussler *et al.* [7] and *implicit geo- graphic forwarding (IGF)* by Blum *et al.* [3] are also implementing similar ideas, focusing on the integration of beaconless routing with the IEEE 802.11 MAC layer. Node, currently holding the packet with known destination, is generally not aware of any of its neighboring nodes and simply broadcasts a data packet. The main idea of beacon-less routing is that each neighboring node, receiving the packet, calculates a small transmission timeout (before forwarding the packet) depending on its position relative to the last node and the destination. The node located at the "best" position introduces the shortest delay and will retransmit the packet first. The remaining nodes then cancel the scheduled packet after detecting this transmission. However, some neighbors with forward progress may not hear the message, and can also retransmit it. Hence, in [9], only nodes within a certain forwarding area are allowed as candidate nodes for the next forwarding step. The forwarding area has the property that each node is able to overhear the transmission of every other node within that area. However, because of this forwarding area this scheme fails to exploit all possible forwarding neighbors, and therefore has reduced success rate.

Fuessler et al [7] propose a technique called *active selection method*. A forwarding node sends to all its neighbors a control packet instead of the full message. Neighbors that provide forward progress respond after a timeout, which depends on their distance to the destination. If a neighbor hears another neighbor's response then it does not respond itself. The forwarding node then sends the full message indicating which of its neighbors shall forward the message. In a similar way, Zorzi [14] proposed a scheme to avoid duplicate forwarding in a beaconless routing scheme by applying the RTS/CTS MAC scheme. The current node sends an RTS signal instead of the message. Afterwards the node waits for a node to respond with a CTS signal. If several responses are received, the node selects one that looks best for forwarding and then sends the packet to that neighbor directly.

However, none of the existing beaconless routing protocols discussed how to guarantee the delivery of the packets. Moreover, they either retransmit the whole data packet immediately [9], potentially generating superfluous additional retransmissions, or have too many messages involved or duplicate messages [7]. The GDBF protocol proposed in this paper guarantees the delivery of the packets and entails less communication overhead by using a special suppression scheme.

2.2 GFG (Greedy-Face-Greedy)

The GFG algorithm [4] is a combination of greedy routing and face (or recovery/perimeter) mode routing. We first describe face routing. Gabriel graph (GG) property is used to preserve only edges that leave connected planar graph from the initial UDG. An edge *PQ* is included in GG if and only if there is no other node in the disk with diameter *PQ*. The construction of planar graph is possible without any messages, assuming each node is aware of positions of its neighbors. Planar graph created by GG divides the plane into faces. Imaginary line from source *S* to destination *D* passes through several faces between them. These faces are traversed, changing faces at intersections of imaginary line *SD* with the faces. Whenever a new face is entered, it can be traversed in one of two possible directions, clockwise (CL) or counterclockwise (CC), and direction could change for a reason, leading to several variants of the protocol (e.g. GOAFR+ variant [12]).

During face traversal, node *U* forwards message to neighboring node *V* together with the selected direction (CL or CC) to follow, which indicates also which of the two possible faces has been traversed. The next neighbor to forward is the one making minimal angle with respect to incoming edge and given direction (e.g. *E* for CL and *H* for CC in Fig. 2). When such rule (called also right/left hand rule for CL/CC direction respectively) is applied repeatedly, selected face can be traversed fully (e.g. face *VGIJKF* in Fig. 2), which guarantees finding the next intersection with the imaginary line and making progress toward the destination. Note that local orientation for neighbor selection and global face orientations are opposite for closed faces (See Fig. 2).

The GFG algorithm begins by routing greedily; that is by forwarding the message at each intermediate node to the neighbor located closest to the destination *D*. Doing so, however, the algorithm can reach a local minimum with respect to the distance from *D*, that is a node *G* none of whose neighbors is located closer to *D* than *G* itself. From this position the algorithm recovers by routing around the *perimeter* of the region by carefully selecting neighbors through the recovery mode protocol. Fig. 3 illustrates the two modes.

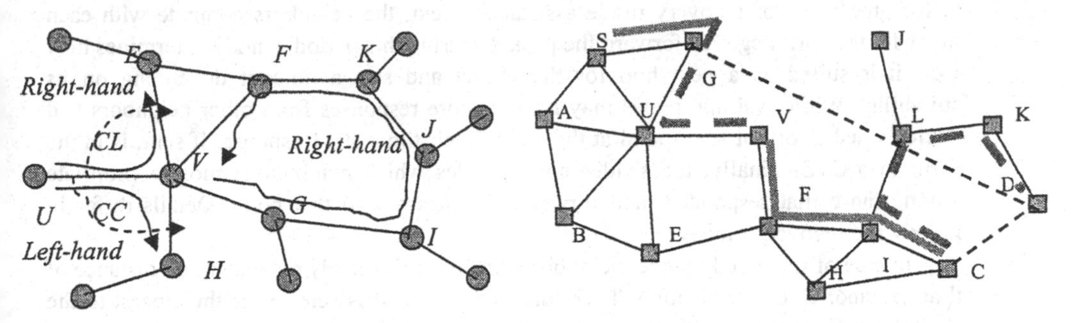

Figure 2. Continuing face traversal

Figure 3. Greedy *SG*, face *GUV*, greedy *VFIC*, face *CILKD* modes in *GFG* algorithm

When a packet enters perimeter mode e.g. at *G* (Fig. 3), GFG records in the packet the location *G*, the site where greedy forwarding failed. This location is used at subsequent hops to determine whether the packet can be returned to greedy mode. GFG returns a packet to greedy mode if the distance from the forwarding node to *D* is less than that from *G* to *D*. Packet also contains source, destination, and position of last intersection *X* with the imaginary line (the next intersection is valid only if it is between *X* and *D*). When entering a new face, packet needs also to carry the first edge on it and the selected direction. If the packet discovers them again later on, a loop has been created which indicates that destination is disconnected from the source. Similar scenario may be created with node mobility, but it can be also then prevented by recording the time face was entered, and ignoring GG edge changes occurring afterwards.

3 GDBF (Guaranteed Delivery Beaconless Forwarding)

The GDBF algorithm proposed in this paper does not require beacons and thus completely eliminates the proactive part of position-based routing. Routes in GDBF algorithm are the same as in the underlying position based routing protocol to which it is applied. More precisely, GDBF is a general framework, with particular instances such as BGFG and BGOAFR+ which are built by applying GDBF on GFG and GOAFR+, respectively. BGFG and BGOAFR+ are beaconless forms of GFG and GOAFR+. Assuming the same neighbors at the same positions, GDBF always selects the same neighbor as the underlying protocol, in both recovery and greedy modes. That is, routes in BGFG (BGOAFR+) are the same as routes in GFG (GOAFR+, respectively) as if 1-hop knowledge was available. GDBF algorithm uses control messages to select the appropriate next neighbor rather than periodic beacons, hence it always selects the neighbor dynamically. Frequent topological changes impact the accuracy of neighborhood information in beacon based protocols, while the proposed protocol resolves this problem with the assumptions stated earlier in section 1. The beaconless protocol GDBF works in three steps. First, the forwarding node transmits the RTS packet as a single-hop broadcast to all neighbors. The packet contains request to forward the message but not the message itself. It also contains one bit indicating whether the request is for greedy or for recovery mode assistance. Next, the neighbors compete with each other for the "privilege" to forward the packet. During this period, a node determines how well it is suited as a next hop for the packet and sets a timeout depending on its suitability. While waiting, nodes may receive more responses from other neighbors and decide whether or not to respond at the end of their timeouts. Response, if sent, is in the form of a CTS. Finally, the sender node decides which neighbor is most appropriate among those that responded, and forwards the message to that node. Details differ in greedy and recovery modes.

In case of the greedy mode, neighbor's timeout is inversely dependent on distance of that neighbor to the destination. Therefore, the node that is selected is the closest to the destination from among all neighbors. Only nodes that are closer to destination than S set such timeout and potentially respond. Once a CTS is received, S transmits the message (data packet) to the neighbor that has just sent the CTS. That message also cancels the transmission by other neighbors. Thus duplicate messages or routes in the network are avoided because a unique CTS is allowed. In Fig. 4, A and B are the greedy nodes because they are closer to the destination D than the current node S. However B is closer to D than A and hence B will have the smallest timeout and will be the first one to send the CTS to S. Nodes overhearing that CTS, like A, will automatically cancel their message. Node S forwards full message to B. This message cancels CTS from other neighbors which did not hear the CTS from B. Therefore, in greedy mode, exactly one neighbor sends CTS message. Note that our GDBF protocol in the greedy mode is similar to the one described in [14].

In a specific MAC implementation, discrete values of timeout are required. It is then possible that two or more of neighbors nearest to D will then respond simultaneously, causing collisions. In such case, node S will issue request for retransmissions to these nodes. They will in turn select new random timeouts, ignoring their positions, to avoid another collision. Similar resolution can be applied in the case of recovery mode.

In case of the recovery mode, the neighbor's timeout is based on the closeness to the current node S having the packet rather than the destination. Closer nodes to S have shorter timeouts. Once its timeout expires, node A responds with a CTS to S. That response subsequently cancels all the transmissions from neighbors X that find A to be located inside in the circle with diameter SX. We now show the basic property of this protocol.

Theorem 1. In described protocol, a neighbor A responds to S with a CTS if and only if SA belongs to the Gabriel graph (GG) of the set of all nodes.

Proof. Suppose that a neighbor X is such that SX is not in GG. Then there exists another neighbor A so that A is inside circle with diameter SX. But then $|AS|<|XS|$ and the timeout of A is shorter than the timeout of X. Therefore A transmits CTS before the timeout at X expires, and CTS transmission of X is therefore canceled. Suppose now that SX belongs to GG. Then there is no other node inside the circle with diameter SX, and transmission from X, at the end of its timeout, is not cancelled, according to the protocol. Note that X may still hear CTS from some other neighbor A which is not inside the considered circle.♦

Therefore the number of CTS responses to the current node S is exactly equal to the number of edges in Gabriel graph, with an endpoint at S. Knowing all edges in GG, sender S (in recovery mode) then follows the corresponding algorithm and makes the decision which of them should receive the message. The message is sent to that node, and routing continues along the same path as if position of all neighbors was known to S. The details depend on particular protocol being followed. Normally, S selects forwarding node that creates the smallest angle toward the incoming packet direction, in decided direction, either clockwise or counterclockwise, following the selected protocol (e.g. GFG or GOAFR+). Initially (in our implementation) it chooses to route the packet to the first edge counterclockwise about S from the line SD (different decision criterion is possible, such as smaller of the two angles) and it continues perimeter traversal till it reaches a point where it shifts back to greedy mode or it reaches the boundary of the enclosing circle/ellipse. In the latter case it reverses its direction of traversal and starts traversing the network in the opposite direction to the present one. Note that, in this case, node receiving packet may simply decide to return it to the previous sender node, in which case no 'competition' is announced, that is, no RTS or CTS messages are sent.

The protocol has details about transition from greedy to recovery and from recovery to greedy modes. The running mode is indicated in the packet from S, therefore each neighbor starts proper timeout.

When the Greedy algorithm reaches local minima, there is no CTS response to the RTS, before the timeout in the source node itself expires. That is, there is no neighbor that is closer to the destination than the current node S, and the algorithm shifts to the recovery mode. S then again transmits a RTS but this time the bit for the selected mode indicates recovery mode. Neighbors then start another timeout, as described for the recovery mode, and the protocol proceeds accordingly.

The shift from the recovery mode to greedy mode in GDBF is dependent on the underlying routing protocol to which the GDBF framework is applied (GOAFR+ & GFG in our case). Beaconless GFG (BGFG) is GDBF framework applied to the GFG routing protocol. BGOAFR+ follows similarly. Sender node S includes, in the RTS packet, the distance of the node that switched to recovery mode from the destinations. If some neighbors detect that they are closer to destination than that distance, they are eligible to respond and convert to greedy mode. Since only one of them is 'allowed' to do so, they start a timeout based on their distance to destination, so that again the closest one wins, that is, responds first with a CTS indicating also transfer to greedy mode. This also means that S needs to wait for all such possible timeouts to expire before proceeding with the recovery mode. Therefore several neighbors may already respond offering 'services' for the recovery mode, before the best neighbor for converting to the greedy mode responded. In case of BGFG, there is immediate fallback to greedy mode, because as soon as a node is encountered that is closer to the destination than the source node where we started the recovery mode, the protocol will shift back to the greedy mode. This is in line with the GFG [4] protocol described earlier, because the paths have to be same to guarantee the delivery of packets.

In case of BGOAFR+, response from a neighbor G offering 'greedy' service does not necessarily imply the change in the mode. If the node that has the packet detects that it is closer to destination than that distance, it increments its counter p (otherwise it increments counter q) and checks for the condition for fallback to the greedy mode. If the condition is satisfied, the protocol shifts back to the greedy mode and the packet is forwarded to *G*.

The value of the timeout is in the interval [0, *Max_Timeout*] and depends on the relative position of current node (node sending the RTS), and destination node. Eventually, the node which computes the shortest timeout as per the formula for greedy and recovery modes, is the first one to send back the CTS. The timeout at a particular node in case of the recovery mode is given by $Timeout = Max\_Timeout*(u/r)$ while in the case of greedy mode it is given by

$$Timeout = Max\_Timeout*((r+d-|SD|)/|SD|)$$

The above timeouts are only defined for neighbors within the transmission region with a radius *r*. Here, *u* is the distance from the node *S* currently having the packet, and *d* is distance from neighboring node to destination *D*.

In case of recovery mode, the current node has to wait for all the neighbors to reply, and hence it has to wait for the complete *Max_Timeout* to elapse, following which it selects the best neighbor out of the CTS's that it has received. In greedy mode, current node will act as soon as the first neighbor responded.

4 Simulations

In this section we present a detailed analysis of GDBF framework applied to GOAFR+ and GFG (before crossing variant of GFG is followed) as the underlying protocols. Our results show performance characteristics in terms of control messages. We measure the number of control messages sent on average by nodes for the whole routing cycle and also the average number of neighbors that send the CTS in the recovery mode. We assume an ideal MAC layer without collisions. Timeouts are real numbers and they are assumed to be distinct.

Table 1 shows the average number of messages that are sent by the neighbors in the recovery mode and in the complete routing cycle. We simply calculate the average on the number of the CTS's sent by the neighbors when the routing is in recovery mode. The count does not include messages offering conversion to greedy mode. As we can observe from the first two columns of Table 1, the number of messages on average from neighbors in Recovery mode slowly increases as the density increases. This is because the number of neighbors eligible as possible next hop nodes will keep on increasing as the density increases. The probability of greedy algorithm getting stuck is very low at high density and hence the protocol rarely invokes recovery mode.

The last two columns of Table 1 present the average number of CTS messages (including both greedy and recovery types of responses) per hop that are sent by the neighbors during the whole routing cycle. This average value increases as we approach the critical density (= 4.71) [12] and then decreases afterwards. For higher network densities, local minimum for greedy routing is occurring with lower probabilities, and greedy routing can be expected to reach the destination with increasing probability. Thus the decrease in average number of CTS messages is observed. For the network of high densities, e.g. over 12 nodes per unit disk, the value approaches 1, since only one CTS from the best host is expected.

Table 1. Average Number of CTS messages from neighbors (RM: Recovery Mode; CRC : Complete Routing Cycle)

Network Density	BGOAFR+ (RM)	BGFG (RM)	BGOAFR+ (CRC)	BGFG (CRC)
3.50	2.423	2.410	1.587	1.599
4.00	2.680	2.645	1.889	1.879
4.50	2.736	2.693	2.050	2.042
4.75	2.742	2.720	2.115	2.099
5.00	2.771	2.745	2.084	2.088
5.25	2.789	2.761	2.161	2.159
5.50	2.810	2.857	2.121	2.106
6.00	2.874	2.851	2.005	1.970
6.50	2.892	2.884	1.892	1.885
7.00	2.934	2.890	1.782	1.820
7.50	2.962	2.926	1.732	1.669
8.00	3.033	2.950	1.570	1.541
8.50	3.065	2.969	1.499	1.455
9.00	3.071	2.986	1.432	1.421
9.50	3.087	2.990	1.350	1.320
10.0	3.103	3.055	1.274	1.260
10.5	3.130	3.194	1.253	1.268
11.0	3.191	3.042	1.224	1.208
11.5	3.166	3.058	1.192	1.176
12.0	3.170	3.079	1.167	1.149
12.5	3.179	3.189	1.139	1.119
13.0	3.269	3.219	1.120	1.108
13.5	3.339	3.243	1.102	1.088
14.0	3.378	3.155	1.083	1.069

5 Conclusions

There are several directions for extending and improving the results presented here. The impact of more realistic medium access layer needs to be studied, and protocol adjusted accordingly. The timeout needs to be discretized, following, for example, IEEE 802.11 standard. That means that obtained timeouts need to be rounded to nearest integer in interval [1, 32], for example. What would be the impact of collisions encountered by CTS messages in the protocol? In greedy mode, it is possible that two or more neighbors are roughly at the same distance from destination, and could select the same slot for reporting. In such case, current node, after detecting collision, should issue request for retransmitting their offer to help. Neighbors whose CTS message collided then need to select new random timeouts and respond again, this time hopefully without collisions. The distance from destination is not needed for setting the second timeout since only few 'winners' that just collided will try again. After the first response is received, others can be suppressed similarly. In recovery mode, neighbors along GG tend to be close to given node, and therefore could frequently be at approximately the same distance. Therefore collisions of messages from them can be expected. Similar retransmission requests from them could be required from current node, which will 'suspend' other timeouts until the collision is resolved. GDBF, in greedy mode, provides clear winner since only one neighbor will respond. On the other hand, about three neighbors respond in recovery mode. It is an interesting open problem to improve this response amount and design a technique that will select proper neighbor with reduced number of CTSs, on average. As an intuition, a different timeout formula could incorporate the angle that neighbors form with last edge on the route (measured in the desired direction), in addition to distance from sender node, so that the desired neighbor on Gabriel graph responds before neighbors on other GG edges. However, the problem is not trivial since canceling the CTS from any GG neighbor may allow other nodes, not on GG, to offer services. This could potentially invalidate the method or cause even more responses than in current method. Therefore the problem is nontrivial and requires careful investigation.

6 References

[1] S. Basagni, I. Chlamtac, V. R. Syrotiuk, and B. A. Woodward. A Distance Routing Effect Algorithm for Mobility (DREAM), MobiCom'98, pages 76–84, Dallas, Texas, October 1998.

[2] L. Blazevic, S. Giordano, and J.-Y. LeBoudec. Self Organizing Wide-Area Routing, Proceedings SCI 2000/ISAS 2000, Orlando, July 2000.

[3] B. M. Blum, T. He, S. Son, and J. A. Stankovic. IGF: A state-free robust communication protocol for wireless sensor networks. TR CS-2003-11, University of Virginia, April 2003.

[4] P. Bose, P. Morin, I. Stojmenovic, and J. Urrutia. Routing with guaranteed delivery in ad hoc Wireless Networks. ACM DIALM, 1999.

[5] T. Camp, J. Boleng, and L. Wilcox. Location Information Services in Mobile Ad Hoc Networks. Proc. IEEE ICC, 3318–3324, April 2002.

[6] G. G. Finn. Routing and addressing problems in large metropolitan-scale internetworks. Technical Report ISI/RR-87-180, March 1987.

[7] H. Fuessler, J. Widmer, M. Kasemann, M. Mauve, Beaconless Position Based Routing For Mobile Ad-Hoc Networks. Ad Hoc Networks 1 (2003) 351–369.

[8] S. Giordano, I. Stojmenovic, Position based routing algorithms for ad hoc networks: A taxonomy, in Ad Hoc Wireless Networking; eds. X. Cheng et al Kluwer,2003,103-136.

[9] M.Heissenbuttel and T. Braun, A novel position-based and beacon-less routing algorithm for mobile ad-hoc networks, ASWN' 03, Bern, 2003, 197-210.

[10] Q. Huang, C. Lu, G.C. Roman, Reliable mobicast via face-aware routing, IEEE INFOCOM 2004.

[11] J. Hou, N. Li, I. Stojmenovic, Topology construction and maintenance in wireless sensor networks, in: Handbook of Sensor Networks: Algorithms and Architectures (I. Stojmenovic, ed.), Wiley, 2005, 311-341.

[12] F. Kuhn, R. Wattenhofer, Y. Zhang and A. Zollinger, "Geometric AdHoc Routing: Of Theory and Practice," PODC, 2003.

[13] I. Stojmenovic, Location updates for efficient routing in wireless networks, in: Handbook of Wireless Networks and Mobile Computing, Wiley, 2002, 451-471.

[14] M. Zorzi. A new contention-based mac protocol for geographic forwarding in ad hoc and sensor networks. IEEE Conf. Communications (ICC 2004), Paris, 2004.

FRAD-HOC: A FRAMEWORK TO ROUTING AD-HOC NETWORKS

Underlea Corrêa[1], Carlos Montez[1], Vitório Mazzola[2], and M.A.R Dantas[2]

Federal University of Santa Catarina (UFSC)

Tecnological Center (CTC)

1 Pos-graduate Program Eletrical Egineering (PPGEEL)
{underlea, montez}@das.ufsc.br

2 Departant of Informatic and Estatistic (INE)
{mazzola, mario}@inf.ufsc.br

Campus Universitário – Trindade 88040-900 – Florianópolis – SC – Brasil

Abstract. *This article presents a routing framework for mobile ad-hoc networks, which was called as FRAd-hoc. The main goal of the contribution was the design and implementation of a structure that could gather generic characteristics from hybrid routing algorithm domains.Therefore, it is possible to offer a specializing framework to produce and make available reusable software components. The results present in this research work indicate that the FRAd-hoc environment has reached a successful level, because it was possible to produce others algorithms starting from the proposed framework.*

1 Introduction

The growing interesting in mobile ad-hoc networks (MANETs), has lead the proposal of many routing algorithms. In the literature [1-6] it is possible to verify that many proposals are oriented to some specific target. It is possible to image that these proposals are not suitable to every MANET. As an example, in [4] it is presented the Distributed Dynamic Routing (DDR) algorithm for mobile ad hoc networks, which is efficient for networks with low traffic density. On the other hand, the Zone-based Hierarchical Link State (ZHLS) [3] is high adaptable for dynamic topology and reduce the communication overheads when compared to pure reactive protocols, exemples are[7, 8]. Therefore, all nodes must have a pre-programmed static zone map. This is not feasible in applications where the geographical

Please use the following format when citing this chapter:

Corrêa, U.C., Montez, C.B., Mazzola, V.B., Dantas, M.A.R., 2006, in International Federation for Information Processing (IFIP), Volume 212, Ad-Hoc Networking, ed. Al Agha, K., (Boston: Springer), pp. 71–82.

boundary of the network is dynamic [9]. The Zone Routing Protocol [10], is an algorithm that it has significantly amount of communication overhead reduction when compared to pure pro-active protocols. It also has reduced the delays associated with pure reactive protocols as DSR [8]. However, it executes perfectly in intermediate networks, because for high density routing zones the protocol can behave in the same fashion as a pure pro-active protocol. On the other hand, for low density zones it behaves as a reactive protocol.

Nevertheless, different network conditions need different routing services [11]. Current routing modes do not allow this feature. It is possible to guess the high level of difficult to change a routing service in a large scale MANET. Characteristcs as conectivity, amount of nodes and mobility are dynamic factors. This aspect illustrates the necessity of new approach to consider different network condictions. In this configuration it is expected that many services are static pre-configured in each node. Therefore, in this paper it proposed the development of a framework that could gather generic characteristic from hybrid routing algorithms domains. As a result, new routing algoritms could be developed from the proposed framework.

The paper is structured as it follows: in section 2, related works are presented. In section 3, the proposal for the MANETs routing framework is described in detail. We present, in section 4, the implementation and specialization of the ad hoc routing framework. Finally, in section 5, the conclusions and expectations for future work are exposed.

2. Related Works

Since its formation, the mobile ad-hoc networks group goals, was to develop the peer-to-peer routing ability in a purely mobile wireless domain. From that, a opportunity was opened for various research groups, interested in the development of researches that approached security, energy management and interaction with adjacent layers protocols. Since then, tens of works have been developed aiming at contributing with the research evolution in the ad hoc mobile networks domain. Some works considered relevant for the development of our research are cited below.

The proposed research by He Yu et al [11], present a programmable routing framework that promotes the adaptative in routing services for sensor networks, including a universal routing service allow the introduction of different services through its tunable parameters and programmable componets.

The work in [9] classifies a series of protocols, providing an overview of the great scale of the routing algorithms proposed in the literature. As a major contribution, we believe this work presents a comparison of all the routing algorithms performances approached by it, indicating which of the protocols is capable of better running in large scale networks.

The research introduced by [12] deals with routing algorithms that incorporate the use of mobile agents for the MANET routing. Through a clustering architecture, mobile agents are used to collect and maintain the intra and inter-clustering routing information. This work is very similar to researches that separates a network into zones. However, its differential is adopting mobile agents for it.

3. FRAd-hoc Model

The dynamic topology nature of MANETs makes the multi-hop routing difficult [2]. Due to this factor, various research works, such as [1, 3, 5 , 13] have been developed to offer, among others, a routing algorithm that defines the network topology, fulfilling the best qualitative and quantitative features demanded. Thus, in [14] we verified that the algorithms aim at proposing different solutions using similar techniques, showing advantages and disadvantages according to specific network situations. Thus, willing to offer a solution, we analyzed the possibility of offering a framework that not only aggregates two or more routing algorithms, but also determines the protocol to be used in according of the network's profile. For that, we introduce the proposal for a structure called FRAd-hoc (Ad-hoc Routing Framework), as shown in Figure 1.

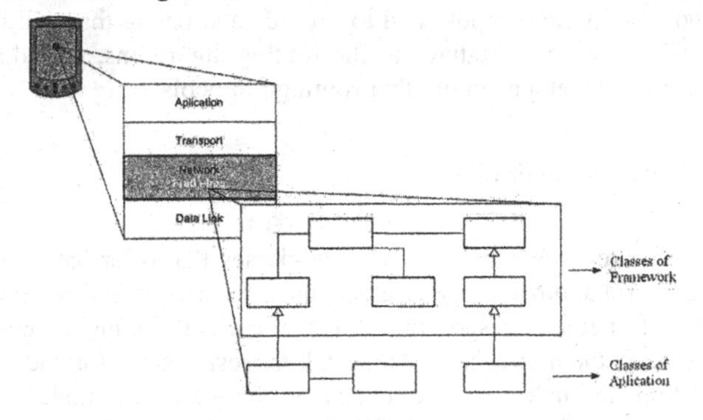

Fig. 1. Ad-hoc Framework Routing

The main goal was the design and implementation of a structure that could gather generic characteristics from hybrid routing algorithm domains.Therefore, it is possible to offer a specializing framework to produce and make available reusable software components.

The development approach for the proposed framework used the example-driven design methodology [15-18], which is threefold. The first stage approaches the domain analysis, where the existing applications are the main information source. The second stage approaches the hierarchy definition of classes that generalize the investigated domain, and the third stage, called framework test, uses it to develop examples of applications that approach the studied domain.

3.1 Domain Analysis

Routing algorithms for MANETs use the routing methodologies quoted above, may be classified, according to [9], in three main characteristics: proactive, reactive and hybrid. In the first case, there are the routing algorithms characterized for trying to continuously evaluate the network keeping updated knowledge of all the routes, for when a package needs to be forwarded, the route is already known. In the second case, there are routing algorithms denominated for establishing routes to be used on demand, that is, only when the route to a destination is required these algorithms initiate the route finding process. In the third and last case, there are algorithms that are proactive and reactive by nature. Designed to increase scalability, allowing the close nodes to work together for forming a kind of backbone to reduce route finding overhead, they are called by [9] the new generation of MANET routing algorithms.

According to the analysis made in [14] we defined, generically, that the domain involves two types of routing protocols: the intra-zone and inter-zone levels routing algorithms and the algorithms that use mobile agents. In the first case, the routing made in the intra-zone relies on a pro-active mechanism, while the one run in the inter-zone relies on a reactive mechanism. In the second case, the routing is initially trusted to mobile agents responsible for both finding and keeping updated the node routing tables, being the nodes able to being finding a route to a certain destination when necessary. Based on this definition, we determine the FRAd-hoc has, as its initial responsibility, to compose and to provide a structure that will work as a base to aggregate the common features to the routing algorithms, providing the support necessary for the development of other routing protocols.

3.2 Class hierarchy definition

FRAd-hoc (Figure 2) is composed by five classes that offer basic mechanisms for developing hybrid approach routing algorithms. Each class in this structure performs a sequence of methods responsible for the correct routing communication and running. Among them, we have: Node Class, responsible for the mechanisms of communication through message exchange between the nodes, made by the *sendMsg()* method. This Node class also has methods that indicate a possible routing failure, in case a route is not valid at the time of a data transmission, for instance. Besides, the framework has methods responsible for updating the route table and for establishing the finding of a path to a certain destination, besides methods that give back an answer from a valid route when asked by a destination node, as it is for the *repRoute(), updateTabRoute(), updateIntraZT()* and *pathDiscovery()* methods. The *IntraZT* and *InterZT* classes are responsible for aggregating methods that run zone construction and updating functions, as it is for the *buildIntraZT(), buildInterZT()* and *updateIntraZT()* methods.

The *Agent* and *TabRoute* classes contain the methods to be used by algorithms that apply the mobile agent paradigm. Both aggregate methods that require and answer the path and maintenance and path update, as established in Figure 2.

The framework dynamics may begin with the Node class, through forwarding messages that allow one node to know other nodes, which share the same frequency channel, calling them its direct neighbors. In case of algorithms that divide the network into zones (see Figure 3), the information received by the neighbor nodes, in a general way, are stored in a table called *intraZT* after the running of the zone building method, *buildIntraZT()*, which can run the inter-zone building method called *buildInterZT()*, in case a gateway node is detected. When a node knows its neighbors, it can run the route requisition method, *reqRoute()*, initially consulting its intra-zone table. In case the route required by the node is not known by its *IntraZT* table, it can run a route requisition method for its *InterZT* table. If *InterZT* cannot obtain information from the node to which one wants to establish a communication, the node may initiate a new message sending process, to check if there is any change in the network.

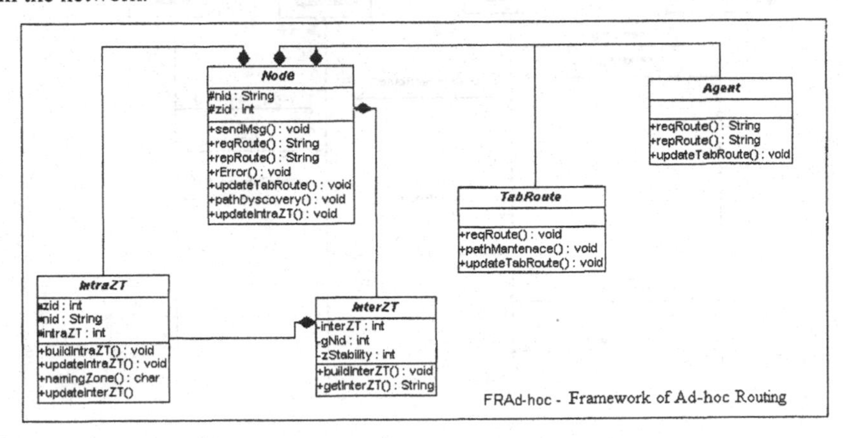

Fig. 2. Class diagram's ad-hoc routing framework

In case of algorithms that use mobile agents, Figure 4 shows that a node, knowing its neighbors, may receive constant visits from mobile agents, which compare their routing table with the visited nodes' routing tables, thus offering the update of the valid routes to a destination. However, if the node needs a route that is not defined in its routing table, it may send a route requisition to its neighbor routes, being able to abort this operation in case a mobile agent updates it before a valid answer is received or if it offers a shorter path route.

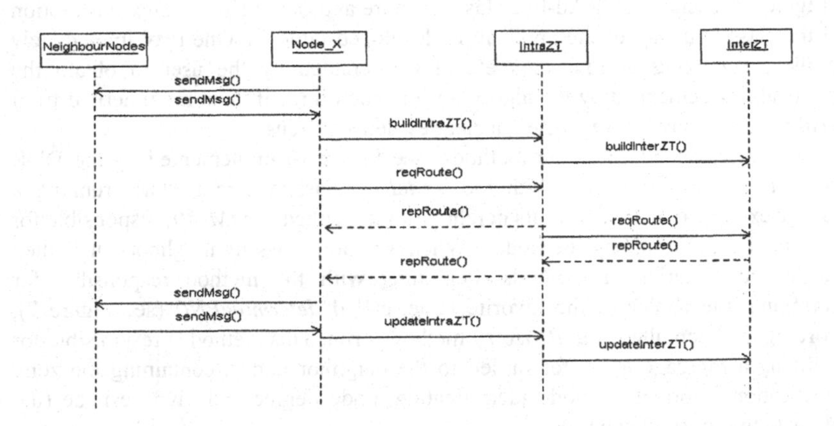

Fig. 3. Sequencial FRAd-hoc diagram of algorithms that divide the network in levels of zones

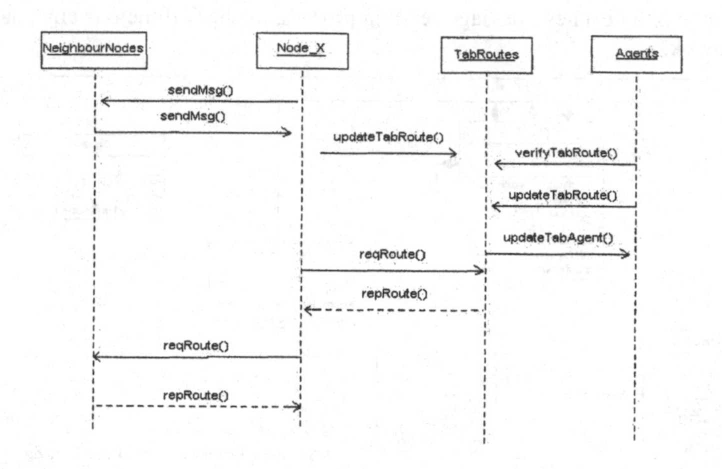

Fig. 4. FRAd-hoc sequence diagram executing algorithms that use mobile agents

4. Experimental Results

In this stage we show the usability of the proposed framework, verifying through the specializing routing algorithms, if it offers the functionalities planned. As a example of developed applications, was implemented the DDR [4], and HARP [5] algorithms among the algorithms studied in [14], because its presents features that may be applied to the other test algorithms.

Figure 5 presents the FRAd-hoc class structure approached in the previous section and the class structure of the application developed under it. One may immediately see the specializing of four concrete classes created by the user to obtain the functionalities demanded by the algorithm, in which three if them are inherited from FRAd-hoc, showing, as we wished, a clear evidence of reuse.

The activity sequence of the methods (see Figure 6) implemented by the DDR algorithm classes [4] begins with the *NodeDdr* class, where it starts running a message exchange method with its neighbor nodes, called *sendMsg()*, responsible for the communication among the nodes. When a node knows its neighbors, it is then able to run a series of methods, beginning with the method responsible for determining the choice of the favorite node, called *determinePN()* (see Figure 7), according to. Then, the *createBeacon()* method is run. This method is responsible for generating a message to be forwarded to the neighbor nodes, containing the zone identification information, node identification, node degree and favorite node (the node with the most neighbors).

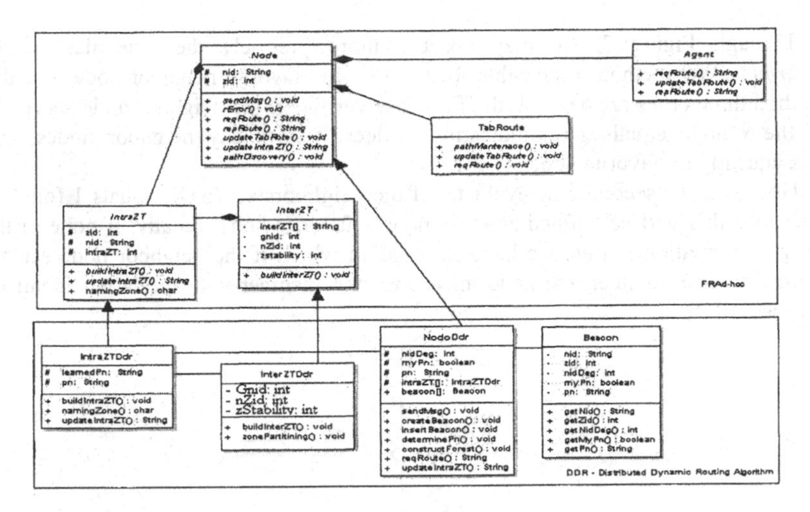

Fig. 5. DDR's implementation algorithm under the FRAd-hoc

The information forwarded by the neighbor nodes through beacon messages are stored in the intra-zone table in each node through the *insertBeacons()* method (see Figure 8). Having this information about its neighbors, a node may then continue building its intra-zone through the *buildIntraZT()* method (see Figure 8). In case the node already has a valid intra-zone table, it will only run an update, adding or removing nodes that no longer belong to this intra-zone table. After building the intra-zone, the IntraZT class runs the method that generates the name of the zone through the *namingZone()* method and consequently builds the inter-zone through the remaining nodes in the intra-zone table, which are called gateway nodes, which can be moved to the intra-zone table whenever they can join an x node tree [7].

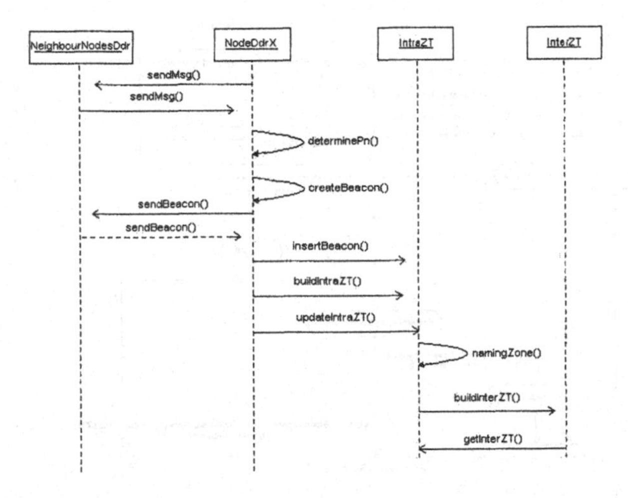

Fig.6. Sequencial diagram algorithm DDR

Through Figure 7, we may observe more precisely the dynamics of the *determinePN()* method responsible for electing the favorite neighbor node. For this method three cases are defined: the first case verifies if the neighbor node set (pnX) of the *x* node equals zero, indicating it doesn't have any neighbor nodes, and consequently no favorite node.

However, the second case evaluates if the neighbors set (pnX) equals 1 (one); if true, then this will be defined as the *x* node's favorite node. Finally, if none of the above information is true, we have the case in which if the neighbor node set has more than one member, the node must elect the member with the larger identifier number (NID).

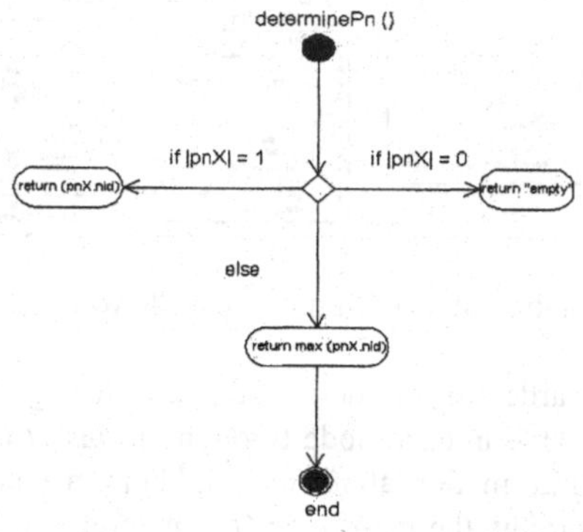

Fig. 7. Preferred neighboring node election method

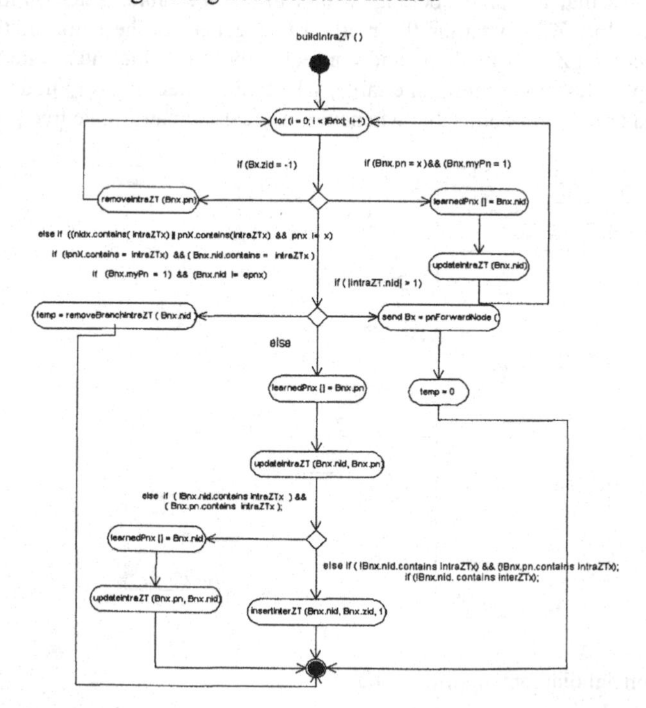

Legend:
X = any node of graph G;
Bx = a beacon of node x;
Nx = Neighbours of node X;
Pnx = Beacons set if Nx;
IntraZT = Intra-zone table of node X;
InterZT = Inter-zone table of node X;
zid = Zone id of node x;
nid = id of node X;

Fig. 8. Construction intra-zone method

Figure 8 represents in a generic way the activity run by the method that establishes the zone construction, as stated by [4]. For its construction, a node needs to know basically two levels: its NID (node id) of neighbors, and the the NID of the elected favorite node neighbors, defined by [4] as *learnedPn* of node.

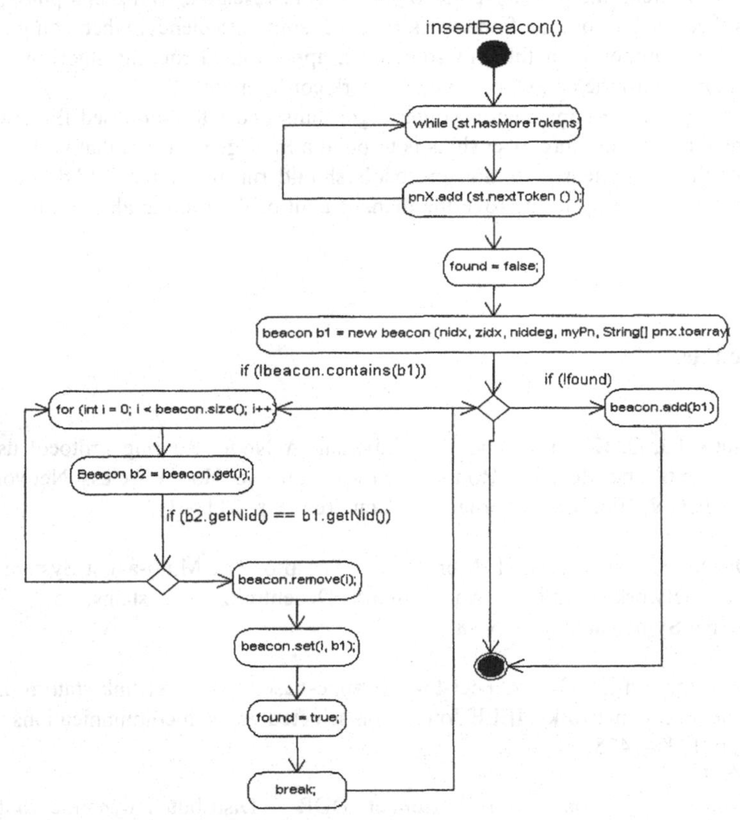

Fig. 9. Beacon insertion method

Figure 9 illustrates the *insertBeacon()* method, responsible for adding the information received through messages forwarded by the nearby nodes.

5. Conclusions and Future Works

In this paper we presented the design and implementation of a framework called FRAd-hoc. The goal of the framework was to create a structure that could offers support to the development of hybrid routing algorithms for mobile ad-hoc networks. The first step was a carefull research related to MANET routing algorithms and analysis. In this phase, was observed the absence of a unique algorithm that aggregates every possible MANET state. Therefore, we presented in this work a new routing approach that uses the oriented-object frameworks mechanism. The next effort was tho design and implement many classes and methods, witch were important to attend the primary goals of the present research. Along this phase, we verified that results from the framework reached some effeciency, when comparede to the native proposal. In this enviroment an appropriated routing algorithm was chosen more approprieted to the related network configuration.

Currently we are implementing other algorithms under the proposed framework structure. One of the future extensions is to build a management tool that will define which of the implemented routing protocols should run under the FRAd-hoc. We find this tool necessary to improve the management of the routing algorithms in the future.

References

1. S. Marwaha, C. K. Tham, and D. Srinivasan, A Novel Routing Protocol using Mobile Agents and Reactive Route Discovery for Ad Hoc Wireless Networks, Networks ICON, 10th IEEE International Conference, p. 311 – 316.

2. R. Onishi, S. Yamaguchi, H. Morino, and T. Saito, The Multi-agent System for Dynamic Network Routing, Autonomous Decentralized Systems, 5th IEEE International Symposium, p. 375-382.

3. M. Joa-Ng, and L. I-Tai, A peer-to-peer zone-based two-level link state routing for mobile ad hoc networks, IEEE Journal on selected areas in communications, vol 17, nº 8, p. 1415-1425.

4. N. Nikaein, H. Labiod, and C. Bonnet, DDR – Distributed dynamic routing algorithm for mobile ad hoc networks, Mobile and Ad Hoc IEEE Networking and Computing. MobiHOC 2000 First Annual Workshop, p19- 27.

5. N. Nikaein, and C. Bonnet, HARP- Hybrid Ad Hoc Routing Protocol, In: IST2001 – International Symposium on Telecommunications http://www.eurecom.fr/~nikaeinn/harp.ps.

6. R. Royclhoudhury, S. K. P. Bandyopadhyay, A distributed mechanism for topology discovery in ad hoc wireless networks using mobile agents, Mobile and Ad Hoc Networking and Computing, MobiHOC IEEE 2000 First Annual Workshop, p. 145-146.

7. S. Das, C. Perkins, E. Royer, Ad hoc On Demand Distance Vector (AODV) routing, Internet Draft, draft-ietf-manet-AODV-11.txt, (2002).

8. D. Johnson, D. Maltz, J. Jetcheva, The dynamic source routing protocol for mobile ad hoc networks, Internet Draft, draft-ietf-manet-dsr-07.txt, (2002).

9. M. Abolhasan, T. Wysocki, Eryk Dutkiewicz, A review of routing protocols for mobile ad hoc networks, Elservier Computer Science, www.elsevier.com/locate/adhoc, (2003).

10. Z.J. Hass, R. Pearlman, Zone routing protocol for ad-hoc networks, Internet Draft, draft-ietf-manet-zrp-02.txt, (1999).

11. Yu He, Cauligi S. Raghavendra, Steven Berson, Roberts Braden, A programmable Routing Framework for Autonomic Sensor Networks, Proccdings of the Autonomic Computing Workshop Fifth Annual International Workshop on Active Middleware Services (AMS'03), (2003).

12. K. Denko Mieso, The use of mobile agents for clustering in mobile ad-hoc networks, Proceedings of annual research conference of the South African institute of computer scientists and information technologists on Enablement through technology, ACM International Conference Proceeding Series. p. 241 – 247.

13. N. Minar, K. H. Kramer, and P. Maes, Cooperating Mobile Agents for Dynamic Networking, Software Agents for Future Communications Systems, Chapter 12.

14. U. C. Corrêa, Vitório B. Mazzola, M.A.R Dantas, Analise Comparativa de Protocolos de Roteamento de Redes Ad–Hoc, Anais da 2a. Escola Regional de Redes de Computadores - ERRC, 149-155 (2004).

15. Ralph E. Johnson, and Brian Foote, Designing Reusable Classes, Journal of Object-Oriented Programming, Volume 1, Number 2, pages 22-30.

16. S. Srinivasan, Design Patterns in Object-Oriented Frameworks, Computer, Vol.:32, Issue: 2, p.:24-32, Jnjornal, (1999).

17. Ralph E. Johnson, Frameworks – Components and Patterns, Communications of the ACM, vol. 40, Number 10.

18. D. Parson, A. Rashid, A. Speck, A. Telea, A Framework for Object-Oriented Frameworks design, Technology of Object-Oriented Languages an Systems, p.: 141-151, (1999).

AN AODV-Based Clustering and Routing Scheme for Mobile Ad Hoc Networks

Mieso K. Denko and Hua Lu
University of Guelph, Guelph, Ontario, Canada, N1G 2W1
denko@cis.uoguelph.ca , hlu@uoguelph.ca

Abstract. A mobile ad hoc network (MANET) is a collection of wireless mobile nodes forming a temporary network without the aid of any fixed communication infrastructure. Due to limited resources, frequent network partitions and unpredictable topological changes, proactive clustering schemes incur high overheads in this environment. In this paper, we propose an on-demand, distributed clustering algorithm for MANETs based on an Ad hoc On-demand Distance Vector (AODV) routing protocol. The use of on-demand routing protocol information for clustering reduces clustering overhead because no clusters are maintained unless they are needed. The clustering algorithm's stability was assessed using clustering metrics such as cluster head and cluster members lifetime. Based on this clustering scheme, a cluster-based routing protocol was proposed to add scalability to the AODV routing protocol. Using simulation, a comparison was made with a pure AODV protocol. Simulation experiments show that the scheme results in stable and scalable clusters and Cluster-AODV routing introduces less overhead than the pure AODV protocol without clustering.

1. Introduction

Mobile ad hoc networking is characterized by highly dynamic network topology and limited system resources. A number of routing protocols have been proposed for routing in MANETs [1, 4, 8, 10]. In MANETs, performance may decrease dramatically when the network's size is beyond a certain threshold. As a result, many routing algorithms perform well only when the network's size is small. To overcome resource limitations such as bandwidth and battery power, and to reduce routing overhead, the organization of the network into smaller and more manageable partitions is necessary [14]. The clustering architecture provides three useful features in a MANET environment: network scalability, fault tolerance and reduction of communication overheads. Most existing clustering algorithms use either geographical regions as clusters or form new clusters proactively even if their

Please use the following format when citing this chapter:

Lu, H., Denko, M.K., 2006, in International Federation for Information Processing (IFIP), Volume 212, Ad-Hoc Networking, ed. Al Agha, K., (Boston: Springer), pp. 83–97.

function is not needed [2, 3, 9]. The algorithm by Chatterjee et al [11] creates clusters on demand. However, this algorithm does not use the information maintained by a routing protocol.

We argue that if the routing algorithm is used as a means of gathering clustering information, the clustering and routing overhead can be significantly reduced. The AODV is one of the reactive routing protocols most commonly used in MANETs. Although the AODV protocol performs well with mobile nodes, it incurs high overhead with an increase in the network's size, the nodal degree or the number of communicating source-destination pairs. By using AODV route construction and maintenance mechanisms, clustering architecture can be constructed on demand. Clusters are maintained when data are to be sent. Such an integrated routing and clustering scheme can improve throughput and reduce routing overhead. The two main contributions of this paper are: (a) we propose a clustering architecture based on an extended AODV routing protocol for cluster formation, maintenance and purging operations; and (b) we propose an adaptive Cluster-AODV routing protocol that uses AODV and clustering information for quick route discovery, maintenance and packet delivery.

The remainder of this paper is organized as follows. Section 2 presents cluster formation and maintenance mechanisms. Section 3 presents the proposed clustering architecture and routing schemes. Section 4 presents performance evaluation and finally, Section 5 presents conclusions and future work.

2. Cluster Management

A clustering architecture provides network scalability and fault tolerance, and results in more efficient use of network resources. It can be used for resource management, routing and location management to reduce communication and computational overhead. In this section, we discuss cluster formation and maintenance mechanisms.

2.1 Clustering Algorithm Design Goal

We intend to integrate clustering with routing functionalities. The main design goals of our clustering scheme are:

1. The algorithm should use a routing protocol's control messages for cluster formation with minimal overhead.
2. The algorithm must operate in localized and distributed manners and interoperate with nodes running only AODV.
3. The algorithm must incur minimal cluster formation and maintenance overhead and support on-demand cluster formation.
4. The algorithm should minimize network-wide flooding and be scalable.

Our proposed scheme constructs or updates clustering architecture only when clusters' service is needed. The on-demand nature emanates from the demand driven nature of the AODV the scheme is based on. Nodes that take part in clustering are known from topological information maintained in the CHs and individual nodes.

2.2 Cluster Formation

The main purpose of clustering is to use the network resources more efficiently, enhance availability, reduce overheads and provide scalable architecture [7, 8, 14]. The choice of a clustering algorithm affects the clusters' stability. Our proposal divides the network into several two-hop clusters. In each cluster, a node can play one of five roles: cluster head, ordinary node, secondary cluster head, undecided node or gateway. A gateway is a node that can directly communicate with two or more clusters.

In each cluster, a cluster head (CH) is elected and responsible for cluster maintenance and inter-cluster and intra-cluster communication. A Secondary Cluster Head (SCH) is also elected to avoid the CH from becoming a bottleneck [5]. The SCH stores backup routing and cluster information. This role is rotated among other ordinary nodes. Its election does not require extra overhead because any node that wishes to serve as a SCH notifies only the CH and the CH informs other members of the cluster. In addition to a routing table, every CH maintains two tables, an intra-cluster node table and a k-hop cluster table. The intra-cluster node table contains the IDs of all nodes within a cluster. The k-hop table stores the IDs of the CHs of all other clusters located in a 2-hop neighborhood. The CHs are coordinators in each cluster and they store shared information. Every node periodically broadcasts a hello message to maintain information about its neighbors. To reduce periodic broadcasting overhead, new nodes or undecided nodes can learn their nearest CH on demand by sending a cluster head request packet. These nodes then act as either an ordinary node or a gateway based on its current location.

2.3 Cluster Head Election

Several distributed algorithms were proposed for CH election in MANETs [2, 3, 7, 9, 11, 14]. Chiang et al [2] have shown that the Lowest ID (LID) algorithm performs better than the cluster head election algorithms based on Highest Connectivity (HC). The proposals in [11, 14] use multiple criteria for CH election. Because a cluster head is responsible for cluster maintenance and intra-cluster and inter-cluster communication, it is expected to function for a long period of time once elected. Nodal mobility and link failure are the main causes of cluster head re-election and cluster membership changes.

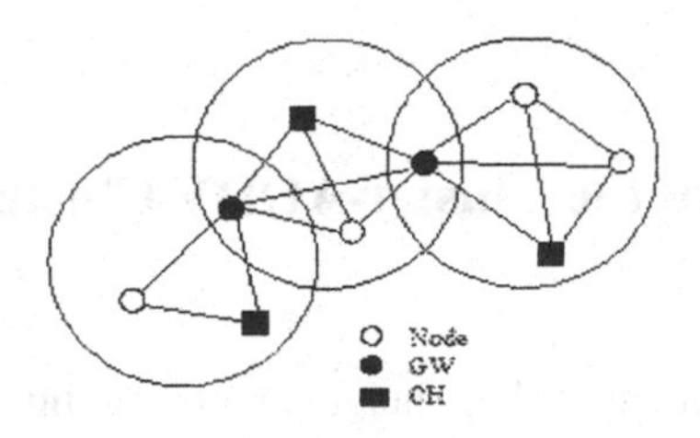

Fig 1. CH election

In [9], a mobility-based clustering algorithm for clustering was proposed. In this algorithm, a node is elected as a cluster head only when its mobility index is below a certain threshold. The mobility index is computed based on cluster membership changes and the number of cluster head changes. In case of a tie, the node with the lowest ID is chosen. In our cluster election algorithm, the lowest ID clustering is initially used for cluster formation. Thus, a node is elected as a CH if it has the lowest ID. This forms initial node configuration. Later on, a node with a lower mobility index than its neighbors [9] is used as a criterion. For example, in Fig. 1, each node broadcasts its mobility information to its neighbors during the cluster head election phase. After collecting information from neighbors, each node checks whether it has the lowest mobility index. Once it confirms this, it sets itself as a cluster head and notifies its neighbors.

2.4 Cluster Maintenance

There are two parts to cluster maintenance: intra-cluster maintenance and inter-cluster maintenance.

2.4.1 Intra-cluster maintenance. In order to keep the neighbor table and CH information consistent, nodes broadcast and exchange hello messages periodically. A hello message contains information about a node's ID and roles. If no hello message is received from a neighbor during the ALLOW_HELLO_LOST interval, the neighbor is considered lost and is removed from the neighbor table. An ordinary node checks its neighbor table to verify whether a CH still exists. If a node finds that no CH exists, a new CH will be elected in the neighborhood. If a CH fails, local maintenance is carried out.

2.4.2 Inter-cluster maintenance. Each cluster head maintains a K-hop cluster table, which contains all k-hop CHs alive in a network. Each CH notifies other neighbor CHs that it is still alive by sending a HeadAlive message. A CH, say, CH1, receives a HeadAlive message from another CH, say, CH2. If CH1 finds out that CH2 already exists in its CH table, CH2's expiration time will be updated. Otherwise, a new CH entry of CH2 will be inserted and its expiration time will be set by adding the CH update time to the current time. If no HeadAlive message is received from a cluster head during a HEAD_UPDATE_INTERVAL interval, that cluster is considered unavailable. If no HeadAlive message is received during an ALLOW_HEADALIVE_LOST interval, the CH is considered unavailable and removed from CH table.

3. Implementation of the Cluster-AODV Clustering and Routing Schemes

A K-hop CH table maintains K-hop neighbor cluster information. We used k=2, where only two hop clusters are considered. The K-hop CH table maintains fields such as CH ID, CH status, cluster size, CH expiration time and number of times the hello message has been lost. The CH's expiration time is the current time plus the HeadAliveUpdate interval. A CH's status could be either "alive" or "not alive." A CH's status will be marked as "not alive" when its HeadAlive message is not received by other CHs within its expiration time. A CH entry will be removed from a K-hop CH table if the number of times that the HeadAlive message has not been received exceeds three. In the following section we will present the various data structure added to the OADV to implement the proposed clustering architecture.

3.1 Hello Message and Neighborhood Maintenance

Before a hello message is sent, the sending node adds its status information to the message. The hello message sender could be a CH, a gateway, an ordinary node or an undecided node. The hello message extension includes source address, lifetime and current status.

We use a neighbor table to store the neighbor's ID, expiration time, status and the number of times the hello message has been lost. When a node receives a hello message from a neighbor, it will check to see whether this neighbor exists in the neighbor table. If the existence is confirmed, the neighbor's expiration time will be updated. Otherwise, a new entry will be added. When a hello message has not been received from a node in three subsequent hello intervals, it is considered not connected and will be deleted from the neighbor table.

3.2 Cluster Management Module

To implement a clustering algorithm based on AODV, we use the following three modules.

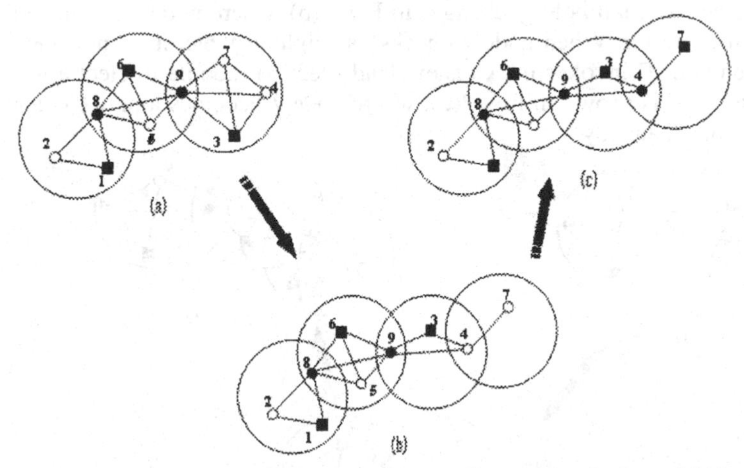

Fig. 2. Cluster re-election when no cluster exists in the neighbor table

3.2.1 Cluster initialization module. The cluster formation module is used to initialize clusters shortly after AODV has been initialized. The module is invoked in the CLUSTER_FORM_PERIOD, which is a predefined threshold. Before the initialization, every node sets its status to "undecided" and broadcasts a hello message to its neighbors. As soon as a node has received all the hello messages from its neighbors, it invokes the Cluster Head Election module to elect a CH. At this stage of cluster formation, an LID clustering algorithm is used. The new CH will then notify its neighbors and other CHs. When a node receives a CH existence notification, it sets its status to an ordinary node and broadcasts a hello message to its neighbors. If one node finds two different CHs in its neighbor table, that node becomes a gateway. After the Cluster Formation Module's execution, every node will belong to at least one cluster.

3.2.2 Cluster head election module. A node will invoke the Cluster Head Election module to elect a cluster head when no CH exists or when multiple CHs come close to each other. The procedure involves three steps as follows: (1) A node checks to see whether it has the lowest mobility index among its non-gateway neighbors. It sets its status to CH and broadcasts its status to its neighbors; (2) If it has the lowest mobility index, it declares itself a CH and notifies other nodes. Otherwise, it sets its own status to ordinary node.

We monitor clusters to avoid both the formation of multiple CHs and the absence of a CH in the cluster. We illustrate this with examples. Fig. 2(a) shows the topology of a hypothetical clustered-network at time t_1. In Fig. 2(a), nodes 1, 3 and 6 are CHs. Nodes 8 and 9 are gateways while nodes 2, 4, 5 and 7 are ordinary nodes. Assume that at time t_2 the network's topology changes to Fig. 2(b), where node 7 has moved out from its original cluster. When node 7 checks its neighbor table, it cannot find a cluster head. Then node 7 invokes the Cluster Head Election module to elect a new CH. The election result is shown in Fig. 2(c), where node 7 becomes a new CH and node 4 becomes a new gateway.

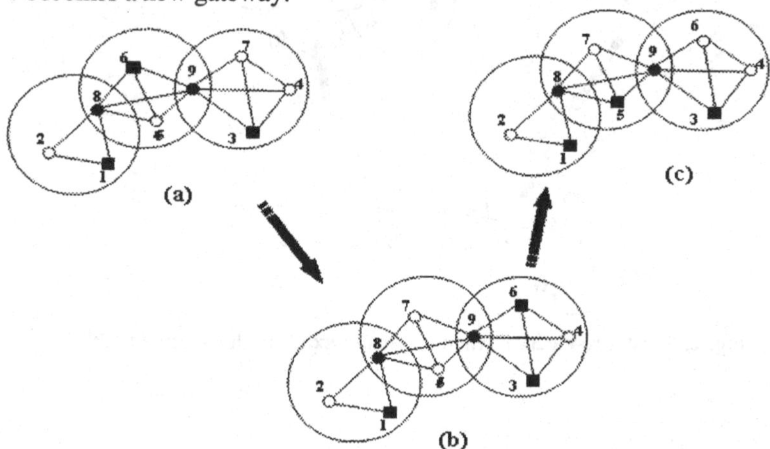

Fig. 3. Cluster re-election when more than one CH exists

Fig. 3 shows a situation where more than one CHs exist in one cluster as shown in (a). If the network's topology changes from Fig. 3(a) to Fig. 3(b) at time t_2, nodes 6 and 7 exchange positions. Nodes 6 and 3 will find that two CHs exist in their neighbors, as shown in Fig. 3(b). Then both nodes 3 and 6 will invoke the Cluster Head Election Module to determine a new cluster head. After cluster election, node 6 abandons its CH status and sets itself as an ordinary node. Node 3 remains as a CH. Also, the cluster with nodes 5, 7, 8 and 9 elects node 5 as a new CH. The network's topology after CH re-election is shown in 3(c).

3.2.3 Neighbor table purge module. Because every node is mobile and the network's topology changes frequently, clusters formed in network may not be stable. Clusters' size and nodes' status may differ at any given time. In order to keep the cluster information fresh and updated, the neighbor table will be purged.

3.3 Cluster-AODV-based Routing

The AODV protocol sends many small packets compared to other reactive protocols such as DSR. Hence when the network's size increases, the degree of node also increases, causing network congestion. The use of clustering reduces this overhead by allowing localized route discovery and maintenance. The proposed Cluster-AODV scheme uses clustering architecture and AODV functionalities to perform routing. In this section, we will discuss the mechanisms used by Cluster-AODV to reduce routing overhead and allow scalability while achieving a good packet delivery ratio.

3.3.1 Intra-cluster routing. Intra-cluster routing involves routing within a cluster. Each node maintains routing information about its cluster. When a node does not have a route to a destination which is also in a cluster, however, it sends a Local Route Request (LRREQ) through the cluster. When there is no RREP due to route failure, local route maintenance is performed within a cluster.

3.3.2 Inter-cluster routing. Inter-cluster routing involves routing between clusters. The CH maintains 2-hop cluster topology. This 2-hop cluster topology is also maintained in a SCH to minimize the problem of one point of failure. When routes cannot be found within a cluster after the issuance of the LRREQ message, a CH uses a traditional RREQ message to search for a destination through a gateway to its 2-hop neighbor clusters. To reduce the overhead caused by the RREQ flooding packet, only gateways and CHs are involved in forwarding the RREQ. No ordinary nodes are involved in RREQ packets in the inter-cluster communication.

3.3.3 Route maintenance. Route maintenance is similar to cluster maintenance. When a route fails within a cluster, it is re-constructed locally using LRREQ and RREQ using the 2-hop topology information. When LRREQ fails, the AODV procedure is invoked and the traditional RERR is sent to the source node to reconstruct routes. The source node also follows a similar procedure to repair the failed routes, first locally and then with incremental scope.

The new node joining and the existing node leaving processes are carried out based on the AODV hello messages. When the CH exchanges neighbourhood information with members of its cluster, any new node in close proximity can register with the CH by using an RREQ message. When a node registers with two

CHs it acts as a gateway. When a node moves away from the current CH, it changes its role to an ordinary node, a gateway or undecided, and it will be removed from the old CH. The old members' routing entry is updated accordingly.

4. Performance Evaluation

4.1 Simulation Environment

The NS2 simulation tool [13] is used for performance evaluation. At the beginning of the simulation, 100 nodes were randomly placed within the simulation area of 1000m x 1000m. The transmission range was set at 250m. The random waypoint mobility model [12] was used for simulating mobility. The pause time was 40 seconds. Other simulation parameters are shown in Table 1.

Parameter	Default values
Node Speed (m/sec)	0-20
Transmission Rate	4 pkts/sec
Traffic Model	CBR, 30 sources
Packet Size	512 bytes
Simulation Time (sec)	1000

Table 1. Simulation parameters

4.2 Performance Metrics

We use three different metrics to evaluate the performance: Clustering stability normalized routing overhead and packet delivery ratio of the proposed clustering and routing scheme.

1. **Clustering stability.** In the first set of experiments, we investigated the clustering stability by monitoring the percentage of CH changes, the CHs' and cluster members lifetime, and variation in cluster size. The less frequently the cluster members change their membership and the longer they stay in the cluster, the more stable the clusters are. These metrics are used to evaluate the clustering architecture's suitability for robust route construction.
2. **Normalized routing overhead.** In the second set of experiments we investigated the normalized routing overhead, which is defined as the ratio of the total number of control packets to data packets. This metric is used to evaluate scalability.
3. **Packet delivery ratio (PDR).** In the third set of experiments we investigated the normalized routing overhead packet delivery ratio, defined as the ratio of the total number of packets successfully delivered to the total number of packets generated. This metric is used to evaluate the routing scheme's transmission reliability.

4.3 Discussion of Simulation Results

In this section we present the results of the experiments based on the above simulation parameters. Each data point in the graph represents an average of ten simulation runs. First, the Cluster-AODV was compared with LID and HC. Then the pure AODV routing was compared with the Cluster-AODV routing scheme.

4.3.1 The stability of the clustering algorithm's effect. The results in Fig. 4 show that the average cluster member residence time is between 90 and 130 seconds in the LID and Cluster-AODV clustering schemes. The minimum value for cluster member residence time was observed as 110 seconds for Cluster-AODV. This is due to the fact that the network's topology changes more frequently when the mobile nodes' speed increases. However, the difference in cluster membership time is similar in all simulated network sizes. Fig. 5 shows that the average CH lifetime is between 128 and 181 seconds in the LID and Cluster-AODV clustering schemes. The minimum value for CH lifetime was observed as 137 seconds for Cluster-AODV. The CH and CH members lifetimes is the longest in Cluster-AODV compared to the other two schemes.

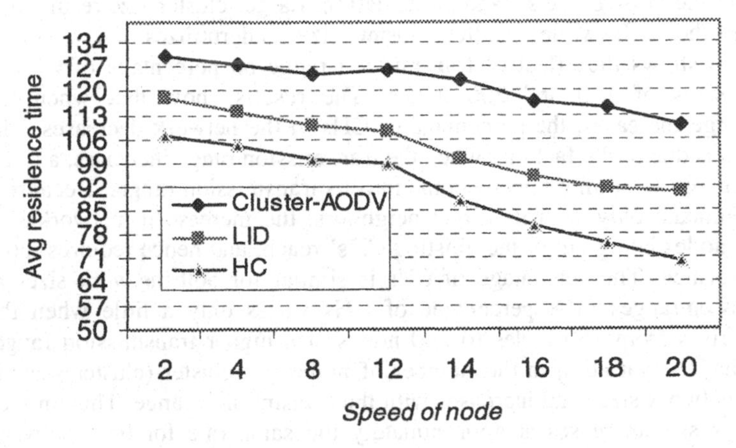

Fig. 4. Average cluster membership time (sec)

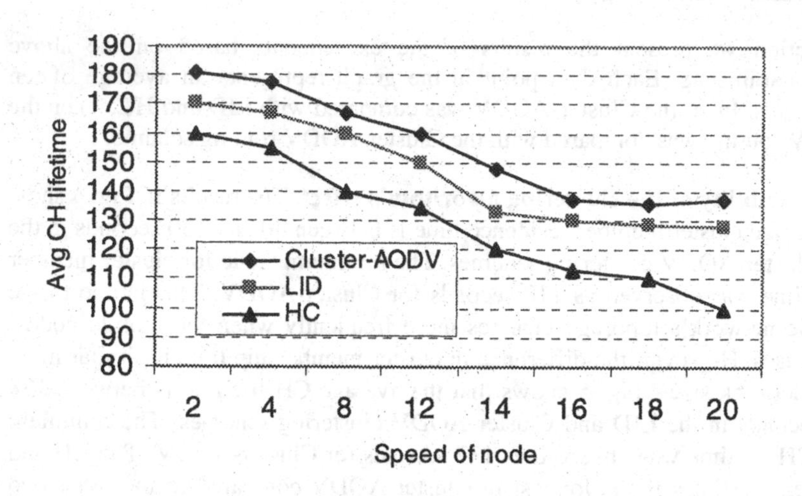

Fig. 5. Average CH lifetime (sec)

We have investigated the clustering algorithm's performance using the percentage of CHs elected and the cluster size's standard deviation. Larger cluster size results in a higher load at the CH, while smaller cluster size underutilizes the available resources. Fig. 6 shows the effect of transmission range on percentage of CHs in network with sizes of 150 and 200 nodes. The results show that when the transmission range increases, the percentage of CHs in the network decreases. The decrease in CHs is due to the fact that when the transmission range increases, a CH's coverage area increases so more nodes come into its transmission range. Because a CH can communicate only with its direct neighbors, the increase in network size results in more nodes being out of the existing CHs' reach, and hence requires more clusters to be formed. The percentage of CHs is similar for both network sizes at higher transmission ranges. The percentage of CHs varies only a little when the network's size rises from 150 nodes to 200 nodes at a higher transmission range. Fig. 7 shows that the variation in the number of nodes per cluster (cluster size) is similar at both network sizes and increases with the transmission range. This implies that the cluster's size increases at approximately the same rate for both network sizes.

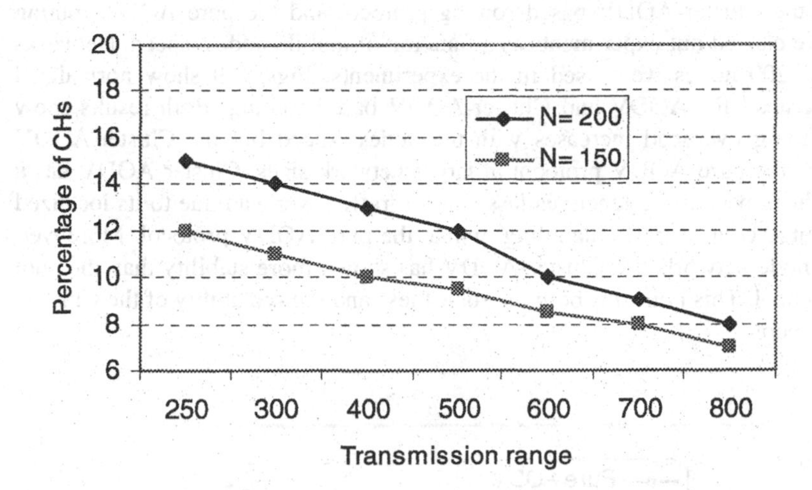

Fig. 6. Percentage of CHs

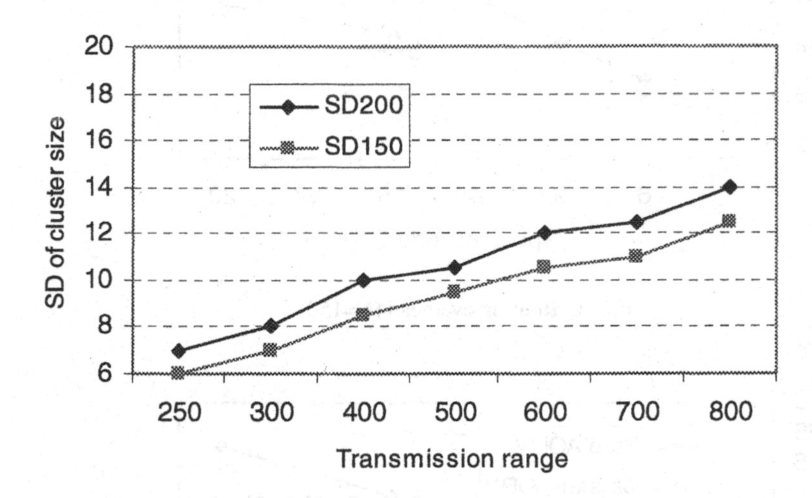

Fig. 7. Standard deviation of cluster size

4.3.2 The analysis of normalized routing overhead. To evaluate the overhead caused by the Cluster-AODV based routing protocol and the pure AODV routing protocol, we carried out experiments as a function of mobile nodes' speed. Networks of 150 and 200 nodes were used in the experiments. Figs. 8-9 show normalized routing overhead for AODV and Cluster-AODV based routing. Both results show that the routing overhead increases with the nodes' speed but the Cluster-AODV outperforms the pure AODV protocol at larger network sizes. Cluster-AODV has a lower overhead because it generates less control traffic overhead due to its localized and distributed control traffic handling, unlike the pure AODV protocol. Moreover, in the 200 node network, the Cluster-AODV has shown more stability than the pure AODV protocol. This confirms both the robustness and the scalability of the Cluster-AODV protocol.

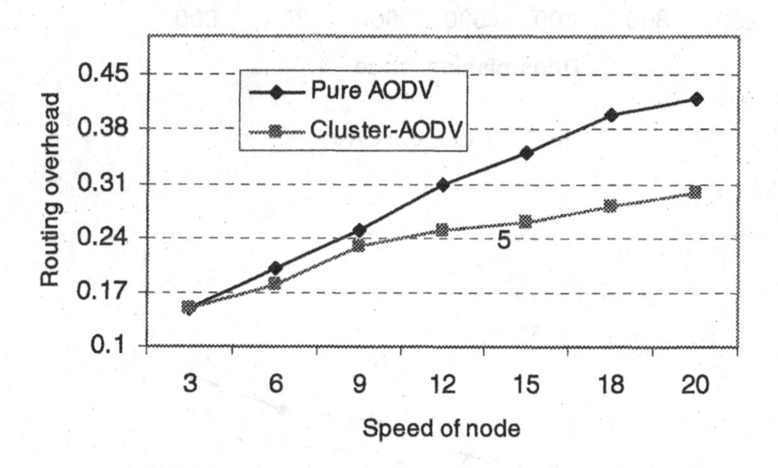

Fig. 8. Routing overhead (N=150)

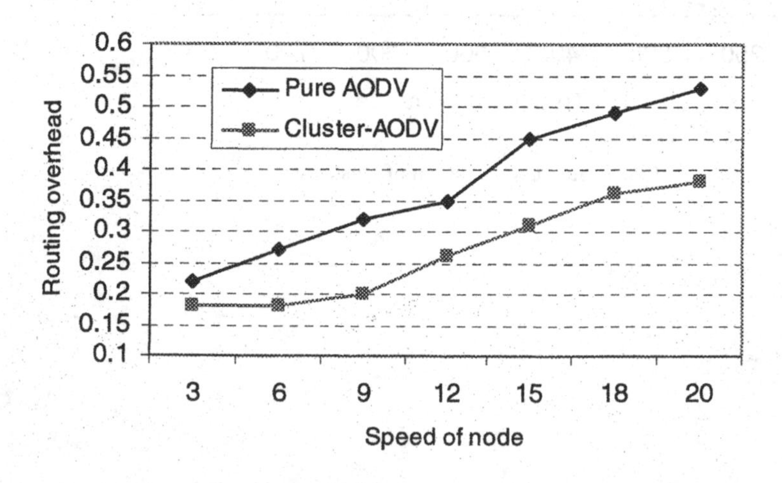

Fig. 9. Routing overhead (N = 200)

4.3.3 The analysis of packet delivery ratio. Fig. 10 shows that the packet delivery ratio is higher for the Cluster-AODV than the pure AODV protocol. The difference in the delivery ratios increases as the network's size increases, which shows the performance gained by the Cluster-AODV based routing scheme. This performance gain is attributed to the localized cluster-based route discovery and maintenance mechanism, and the effective use of AODV control messages in the Cluster-AODV protocol.

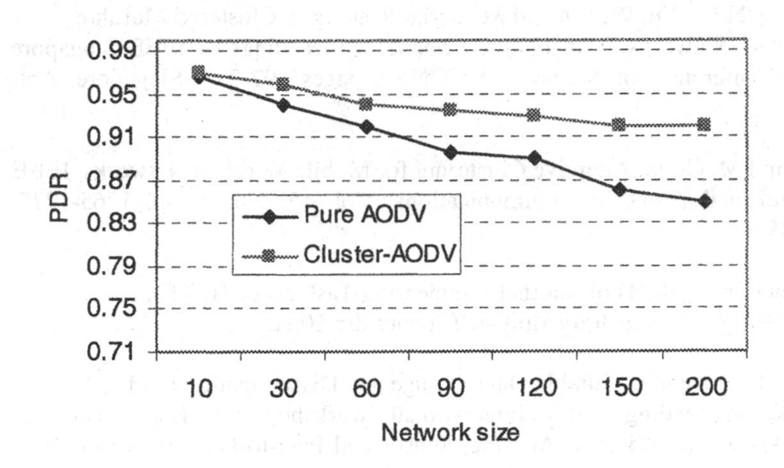

Fig. 10. Packet delivery ratio (N=200)

5. Conclusions and Future Work

This paper presents an AODV-based clustering and routing scheme for MANETs. The scheme is used for integrated routing and message delivery in clustered networks. A clustering architecture improves the network's scalability and fault tolerance, and results in a more efficient use of network resources. We evaluated the purposed clustering architecture using simulation experiments. The simulation results show that the algorithm builds stable clusters with low communication overhead due to its localized, distributed and reactive nature.

Our current study has built a basic framework for reactive clustering. Our future work includes building a cluster-based middleware for data dissemination and replica management among clusters. We also intend to extend the clustering architecture to support multihop clustering in MANETs.

References

1. I.D. Chakeres and E.M. Belding-Royer, AODV Routing Protocol Implementation Design, Proceedings of the International Workshop on Wireless Ad hoc Networking (WWAN), Tokyo, Japan, March 2004, pp. 698-703.

2. C.C. Chiang, H.K. Wu, W. Liu and M. Gerla, Routing in Clustered Multihop, Mobile Wireless Networks With Fading Channel, Proceedings of IEEE Singapore International Conference on Networks SICON'97, pages 197-211, Singapore, Apr. 14-17, 1997.

3. C.R. Lin and M. Gerla, Adaptive Clustering for Mobile Wireless Networks, IEEE Journal on Selected Areas in Communications, Vol. 15, No. 7, pp. 1265-1275, September 1997.

4. DSR internet draft (2004) of Internet Engineering Task Force (IETF); http://www.ietf.org/internet-drafts/draft-ietf-manet-dsr-10.txt.

5. H. Lu and M. K. Denko, Reliable Data Storage and Dissemination in Mobile Ad hoc Network, Proceedings of International workshop on Theoretical and Algorithmic Aspects of Wireless Ad Hoc, Sensor and Peer-to-Peer Networks, June 2004, Chicago, USA.

6. I. Stojmenovic I. and J. Wu, Broadcasting and Activity Scheduling in Ad Hoc Networks, in: Ad Hoc Networking, S. Basagni, M. Conti, S. Giordano and I. Stojmenovic, eds., IEEE Press, 2004.

7. M. Gerla and J. Tsai, Multicluster, Mobile, Multimedia Radio Network, Wireless Networks, vol. 1, no. 3, 1995, pp. 255-65.

8. M. Jiang, J. LI, Y. C. Tay, Cluster Based Routing Protocol (CBRP) Functional Specification Internet Draft, draft- ietf-manet-cbrp.txt, work in progress, June 1999.

9. M.K. Denko, Analysis of Clustering Algorithms in Mobile Ad Hoc Networks, Proceedings of International Conf. on Wireless Networks, pp. 98-105, 2003.

10. P. Jacquet, P. Muhlethaler, A. Qayyum, A. Laouiti, L. Viennot, T. Clausen, Optimized Link State Routing Protocol Internet Draft, draft-ietf-manet-olsr-04.txt, work in progress, June 2001.

11. M. Chatterjee, S. K. Das and D. Turgut, An On-Demand Weighted Clustering Algorithm (WCA) for Ad-Hoc Networks, Proceedings of IEEE GLOBECOM 2000.

12. J. Broch, D. A. Maltz, D. B. Johnson, Y.-C. Hu and J. Jetcheva, A performance comparison of multi-hop wireless ad hoc network routing protocols, Proceedings of Mobile Computing and Networking (MOBICOM), 1998, pp. 85–97.

13. S. McCanne and S. Floyd, NS2; http://www.mash.cs.berkeley.edu/ns/.

14. F. Garcia, J. Solano and I. Stojmenovic, Connectivity based k-hop clustering in wireless networks, Telecommunication Systems, 22: 1-4, 205-220, 2003.

Adapting SLP To Ad-Hoc Environment

Janne Pietiäinen, Jussi Saarinen, Pekka Vuorela, and Tommi Mikkonen

Institute of Software Systems, Tampere University of Technology
P.O.Box 553, FIN-33101 Tampere, Finland
{pietiain,saarin24,pvuorela,tjm}@cs.tut.fi

Abstract

Ad-hoc networking, where network structure is created dynamically as nodes enter and leave the network, has recently become an active reseach subject. As majority of existing network protocols has been targeted to be used in an environment, where a static network configuration and the option of using registry repositories is enabled, they need tailoring for ad-hoc networking. In this paper, we discuss how Service Location Protocol (SLP) can be modified for such a dynamic environment starting from the requirements of applications that are to be run, and user's intentions. The adaptations we have implemented include passive service discovery where the amount of network traffic needed for service discovery can be reduced, security related features for improved privacy, gateway function that offers connectivity to external networks, and service discovery proxies that assist in the discovery of services between ad-hoc and fixed networks. The paper also addresses implementation of these features.

1 Introduction

While a majority of application level protocols that are readily available for networking are based on an assumption that a fixed structure exists, it is often possible to augment the protocols with extensions that enable ad-hoc networking. This approach is further supported with the option to use the same protocol in both ad-hoc and infrastructure assisted network, e.g. the Internet [8]. Furthermore, application requirements and the convenience of the user should be the driving force for new features.

One crucial issue in ad-hoc networking is the ability to locate services in the network. In this paper, we will use Service Location Protocol (SLP) [2] as a vehicle for studying the modifications needed for ad-hoc networking in

Please use the following format when citing this chapter:

Pietiäinen, J., Saarinen, J., Vuorela, P., Mikkonen, T., 2006, in International Federation for Information Processing (IFIP), Volume 212, Ad-Hoc Networking, ed. Al Agha, K., (Boston: Springer), pp. 99–117.

a fashion that is adequate for applications and convenient for the user. The extensions we have implemented to SLP for supporting operation in ad-hoc network include the following:

- Passive service discovery where network traffic can be reduced;
- Security related features for improved privacy;
- Gateway function that offers connectivity to external networks;
- Service discovery proxy function that assists in the discovery of services between ad-hoc and fixed networks.

The run-time environment of our implementation consists of laptop computers with built-in WLAN connectivity and 2.6 Linux kernels.

The rest of this paper discusses these issues as follows. Section 2 introduces SLP and its most relevant features from the viewpoint of ad-hoc networking. Sections 3, 4, 5, and 6 discuss the above improvements we have implemented using OpenSLP [9] as the baseline system. Then, Section 7 concludes the paper.

2 Service Location Protocol v2

The goal of Service Location Protocol (SLP) version 2 is to enable effortless autoconfiguration in fixed networks. In addition to discovering services of a certain type SLP also allows discovery based on service attributes. SLP also provides means for service browsing: a user may discover all available service types, search for attributes associated with a certain service type, and also issue a request for attributes of a single service. The use of DHCP and multicast in the initialization of SLP framework enable it to scale from a single local area network to an enterprise network. SLP supports also administrative grouping of services with so-called scopes.

SLP has three types of entities: User Agents (UA), Service Agents (SA), and Directory Agents (DA). UA represents a client that searches for services, SA represents a service provider, and DA operates as a centralized service repository. The most general operations and messages associated with them are illustrated in Figure 1.

UAs issue three multi- or broadcast Service Request (`SrvRqst`) messages during each discovery operation, to which SAs that have a matching service in their local databases respond with unicast Service Reply (`SrvRply`) message. If DAs are present SAs must register their services to them with unicast Service Registration (`SrvReg`) messages that DAs respond to with unicast Service Acknowledgement (`SrvAck`) messages. UAs are required to request services from them with unicast `SrvRqst` messages that DAs respond to with unicast `SrvRply` messages. UAs and SAs may actively search for DAs by issuing multi- or broadcast `SrvRqst` messages. DAs respond to these messages with unicast DA Advertisement (`DAAdvert`) messages. DAs may also periodically send multi- or broadcast `DAAdvert` messages to enable UAs and SAs to passively discover them.

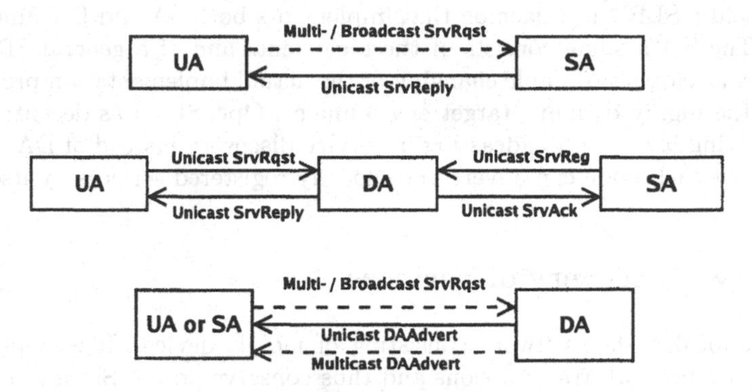

Fig. 1. SLP agents and most common messages in the protocol.

SLP has a security scheme that enables UAs to verify authenticity of SAs. It is aimed at preventing forged service information from being propagated in the framework. The scheme relies on signatures generated with public key cryptography. They are carried inside authentication blocks along with Security Parameter Index (SPI) strings that indicate which public key can be used to verify the signature. The signature is generated by forming a hash from relevant fields of a message with SHA-1 [3] and then encrypting it with the private DSA [4] key of the sender. These fields depend on the message type. The authentication block structure is illustrated in Figure 2.

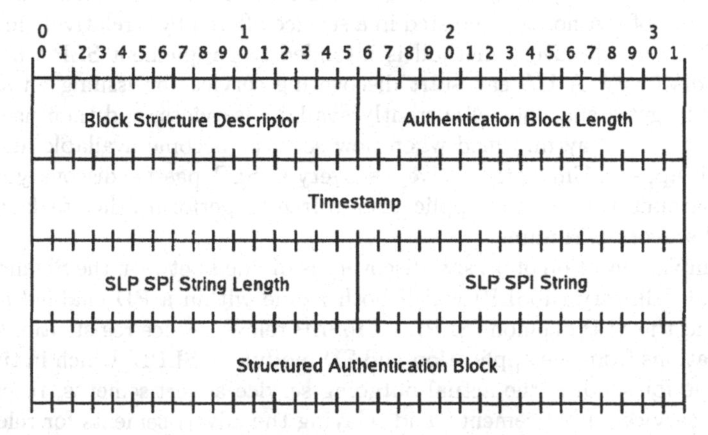

Fig. 2. The SLP Authentication Block.

We chose version 1.0.11 of OpenSLP C language implementation as the basis for our Service Discovery (SD) module. OpenSLP is an open source implementation of SLP version 2. It is divided to two main elements: libSLP and SLPD. LibSLP implements Service Location API [6] and provides UA functionality. SLPD is a daemon that implements both SA and DA functionalities. The SD module consists of these elements and of a general SD API that was developed to enable changing of the actual implementation protocol. Due to the highly dynamic target environment, OpenSLP was decentralized by modifying it to use broadcasting in service discovery instead of DAs. This means that each node can advertise its locally registered services by itself.

3 Passive Discovery of Services

In a link-local ad-hoc network consisting of mobile devices, it is important to minimize network transmissions and thus conserve power. Since the set of available services in an ad-hoc network is constantly changing as nodes enter and leave, a UA must repeat service discovery periodically to maintain an up to date list of available services. As we discarded the use of SLP DAs as such in the ad-hoc network, UAs can only discover new services by performing a service discovery and waiting for replies from SAs. In a limited bandwidth network with a large number of UAs, this may result in a significant constant network traffic, since each SLP service request consists of three broadcast messages from the UA and possibly a unicast service reply message from an SA.

Passive Discovery (PD) is an extension to SLP that was designed to ease the problem discussed above. It allows SAs to broadcast advertisements of their services so that UAs can passively accumulate a list of services they are interested in. A typical scenario for using PD would consist of a relatively large number of UA nodes interested in a service offered by a relatively few SA nodes. This new discovery method is intended to supplement SLP's normal "active" discovery. A UA can start discovering services by issuing an active discovery to get a snapshot of currently available services, and then use passive discovery to stay informed when new services become available and old services disappear. Unlike the active discovery in SLP, passive discovery is not a blocking operation, so the application is free to perform other tasks while passive discovery is running.

The implementation of passive discovery is divided between the SD module and the SLP library (libSLP) which both reside within a PD enabled application, and the SLP daemon (SLPD). LibSLP relays service registrations and deregistrations from the application and SD module to SLPD, which in turn is responsible for sending the actual outgoing service advertisements, receiving incoming service advertisements, and relaying the advertisements for relevant services back to the application via libSLP and SD module. LibSLP and local SLPD communicate through a TCP connection on the loopback interface.

LibSLP sends to SLPD special control messages encapsulated in a custom SLP message type (`CtrlMsg`) using SLPD's existing messaging infrastructure. SLPD communicates back to libSLP with similar control messages, but without the SLP encapsulation. These communications are all initiated by libSLP. One of our goals was to minimize the necessary changes to OpenSLP during the implementation process and furthermore, PD works very differently from its design, therefore libSLP was not directly modified. Parts of PD that are related to libSLP are implemented as a parallel system and compiled to the same library as the original OpenSLP implementation. SLPD was modified by adding a custom SLP message (`SrvAdvert`) for service advertisements and a new subsystem, which manages service listener registrations from libSLP, processes the incoming service advertisements, and sends the outgoing service advertisements as broadcast messages. The subsystem also contains two databases, one for outgoing service advertisements, i.e. services registered by local libSLP instances, and another for the service types that local libSLP instances are interested in so that received advertisements for matching services can be relayed to them. A single process can initiate multiple simultaneous passive discoveries, and multiple processes are able to utilize passive discovery within one device. Despite the modifications, PD enhanced OpenSLP should be able to interwork with other nodes running rfc2608 compliant SLPv2 implementations.

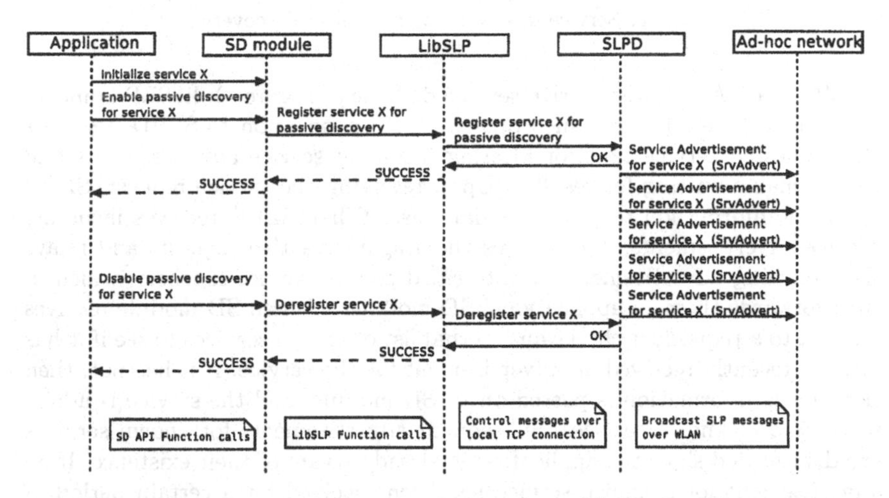

Fig. 3. Registering and deregistering services with Passive Discovery.

When a PD enabled application proceeds to register a service for passive discovery (Figure 3), it must first initialize a data structure representation of the service and then advice the SD module to enable passive discovery for the service. SD module relays the registration to libSLP which prepares a registration message, connects to SLPD, and transmits the message. It then waits for a reply message containing an error code from SLPD, which is returned to SD module and finally to the application. SLPD processes the service registration message, and, if all is in order, it stores the registration in a database for outgoing service advertisements. Services in the database are advertised at predefined intervals until either their lifetime expires or they are deregistered.

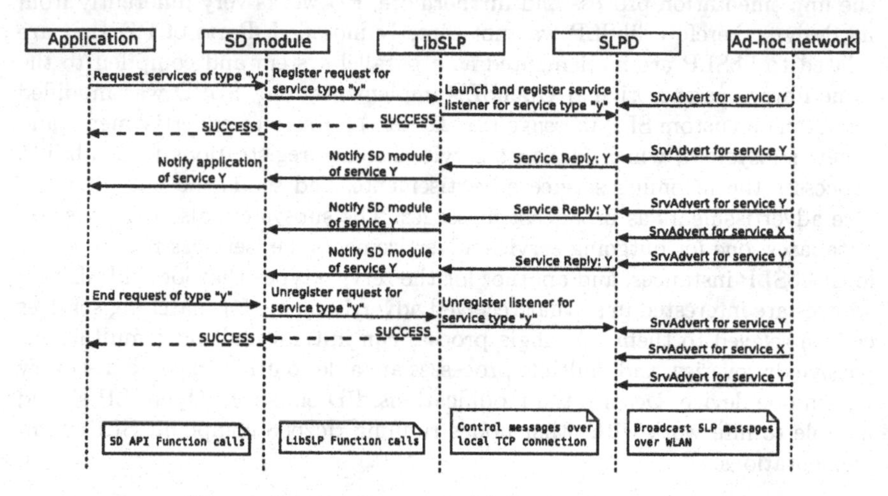

Fig. 4. Service discovery with Passive Discovery.

When a UA initiates passive service discovery (Figure 4), libSLP launches a service listener thread, which opens a TCP connection to SLPD, registers the requested service type for filtering incoming service advertisements and then remains waiting for results. Upon receiving the service request, SLPD adds the information to a request database. When SLPD receives incoming service advertisements, it compares them against active requests and relays the matching advertisements to interested parties service listeners, which in turn forwards them to applications' SD modules. When SD module receives a result to a request, it checks an internal list of known services to see if it has already recently received an advertisement for the service. If it has not, then the service information is passed on to SD module, and the service is added to the list of known services. Subsequent advertisements for known services are disregarded since the application is already aware of their existence. If no advertisement for a known service has been received for a certain period of time, SD module removes its information from the list of known services and notifies the application that the service disappeared.

In our tests PD worked well. However, due to time and resource constraints, the implementation contains some restrictions. Actively and passively advertised services are currently completely separate, i.e. two services can have an identical name but different attributes, lifetime etc. if one is made available for active discovery and the other for passive discovery. In a typical use scenario for PD there would be a large number of UA nodes looking for a service, such as a printer or a gateway, advertised by a relatively few SA nodes. Let us assume that we have an ad-hoc network with 3 SA nodes offering a gateway service, and 50 UA nodes interested in such services. If the nodes would try to discover the services using active model once every 30 seconds, the traditional SLP solution would consist of each UA node broadcasting an SLP service request message three times and SAs sending a unicast service reply message to each UA which amounts to 300 sent messages per discovery cycle. In contrast the same scenario with passive discovery, SA nodes advertising every 30 seconds, results in 3 sent messages per discovery cycle. If we assume that the sent messages are approximately 110 bytes in size per message, the passive model generates only 1% of the messages and data to be sent in this scenario in comparison to active model.

4 Secure Service Discovery

When compared to traditional fixed networks, an ad-hoc network imposes new security requirements for service discovery protocols. It is highly dynamic, more open and unsecure. Therefore protocols used in such environment need to be augmented with effective security features. We enhanced OpenSLP by enabling two security levels, "Authentication" and "Confidentiality". This system allows the whole scheme adapt to varying resource constraints of mobile nodes.

The implementation uses Authentication and Authorization (AA) module to store access control rules, certificates, and related keys. The AA module is together with cryptographic helper module that utilizes OpenSSL library 0.9.7d or later [10], used to perform all required cryptographic operations. It is described more thoroughly in [7]. To establish connection between each service and required security properties, we use abstract part of the SLP service type as a service ID. Due to this design choice, service browsing capabilities of SLP were disabled.

Authentication level enables two-way role based access control, authentication, and authorization between UA and SA. Furthermore, it protects integrity of most fields in the SLP messages and uses a logical timestamping system instead of the real-time system used by the original SLPv2 security scheme described in Section 2. This level was enabled for both active and passive discovery by adding SLP Extension blocks that carry modified SLP Authentication blocks to the end of `SrvRqst`, `SrvRply`, `AttrRqst`, `AttrRply` and `SrvAdvert` messages. Each modified SLP Authentication block contains sender's role dependent user ID. It is used together with the ID of the requested service by the receiver to determine which keys and access control rules should be used. The signature attached to the modified block is generated the same way as the signature in the original SLPv2 security scheme but it covers all fields of the message excluding the message length. The logical

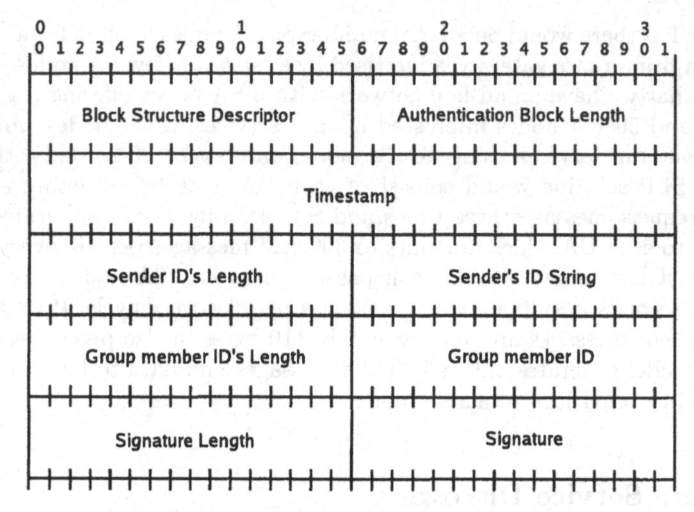

Fig. 5. The Modified SLP Authentication Block.

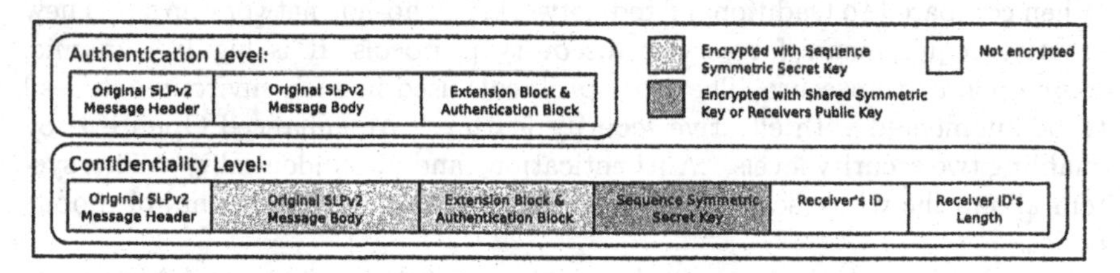

Fig. 6. The Message Structures on Authentication and Confidentiality Security Levels.

timestamping system uses positive integer valued timestamps that are increased each time a message is sent. All user ID and timestamp value pairs of each sent and received message are stored in a database for a limited lifetime. Since the timestamp and the sender's user ID are both signed this method enables nodes to detect replayed messages without synchronized clocks. They just need to compare user IDs and timestamps of received messages to the ones stored previously in its database. The limited lifetimes of timestamps also enable them to resolve situations in which one of them resets and thus loses its timestamp database. The structure of the modified Authentication block is illustrated in Figure 5.

Confidentiality level adds a partial message encryption on top of the features of the Authentication level. It was enabled only for active discovery and is therefore used with the same messages as the Authentication level excluding `SrvAdverts`. Message body and the Extension block are encrypted with a symmetric AES [5] key that is different for each message exchange sequence

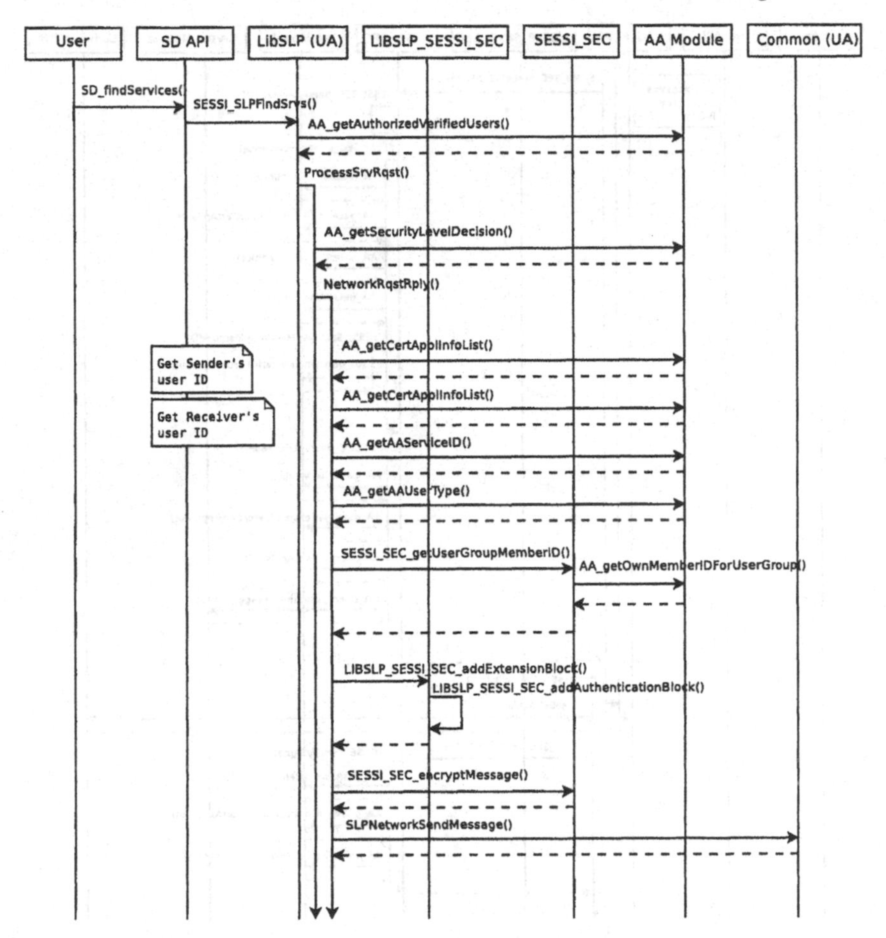

Fig. 7. The Secure Service Discovery Operation on UA Side Part 1.

consisting of one Request-Reply message pair. The symmetric key is then encrypted with the intended receiver's asymmetric RSA [11] public key. This lessens the computational load caused by the encryption process. Receiver's user ID is finally added to the end of the message accompanied by its length enabling receivers to identify messages intended for them and thus avoid unnecessary decryption attempts. The SLP header is not encrypted because it contains message length information that is required in message transmission over TCP connections. Furthermore information in it was not regarded too sensitive. The message structure is illustrated in Figure 6.

A detailed description of the Confidentiality level functionality on UA is described in Figures 7, 8, and 9. The first diagram shows how user initiates service discovery by calling function `SD_findServices`. Then users

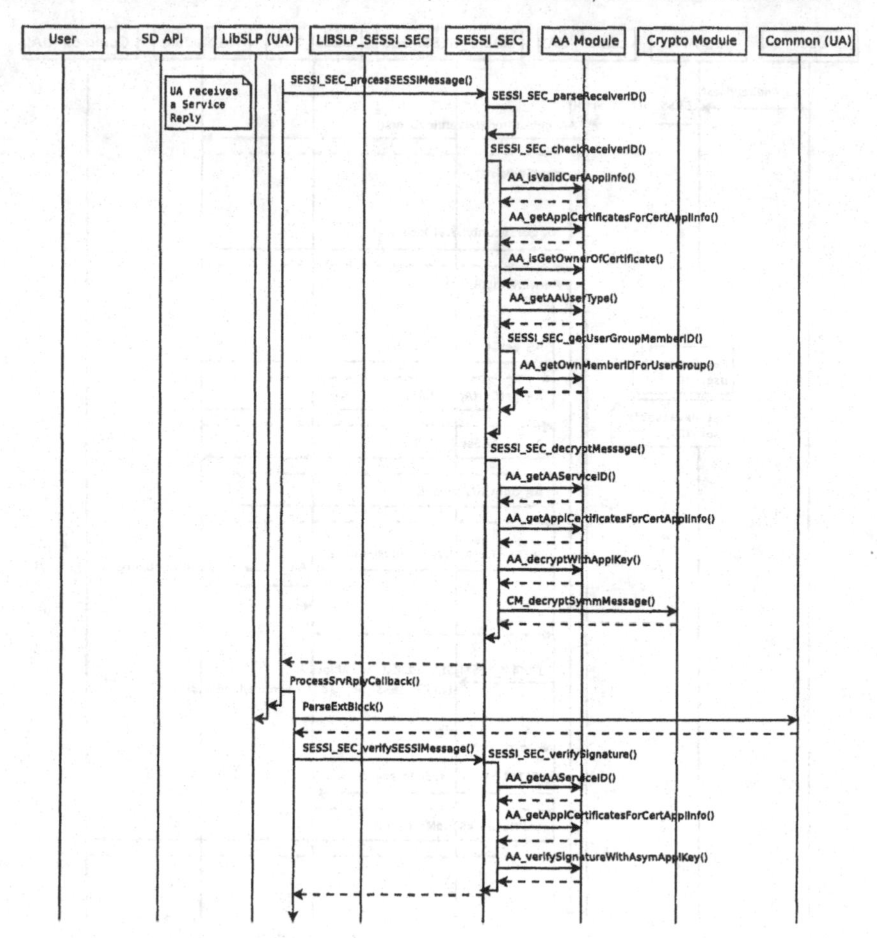

Fig. 8. The Secure Service Discovery Operation on UA Side Part 2.

who are authorized and verified are retrieved from AA module by calling `AA_getAuthorizedVerifiedUsers` and for each of them a security level is decided by calling for `AA_getSecurityLevelDecision`. Finally the Extension block is added to the message, it is then encrypted and receiver's user ID is attached to the end before transmission. The second diagram shows how `SESSI_SEC_processSESSIMessage` is used to determine the message security level and decrypt it. After this the signature of the message is verified with `SESSI_SEC_verifySESSIMessage`. The final diagram shows how the message timestamp is verified with `LIBSLP_SESSI_SEC_verifyTimestamp`, the sender's authorization to provide the service is checked with `SESSI_SEC_isAuthorizedForService`, and

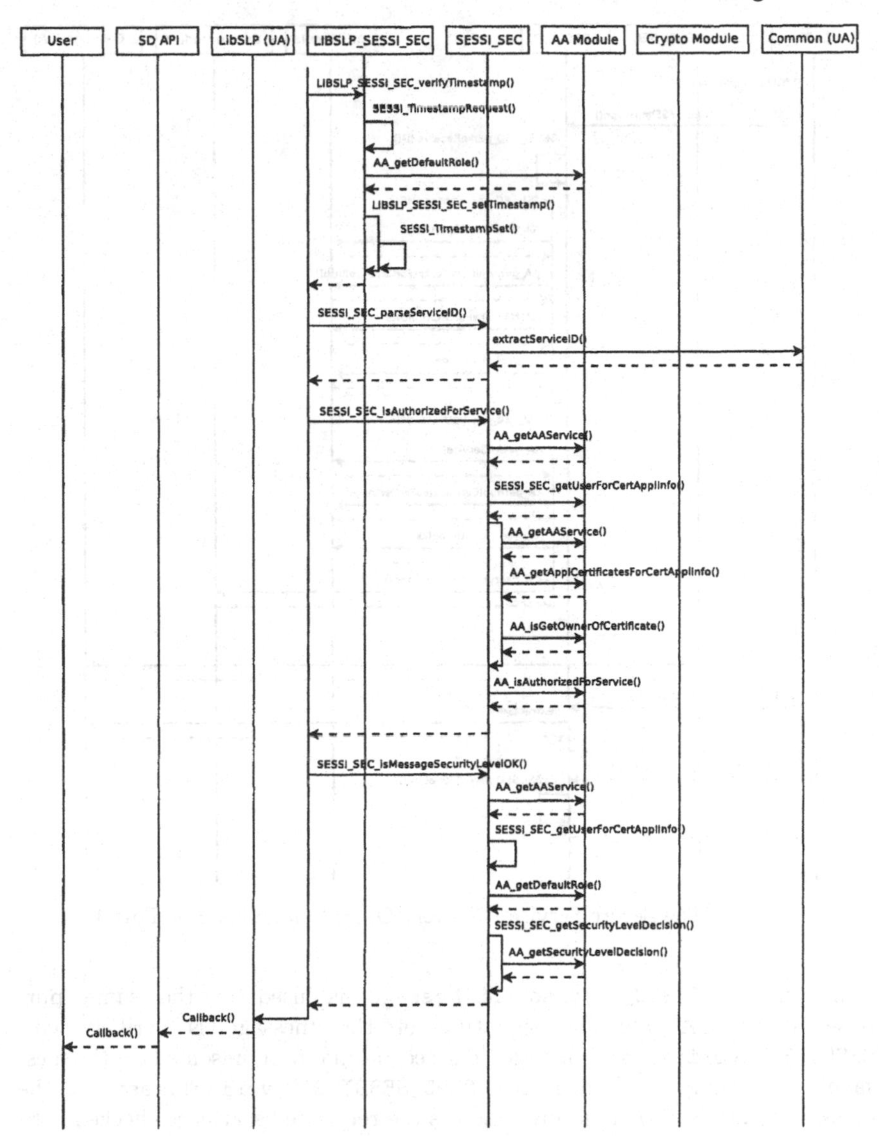

Fig. 9. The Secure Service Discovery Operation on UA Side Part 3.

`SESSI_SEC_isMessageSecurityLevelOK` is finally used to verify that the received message's security level is sufficient.

A detailed description of the Confidentiality level functionality on SA is described in a similar manner in Figures 10, 11, and 12. The first diagram shows what happens when SA receives a SLP message.

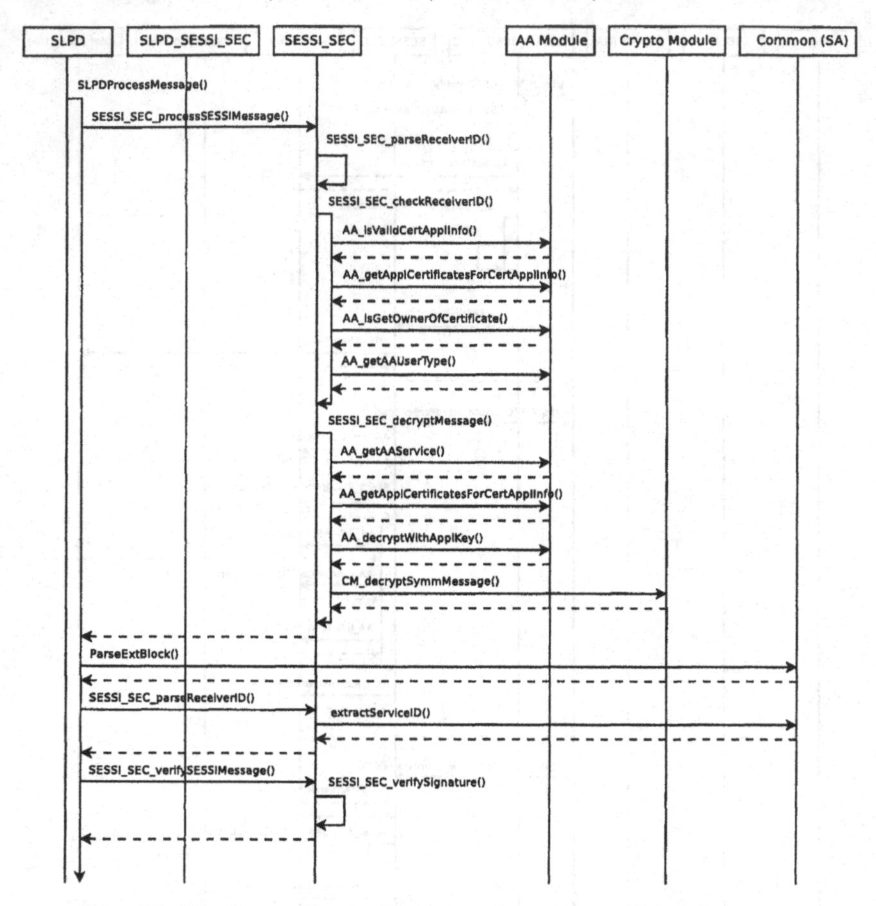

Fig. 10. The Secure Service Discovery Operation on SA Side Part 1.

Function `SESSI_SEC_processSESSIMessage` is used in the same purpose as in UA and the signature of the message is verified with `SESSI_SEC_verifySESSIMessage`. The second diagram presents how the message's timestamp is verified with `SLPD_SESSI_SEC_verifyTimestamp`, the message sender's authorization to access the requested service is checked with `SESSI_SEC_isAuthorizedForService` and the message security level is again verified with `SESSI_SEC_isMessageSecurityLevelOK`. After these steps the SA will check if the service is found in its database. The final diagram shows how `SLPD_SESSI_SEC_processOutgoingSESSIMessage` is called to perform necessary actions for the SA's reply message before it is transmitted. It adds the Extension block to the message, encrypts it, and adds the receiver's user ID to the end of the message.

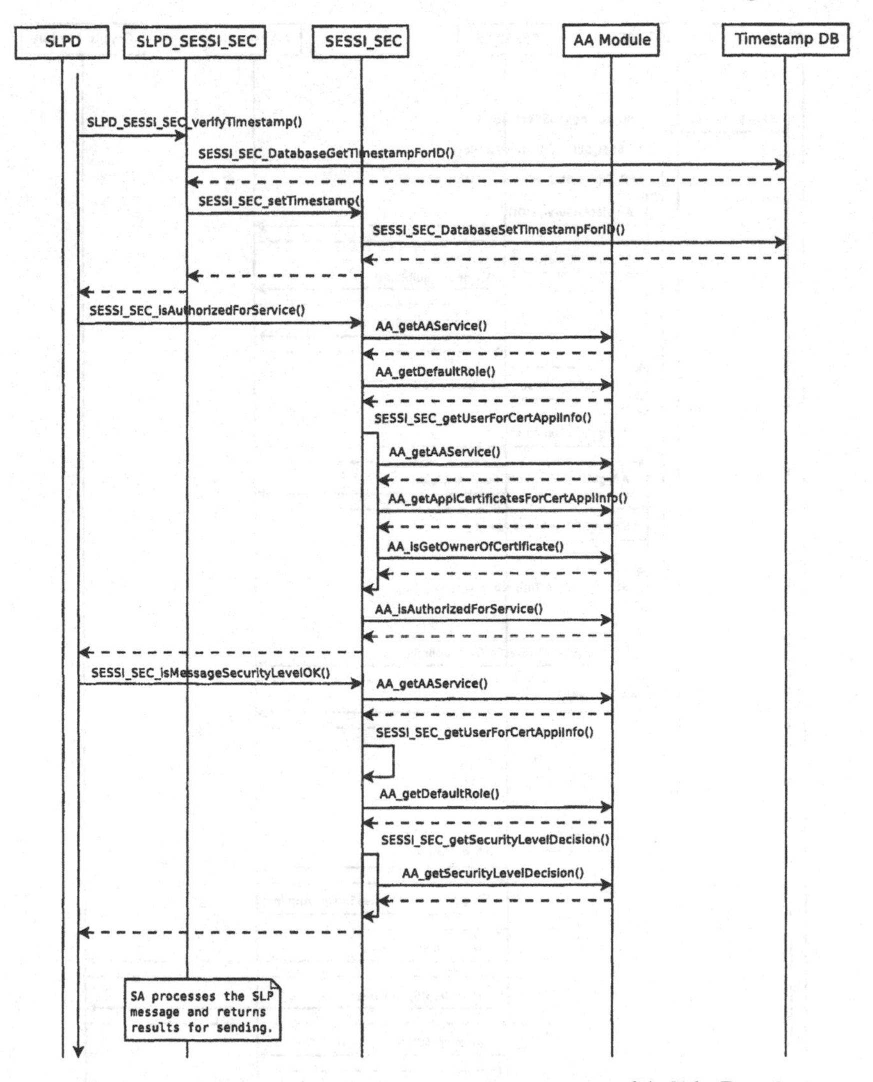

Fig. 11. The Secure Service Discovery Operation on SA Side Part 2.

Our implementation of the security extension achieves the goals we set and has been identified to cooperate with other components of our framework i.e. Passive Discovery and Gateway. It should also maintain interoperability with nodes running rfc2608 compatible SLPv2 implementations when no security features are used. On the downside the cryptographic operations can be fairly heavy for mobile devices with limited resources. However, since their capabilities are constantly expanding, this will most likely cease to be an issue in the near future. Our security scheme relies on predistributed certificates and

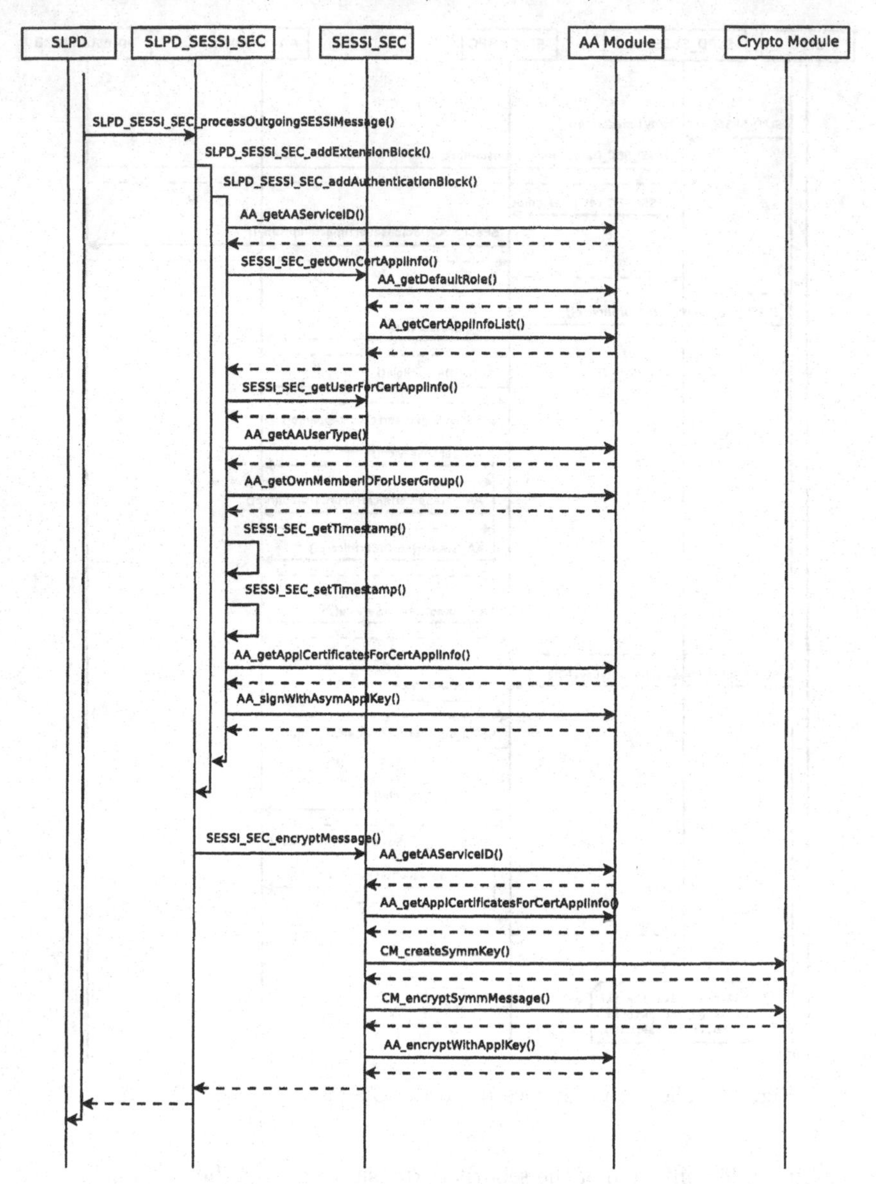

Fig. 12. The Secure Service Discovery Operation on SA Side Part 3.

keys due to the fact that use of distribution servers in ad-hoc network is not feasible. This characteristic imposes some flexibility constraints on our system that could be averted by relying on servers located in the fixed network. The approximate average message sizes in a typical ad-hoc network with 15 nodes are the following: 110 bytes when no security features are used, 300 bytes on Authentication level, and 480 bytes on Confidentiality level. The SHA-1 signature is 64 bytes long and represents almost half of the overhead on Authentication level. The rest of the overhead on that level is due to the Extension block and Authentication block structures. The additional overhead generated on the Confidentiality level is due to the AES encrypted data, the RSA encrypted 16 bytes long AES key, and the 10 bytes long receiver's ID that is added to the end with two byte length field.

Different approaches to create a secure service discovery infrastructure have been presented in several papers. Many of them rely on servers located in the fixed network which is an infeasible option in our target environment. Czerwinski et al. [1] present a scheme that relies on servers that form a dynamic hierarchy. Use of external servers to distribute certificates and provide access control information also suggests that all ad-hoc nodes should always have connection to the fixed network. Zhu et al. [12] have developed a scheme that supports also privacy protection and location dependent service discovery. Their solution uses proxies to support the mobile nodes which therefore must have a stable connection to the fixed network.

5 Gateway

Ad-hoc users may want to communicate with users in the fixed network or use the services available there. To achieve this goal a network gateway is needed. Due to the dynamic nature of ad-hoc environment, the gateway should not be a static entity, but rather any node willing to provide the service to others should be able to act as one. Therefore the gateway should itself be a service, discoverable in the ad-hoc network, and the client nodes should be able to easily start using it. The gateway should also be able to enforce access control on users. Furthermore, the nodes that have not been authorized for external connectivity should not be able steal it from authorized nodes. These requirements were addressed in our design of the gateway service.

Our implementation consists of two main components. Gateway Manager (GM) resides in the gateway node, and is responsible for initializing the gateway service along with negotiating and managing incoming client connections. Gateway Client (GC) resides in an ad-hoc node that wants to use the gateway, and takes care of automating the steps necessary for locating a suitable gateway, negotiating the connection parameters and configuring the node for external connectivity via the gateway. An example of an ad-hoc network with three gateways, one hosted by a mobile operator and the other two by nodes in the ad-hoc network, and client nodes is presented in Figure 13.

The gateway is highly customizable. Its modular design makes it enabled to launch and manage other related services, such as various proxy servers, DNS server etc. The method in which the connection between GM and GCs is established is defined as a gateway mode. GM can offer many different modes

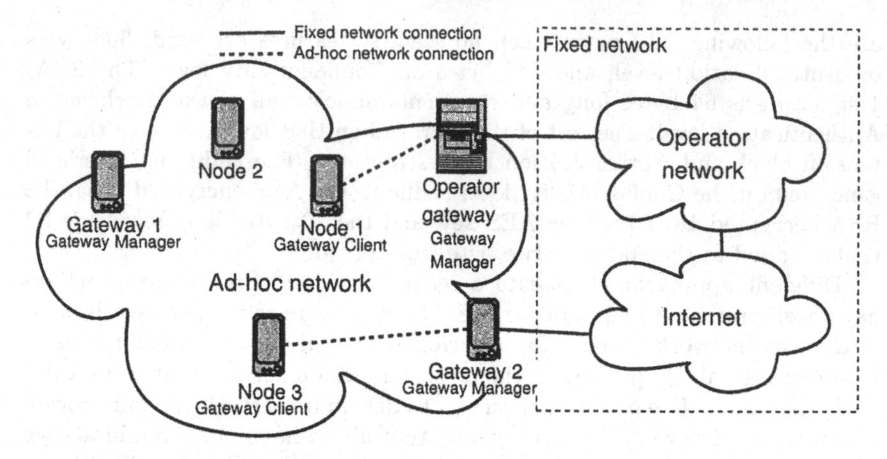

Fig. 13. An example of the gateway service.

which are then listed as attributes of the registered service. GC chooses one mode that it also supports, and begins the connection negotiations with GM. We implemented two modes. The first mode, named "open", is simply an open gateway without any access control. Any ad-hoc node can be configured to use the gateway operating in this mode. The second mode is named "secure". It implements a secure, encrypted tunnel from GC to GM, and requires users to be authenticated and authorized. All security features are implemented with the AA module. Gateways can be tagged with an operator string, which can then be used to target the gateway discovery to those that belong to a given operator. Commercial gateway services could authenticate and authorize customers using the security features in AA module.

Both GM and GC are command line tools, implemented as C language programs with shell script frontends. They both require an SLPD with our modifications to be running on the node. The gateway service worked well in our tests and supported other components, such as SD Proxy. It is also a good example of a service implemented with our platform.

6 Service Discovery Proxy

Connectivity established with our gateway between ad-hoc and fixed infrastructure network, allows using services from the other network. This creates a need to locate the services and therefore support from the service discovery service is necessary. To enable searches across the networks, we introduced a new entity called SD Proxy to the SLP network.

The first step in the implementation of searches between the networks was separating the services using SLP scopes. One scope was specified for the services that are globally available and another one for the services that are available to the ad-hoc network.

The SD Proxy was based on the Directory Agent of the basic SLP, and it resides on the gateway node. Ad-hoc nodes willing to use or offer services to the fixed network can set the gateway node to be used as a DA for the global SLP scope. DA Advertisement messages were not used because the information on SD Proxy availability is obtained in the search for gateways. Further, rogue nodes could advertise DA service for the ad-hoc scope and unwary nodes would direct their ad-hoc searches to them. When a DA for the global scope is set to be used by the UAs, queries using that scope will be unicast to the DA, while queries using ad-hoc scope are still broad- or multicast to the ad-hoc network. On the fixed network side it was assumed that the nodes willing to access ad-hoc network or offer services to it are configured with the address of the SD Proxy.

The use of an SD Proxy enables service registrations and searches to be made from both ad-hoc and fixed networks. However, the address space of the ad-hoc network is commonly link-local and non-routable. This means that services cannot be offered to the fixed network using the ad-hoc addresses. There are two solutions for this problem: giving nodes in the ad-hoc network additional global addresses which can be used to register services, or using Network Address Translation (NAT) for the services. Both of these solutions can be used simultaneously. In our implementation global addresses can be acquired from the gateway service when forming the connection to the fixed network, but the focus was on the NAT support.

To enable NAT for the ad-hoc services the SD Proxy was modified to create port forwards. This requires that the NATted service URLs include both address and port number, i.e. `<IP_address>:<port>`. The port number needs to be explicit so the SD Proxy knows where to forward the incoming traffic. The services made available to the fixed network have their original ad-hoc address replaced with the SD Proxy's fixed network address and the forwarded port number.

Separate scopes and the SD Proxy provided an elegant solution for service discovery support in heterogenous environment. Also compatibility with basic SLP was preserved from the fixed network side. A known problem with the current network setup is the need to configure fixed network nodes to use the SD Proxy. Also, the NAT support has limitations, e.g. services using multiple ports are difficult to advertise.

7 Conclusions

Many research papers on ad-hoc networking have contributed to low-level problems. However, the effect of ad-hoc environment on application level aspects and the convenience to user has been studied less. Further motivation for our work is on the option to use the same protocols in ad-hoc and infrastructure organized networks, but with certain new functions that are of crucial importance for ad-hoc networking. In this paper, we have addressed service discovery from this viewpoint.

As the sample service discovery protocol, we used SLP. Furthermore, we started with an assumption that link-local communication will be used to focus the work to the actual service discovery. The extensions we have identified are:

- Passive service discovery in order to avoid excessive communication when a group of nodes look for services;
- Security considerations restrict the visibility and availability of services;
- Connectivity to an external network via a node in the ad-hoc network;
- Service discovery proxy function that can be used for locating services in the ad-hoc network from some other network, and vice versa.

Furthermore, we discussed how we have implemented these features in an open source SLP implementation.

Like in any research, there are a number of topics that could be further studied. One option is how to enable the use of several nodes as a gateway at the same time or in turns for improved bandwidth. This would then allow the users to offer connectivity in turns to e.g. share the costs of the external connectivity. Also the SD Proxy could be enhanced by making it more proxy-like with a static DA in the fixed network. This would allow dynamic fixed network addresses for SD Proxies and ease having several SD Proxies on the network. No changes would be needed to the nodes in the ad-hoc network. Another direction for future study is to widen the scope of the approach to e.g. multihop networks.

References

1. Steven E. Czerwinski, Ben Y. Zhao, Todd D. Hodes, Anthony D. Joseph, and Randy H. Katz. An architecture for a secure service discovery service. In *Mobicom '99*, Seattle, Washington, USA, August 1999. ACM.
2. Guttman E., Perkins C., Veizades J., and Day M. Service location protocol, version 2. Technical report, The Internet Engineering Task Force, June 1999.
3. D. Eastlake and P. Jones. US Secure Hash Algorithm 1 (SHA1). RFC 3174, The Internet Society, September 2001.
4. FIPS. Digital Signature Standard (DSS). Standard 186, National Institute of Standards and Technology (NIST), May 1994.
5. FIPS. Advanced Encryption Standard (AES). Standard 197, National Institute of Standards and Technology (NIST), November 2001.
6. Kempf J. and Guttman E. An API for service location. RFC 2614, The Internet Engineering Task Force, June 1999.
7. L. Källström, J. Saarinen, and S. Liimatainen. Secure service discovery protocol implementation for wireless ad-hoc networks. In *1st International Wireless Summit, Aalborg, 17-22 September*, 2005.

8. S. Leggio, S. Liimatainen, J. Manner, T. Mikkonen, J. Saarinen, and A. Ylä-Jääski. Towards service interworking among ad-hoc networks and the internet. In *14th IST Mobile and Wireless Communications Summit, Dresden, 19-23 June*, 2005.
9. OpenSLP Project Group website. At `http://www.openslp.org`, April 2004.
10. The OpenSSL project. OpenSSL: The open source toolkit for SSL/TLS.
11. R.L.Rivest, A.Shamir, and L. Adleman. A Method for Obtaining Digital Signatures and Public-Key Cryptosystem. *Communications of the ACM*, 21(2):120–126, 1978.
12. Feng Zhu, Matt Mutka, and Lionel Ni. Splendor: A secure, private, and location-aware service discovery protocol supporting mobile services. In *First IEEE International Conference on Pervasive Computing and Communications (PerCom'03)*, pages 235–242, March 2003.

A Design Framework for Wireless Sensor Networks

Mats Neovius, Lu Yan
Åbo Akademi University, Department of Information Technologies,
Lemminkäisenkatu 14, FIN-20520 Turku Finland.
{mneovius, lyan}@abo.fi

Abstract. Wireless sensor networks (sensornets) are wirelessly communicating smart gadgets with the capability of sensing the environment. With the immense applicability of sensornets, there is an increasing need of a general organisational and architectural development framework for sensornet systems. This paper outlines an abstract framework for modelling responsibilities and tasks to sets of nodes according to their vocation. These guidelines are presented with the intension to ease reasoning about a sensornet as a system, and its applications.

1. Introduction

The amount of research conducted regarding wireless sensor networks (sensornets) is emerging. The concept of sensornets envisions a new ambitious paradigm of computing, brought forth by Weiser in 1991 [1], usually referred to as ubiquitous or pervasive computing.

Large scale sensornets are complex and challenging environments in which to develop software. The applicable areas for ubiquitous sensors providing raw unprocessed data about the environment are vast. Moreover, sensornets constitute several Internet-era challenges, making them interesting for the research community as well as for industry.

Typically, a sensornet comprises a set of energy constraint nodes which, in addition to amorphous Ad Hoc networks, relies on collaboration with each other. The main advantage, from a research point of view, compared to more efficient computing units is that the sensornet node has only a limited number of reasonably executable tasks, which it is designed for.

Please use the following format when citing this chapter:

Neovius, M., Yan, L., 2006, in International Federation for Information Processing (IFIP), Volume 212, Ad-Hoc Networking, ed. Al Agha, K., (Boston: Springer), pp. 119–127.

The future potential of sensornets is immense. Sensornets provide a sensible transition towards ubiquity and pervasiveness, which might very well be the next step in the development of computing gadgets. If so, sensornets might trigger a new "era" in computing, like the one entered when the computers shrank to desktop size.

Only human imagination is the limit for what sensornets ubiquity can assist in and/or do for us when brought around and integrated to our environment and daily life. In order for this to happen, the units must be miniaturised. In minimised gadgets, the energy supply constitutes a significant portion of the total size. Hence, there are two ways to proceed; decreasing either energy consumption or battery size.

Many ideas and implementations utilising the ubiquity of a sensornet have already been presented, one of the most well known is the smart home with the example refrigerator automatically composing the shopping list [2]. Technically, this has been done and is available. The questions arising today address what humans are willing to learn, use and long for. Consumers have comprised as the test bed for the past era of computing development and a kind of technical saturation might come up. Consequently, a transition towards ubiquity, where the system filters relevant from irrelevant data, and assist in decision making is likely to be about.

The sensornet could thereby be viewed as a wirelessly inter-communicating encapsulated environment harvesting raw data with its sensors. The sensors extract measurements from its surroundings, that might be further refined in others, for that specific task dedicated units. The sensornet, as an architecture, ends where the data is passed to gadgets not fulfilling the criterions of a wireless sensor. Because the encapsulated nature and limited functionality, it is also attractive to make an effort to reuse code or parts of it.

Research regarding sensornets is often interdisciplinary, usually concerning at least the areas of computer science and electrical engineering. There are plenty of unsolved issues in various fields of study within the area. From a software point of view, there is a demand for novel ideas in areas concerning human-computer interaction, energy-saving, optimisation, self-organisation, information composition, query propagation and miniaturisation to mention a few. Consequently, sensornets assert the extreme of many problems in computing related disciplines.

We argue that in order for achieving a breakthrough in sensornets, a consensus regarding a general system framework for declaring which computations are performed on which parts of the network is necessary. If done, the network could apply the most suitable existing method for each situation.

The organisation of this paper is as follows. In section 2, we discuss the fundamental building blocks, identifying sensornets, from a perspective of hardware, functionality and middleware. The proposed system design framework is presented in section 3. Finally, we conclude the paper in section 4.

2. Fundamental building blocks of sensornets

The amount of separate building blocks of any system depends on the level abstraction it is viewed at. In this paper, we take a high-level of abstraction in order to keep the ideas scalable and as general as possible, to fit sensornets from small stationary static environments to vast dynamic mobile networks.

A sensornet can be viewed as an encapsulated end-to-end mini-world with limited energy. The nodes energy capacity varies within the network. Moreover, for a sensornet to supply any service, it must have an interface for external data consumption. If the system provides means for bidirectional data flow, an overlay structure to organise query propagation is required.

The aim of the system is providing a method to obtain raw data and fuse it with appropriate context. Because the sensornet is a raw data provider for a service, it must address all the different parts; interface, propagation, data extraction and so forth. Moreover, each node must be able to function independently and collaborating when suitable. Thereby, dynamicity is a core issue to address. The highest priority for the system is to reply any proper query origin and deliver the requested service to the inquirer.

2.1 Hardware blocks in sensornets

Unfortunately, there is no commonly agreed definition for what a wireless sensor is, and what it is not. In order for providing a system framework for the sensornet to be applied on, an explicit definition is demanded. Deducing a definition from the meanings of the words wireless, sensor and network seems right, [3] described the concept as a simple equation which is supported by [4]:

"Sensing + CPU + Radio = Thousands of potential applications" [3]

[5] adds to this equation a power unit. However, this definition covers, for example, a laptop with WLAN capability that adjusts its display contrast to the environments luminosity, which was not the original idea of the equation.

With the compelling need of a definition, we agree on the equation, except for the term "radio" which we would like to replace with "wireless transceiver". The reason is that wirelessness does not necessarily equal radio-transmission. Moreover, we would like to add that a wireless sensor is usually a stand-alone small-scale device. Hence, this is the definition to be used throughout this paper.

The constituting compulsory blocks are thereby the clear-cut power unit, sensor(s), CPU (and consequently some memory) and the transceiver(s). Sensing capabilities are restricted by energy consumption and the physical size. The CPU power is restricted by the energy source capacity and should respond to the given sensor's needs, e.g. measuring temperature do not require much CPU power. The transmitter is the single device usually consuming the majority of the available energy. Consequently, energy efficient routing in self organising mesh networks attracts researchers focus. All of these units are connected to each other on a motherboard-like circuit, usually referred to as the *mote*.

2.2. Functional classification of sensornets

As described earlier, the sensors sense the environment and produce raw data, for example, "+20°C". Naturally, the amount of information this data provide without the context of location is limited. The context is added by another sensor connected to the same mote or by data composition[1] with data from another device. Regardless of the extent the data is composed of and refined to, it must finally be representable and becomes relevant only when it is sufficient enough to influence a decision. However, still at this era of ubiquity, the decision is often made by a human, on the top of the system hierarchy.

As stated, data without context destitute information and distinct raw data seldom have context. Considering sensornets, the context of the specific data becomes crucial. Any unit composing the data possesses additional knowledge that combined increases the amount of information. For example, in a simplified case, three distinct measurements are composed to provide relevance, temperature, location and time that might origin from distinct nodes. Unless this device is the gateway, there is a system hierarchy consisting of at least two levels.

In order to efficiently utilise available energy, moderate sized sensornets routing employs multi-hop protocols [6, 7, 8]. In many ways, the protocols resemble ideas used in decentralised mesh networks. The network is often fragmented and "cluster heads" are appointed [9]. Consequently, the framework must handle systems that are hierarchical to an undefined depth as well as flat networks, in order to preserve scalability and generality.

If the sensornet nodes are heterogeneous, with nodes dedicated for a specific tasks such as communication (more energy), locating (for example, GPS), their special capabilities should be taken into account when initialising the network. Thereby, we classify nodes in a sensornet as follows:

1) Sensing node(s)
2) En route node(s)
3) Gateway node(s)

The sensing nodes are the "bottommost" nodes in the system hierarchy, the ones sensing the environment. The en route nodes are devices that act as cluster heads or forwarders of the data between its endpoints, and possibly aggregate[2] or/and compose the raw data. The obligation of acting as an en route node is, due to energy capacity, traffic load and network lifetime, in some cases altered between nodes according to the routing method. Consequently, the nodes classified in class 1 and 2 should vary for efficient utilisation of network resources. The gateway node(s)[3] is responsible for the "topmost" level of a sensornet and according to the definition, the upper boundary. This node acts as the interface towards an external data consumer, for example, the Internet.

[1] Composition: Two distinct parts of data combined to be one.

[2] Aggregation: Two distinct parts of data embedded with their key characteristics into one packet in order to save energy consumed in transmission.

[3] Gateway node: Considered written singular though possibly plural occurrence.

The gateway is the interface to the outside. Any node can belong to one or more classes at the same time. In special cases, one node can constitute in all taxonomy, meaning that the gateway's underlying network size is one.

2.3. Middleware and components

Middleware technologies in a broad sense, which covers operating systems and virtual machines, query processing, data composition and aggregation, resource awareness and energy harvesting, overlay routing and communication management, etc., have the potential to ease and accelerate software development in sensornet environments by offering simplified application-level views that abstract over factors such as the above.

As a supporting example, as well as prevailing paradigm, lots of experimental sensornets today run on top of TinyOS [10] and TinyDB [11]. The first, TinyOS, is an open-source operating system specially trimmed for sensornets. It features a component-based architecture which enables rapid prototyping and implementing sensornet applications via providing higher-level programming abstractions. The latter, TinyDB, is a query processing system for extracting information from sensornets made from sensors running TinyOS. It features a SQL-like query interface technology which alleviates the complex of writing low-level C codes and supports traditional database queries with auxiliary sensornet parameters.

3. The design framework

A system design framework for sensornets is longed for, as Culler et. al. conclude: "We contend that the main obstacle limiting progress in sensornet work is the lack of an architecture. A sensor network architecture would factor out the key functionalities required by applications and compose them in a coherent structure, while allowing innovative technologies and applications to evolve independently" [12]. [5] describes the sensor networks protocol stack as 2-dimensional with six communication layers and three management planes.

We agree with both, but in addition tackle the issue from a "horizontal" view of node vocation, making the framework 3-dimensional. The 3-dimensionality is necessary in order to give the sensornet an overview of the system's status and adapt to it. Adjustment to prevailing situation is made by altering the routing method, changing functionality between reactive, proactive and hybrid protocols or by any other modification.

The strength is the utilisation of the core quality of each node, "because any specific context can often be provided by a variety of different types of sensors and used by different applications" [13]. We describe a general system framework for implementation on any sensornet platform that meets with the constraints described in section 2.

3.1. The layers

To factor out the key functionalities, a viable sensornet system design framework must partition the model to a structure with "black-boxes". This way the developer needs to know only the task and the interface of the box in order to develop a replacement, use, test or evaluate it. "To become a reusable asset, it is not enough to start with a monolithic design of a complete solution and then partition it into fragments Instead, descriptions have to be carefully generalised to allow for reuse in a sufficient number of different contexts" [14]. Thus, developers are able to tune the sensornet upon the system framework according to their preferences.

As described in section 2.2 and 3, the framework have *n* horizontal and at least 3 vertical layers. Figure 1, deduced from [15], illustrates the vertical layers and horizontal node classes combined with the diagonal execution ellipse. [5] motivated the 2-dimensionality on each sensor, which is considered.

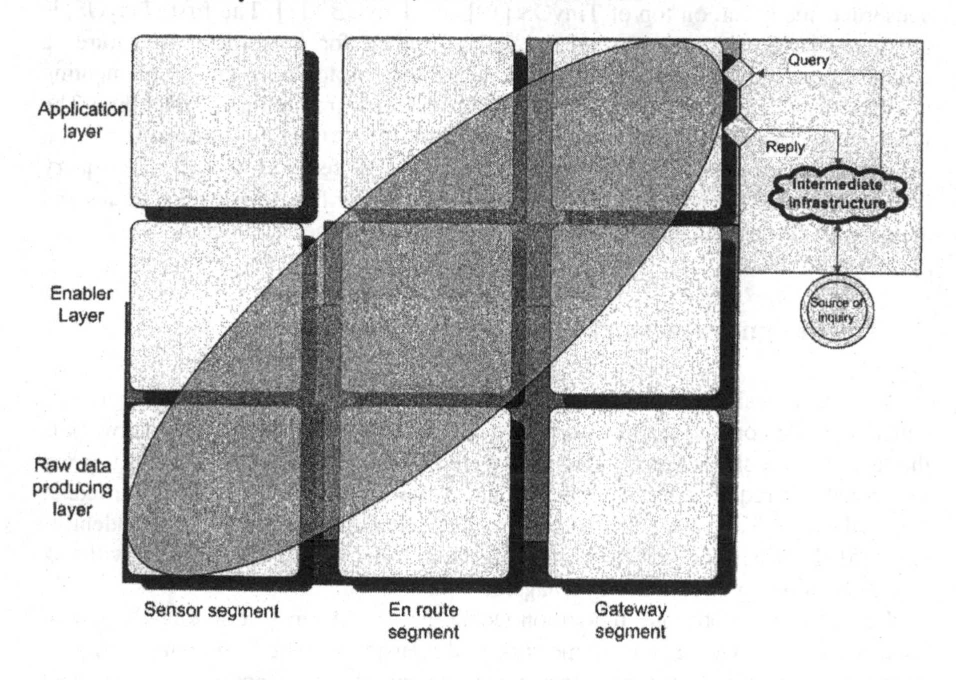

Figure 1. The sensornet system framework

The grey-shaded angular areas illustrate the main responsibility for the sensors belonging to them, where the dark grey area constitutes the sensing nodes, the grey the en route nodes and the light-grey the gateway node. Moreover, Figure 1 should be interpreted so that each item is considered belonging primarily on the "layer" and secondarily to the "segment". The unified sensing system model presented in [16] supports the idea, layers and tasks meet in the ellipse.

A contribution in this framework is that all sensors do not necessarily provide data needed for replying a query, nor does all function as en route nodes. Consequently, the en route nodes can decide based on the query whether their underlying sensing nodes can provide relevant information and thereby, decide to forward or not.

Moreover, the framework in Figure 1 could, if needed, illustrate a subset of a complete sensornet system and there might potentially be several such models in parallel interconnected by, for example, the Internet. As an example, one subset might concern the heating adjustments in a building whilst another is responsible for logging the temperature near by. Combining the data from these two completely distinct systems refines the information.

The ellipse describes issues the system framework emphasises on the different classes. Vaidya et al. [16] present a strict hierarchy for sensor management and configuration used for solving a tracking problem. The model is applicable with minor modifications for different applications and supports the ellipse. Huebesher and McCann describe a middleware's context provision, which is a three level hierarchy [13]. Additional service providers and refiners could easily be added in this scenario supporting the ellipse of node vocation.

3.2. Query propagation and reply composition

Query propagation and reply composition are the things affecting QoS (quality of service) and quality of context the most. Consequently, the system robustness is preserved during these phases. In addition to providing QoS, propagation and composition should preserve energy by merging into packets payloads, reducing transmission. According to studies, the ratio of sending one bit compared to one CPU-instruction is in WINS NG 2.0 nodes around 1 to 1400 [17] and usually considered to be approximately 1 to 1000. Hence, it is motivated to emphasise the critical parts affecting consumption of the scarce resources, the en route nodes.

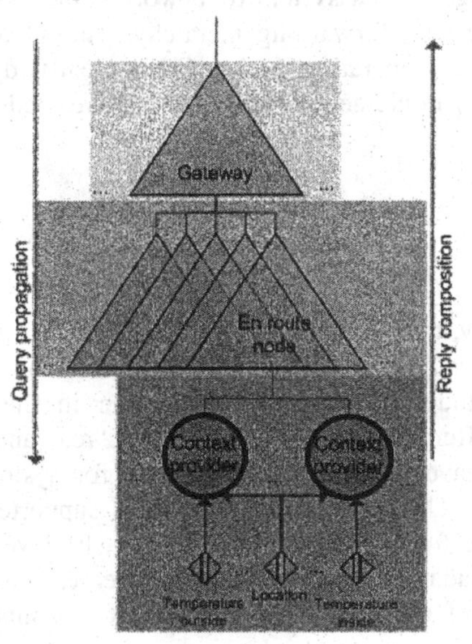

Figure 2. Data propagation / composition

Query propagation and reply composition are opposite to each others and can theoretically take place anywhere en route, see Figure 2. Fundamentally, the inquirer expects providing of announced service, whether it is a user or a layer above. The query must be properly propagated down the layers until replied or reaching the "bottom" and the raw data replied composed with context, providing relevance.

Figure 2 illustrates how data is propagated and composed in a 3-level hierarchical system. The context providers provide distinct raw data that is in the en route node composed to increase information. The gateway finally functions as the interface. Placing this figure diagonally on the framework provides an illustration of node vocation and executing tasks.

A reply for the query can also be processed at any node en route. This depends on the context-awareness method used. According to Chen and Kotz [18], two different kinds exist and they defined them as following:

> Active context awareness: an application automatically adapts to discovered context, by changing the application's behavior.
>
> Passive context awareness: an application presents the new or updated context to an interested user or makes the context persistent for the user to retrieve later.

[18]

The similarity of these to reactive and proactive data passing modes in sensornets is evident. Recalling the examples mentioned in section 3.1, adopting the heating to temperature variations would be active context awareness whilst logging outside temperature is an example of passive.

An additional strength of our system framework is the possibility to differentiate between layers in the data forwarding hierarchy. The advantage is that different layers can adopt different operating modes. Consequently, dynamically adapting to application demands by implementing active or passive modes in a system can save energy.

4. Conclusions

We argue that today, the main task is to harvest as much information as possible. However, with the development and ubiquity of processing units, we anticipate an overwhelming magnitude of available information in the future. Thereby, the challenge will be to differentiate between "data" and "relevant data".

In this work we have presented a framework for systematic development of sensornet applications. The proposed framework is supported by numerous works and binds together the fundamental points in them. Its level of abstraction covers known demands and adapts to new situations. It eases reasoning and provides a method upon which to facilitate the development of new innovative applications in sensornets.

References

1. M. Weiser, The Computer for the Twenty-First Century, Scientific American, Sept., 1991.
2. A. C. Huang, B. C. Ling, S. Ponnekanti, A. Fox, Pervasive Computing: What is it Good for?, In Workshop on Mobile Data Management (MobiDE) in conjunction with ACM MobiCom, 1999.
3. J. Hill, System Architecture for Wireless Sensor Networks, Ph.D. Thesis, UC Berkeley, 2003.
4. A. Wadaa, S. Olariu, L. Wilson, M. Eltoweissy, K. Jones, Training a wireless sensor network, Mobile Networks and Applications, Volume 10, Issue 1-2, February 2005, Pages: 151 – 168.
5. I. Akyildiz, W. Su, Y. Sankarasubramaniam, E. Cayirci, A survey on sensor networks, Communications Magazine, IEEE, Volume: 40, Issue: 8, Aug 2002, page(s): 102- 114, ISSN: 0163-6804.
6. A. Woo, T. Tong, D. Culler, Taming the Underlying Challenges of Reliable Multhop Routing in Sensor Networks, In Proc. ACM Conference on Embedded Networked Sensor Systems (SenSys'03), 2003.
7. W. Ye, J. Heidemann, D. Estrin, An Energy-Efficient MAC Protocol for Wireless Sensor Networks, In Proc. IEEE INFOCOM'02, 2002.
8. W. R. Heinzelman, A. Chandrakasan, H. Balakrishnan, Energy-efficient Communication Protocols for Wireless Microsensor Networks, In Proc. IEEE HICSS'00, 2000.
9. Jamal N. Al-Karaki, Ahmed E. Kamal, Routing techniques in wireless sensor networks: a survey, IEEE Wireless Communications, ISSN: 1536-1284, Dec. 2004, Volume: 11, Issue: 6, page(s) 6- 28.
10. TinyOS: http://www.tinyos.net/ .
11. TinyDB: http://telegraph.cs.berkeley.edu/tinydb/ .
12. David Culler, Prabal Dutta, Cheng Tien Ee, Rodrigo Fonseca, Jonathan Hui, Philip Levis, Joseph Polastre, Scott Shenker, Ion Stoica, Gilman Tolle, Jerry Zhao, Towards a Sensor Network Architecture: Lowering the Waistline, Tenth Workshop on Hot Topics in Operating Systems (HotOS X), Eldorado Hotel, Santa Fe, NM, USA, June 12–15, 2005.
13. Markus C. Huebscher, Julie A. McCann, Adaptive middleware for context-aware applications in smart-homes, ACM International Conference Proceeding Series; Vol. 77 archive, Proceedings of the 2nd workshop on Middleware for pervasive and ad-hoc computing, Toronto, Ontario, Canada 2004, Pages: 111 – 116, ISBN:1-58113-951-9.
14. Clemens Szyperski, Dominik Gruntz, Stephan Murer, Component Software - Beyond Object-Oriented Programming, Second Edition Addison-Wesley / ACM Press, 2002. ISBN 0-201-74572-0.
15. Jurgen Ziegler, End-to-End Concepts Reference Model, Nokia, 2003.
16. D. Vaidya, J. Peng, L. Yang, J. W. Rozenblit, A Framework for Sensor Management in Wireless and Heterogeneous Sensor Network, ecbs, 12th IEEE International Conference and Workshops on the Engineering of Computer-Based Systems (ECBS'05), 2005, pp. 155-162.
17. V. Raghunathan, C. Schurgers, Sung Park, M.B. Srivastava, Energy-aware wireless microsensor networks, Signal Processing Magazine, IEEE Volume 19, Issue 2, Mar 2002 Page(s):40 – 50. 2002.
18. Guanling Chen, David Kotz, A Survey of Context-Aware Mobile Computing Research, Department of Computer Science, Dartmouth College, Dartmouth Computer Science Technical Report TR2000-381.

IEEE 802.11 Throughput and Delay Analysis for mixed real time and normal data traffic

Matias Arenas P. and Walter Grote H.
Department of Electronic Engineering, Federico Santa Maria Technical U.
Avenida España 1680, Valparaíso, Chile

Abstract. IEEE 802.11 based network analysis has been largely focused on throughput performance. There has been a growing concern to provide quality of service (QoS) to this protocol suite, the result of which has been the considerable work towards the formulation of the IEEE 802.11e and IEEE 802.11n versions. One important aspect to consider is performance for real time applications like voice over IP (VoIP). In this paper we focus on performance issues of delay and throughput as a function of packet size, initial contention window size settings and the number of active terminals competing for access to the network, when some terminals provide VoIP services, while others transfer data. The simulation model developed using Network Simulator 2 (ns-2) is first validated comparing published results for throughput and delay, to then proceed to perform analysis on Ad hoc networks that will carry mixed VoIP and data traffic. We determine that tuning the initial and final contention window settings on the real time terminals does have a great impact on delay, throughput and packet loss in individual and on the network performance when in congestion.

1 Introduction

Wireless access technologies have experienced a tremendous growth in the last decade. End users have been attracted by various aspects of it, the most important being mobility. The IEEE 802.11 protocol provides wideband data services using small coverage cells, with distances ranging from 50m in in-building applications to about 300m in open spaces. These networks may work as pure random access networks using the DCF – Distributed Coordination Function – mode. Another possibility is to combine random access (DCF) and transmission scheduling (PCF:

Please use the following format when citing this chapter:

Arenas P., M., Grote H., W., 2006, in International Federation for Information Processing (IFIP), Volume 212, Ad-Hoc Networking, ed. Al Agha, K., (Boston: Springer), pp. 129–139.

Point Coordination Function) for delay sensitive information. Unfortunately, most implementations only consider DCF operation. Therefore it is interesting to analyze if delay sensitive information like VoIP can be delivered satisfactorily in networks that will supply data and voice transmission services using DCF. Random access can be used in peer to peer - also known as Ad Hoc – or centralized – also known as infrastructure – kind of networks, [1]. Considerable effort has been made to develop analytical and simulation models to establish throughput performance for random access networks to transport low-bandwidth, data application traffic, [2, 3, 4, 5, 6]. Today's requirements for wireless transmission for data applications requiring large bandwidth in conjunction with time-sensitive multimedia applications with quality of service (QoS) puts the focus on performance issues like delay, throughput and packet loss performance as a function of packet size, initial contention window size settings and the number of active terminals competing for access to the network, [7]. Reducing initial and final contention window settings, as well as the number of retransmissions at terminals running time sensitive applications will reduce delay and its jitter. However these adjustments come at a price, affecting overall delay and throughput, when in congestion. This publication aims to provide some further insight on these issues. Specifically we want to establish how to set the initial contention window size in terminals that will provide VoIP services in order to reduce delay in packet delivery, while not affecting global throughput and delay significantly.

Networks covering indoor spaces span short distances and problems like the hidden terminal and capture seldom occur. When the hidden terminal problem is present, a transmission or a collision of 2 or more transmissions may not be detected by some terminals that in turn may start to broadcast on their own, either creating a collision or contributing to an existing one [2]. Capture may occur when the received power from two terminals differ by a large amount due to the fact that one terminal experiences larger propagation losses than the other, [3]. In our analysis we consider that neither the hidden terminal nor the capture effect are present, and therefore consider only the basic access mechanism.

In [4], a simple but accurate, analytical model has been developed to compute the 802.11 Distributed Coordination Function (DCF) throughput in the assumption of finite number of terminals and ideal channel conditions. By means of the proposed model, an extensive throughput performance evaluation of both access mechanisms of the 802.11 protocol is provided. This analysis is a good starting point to develop an understanding of how the initial contention window (*CWmin*) size affects network performance. However it assumes that all terminals are configured the same way and it pays no attention to the effect of setting the maximum contention window (*CWmax*) size.

DCF uses a contention window (CW) to control the random access to the channel. Basically, it consists of a backoff counter that inhibits a terminal from immediate transmission, by delaying that instant to the moment the counter reaches zero, starting from an initial value that is being set upon arrival of the packet. The contention window is defined by two parameters: *CWmin*, *CWmax*. The random number used in the random backoff is initially a number between 0 and *CWmin*. If the initial backoff expires without successful broadcast of the packet, the terminal doubles the value random backoff window size ($CW = 2 \cdot CWmin$) and picks a new value at random between 0 and (*CW*-1). This doubling in size will continue with each additional retry until *CW* = *CWmax*. Once this value has been reached, further retries will be made picking a random number in the range [0, *CWmax*-1]. Retries continue until the maximum retries has been reached. This process of doubling the backoff window is often referred to as a binary exponential backoff. The influence of the backoff algorithm has been studied analytically and by simulation by [4, 5, 6, 7 and 8]. In [5, 6] Wu, et. al. enhance the analytical model developed by Bianchi, [4], limiting the maximum number of retries and define new metrics like goodput, fairness and average delay. Ziouva and Antonakopoulos obtain average delay measures, [7]. Xiao shows that a throughput upper limit and a delay lower limit exist since the overhead in the MAC magnifies itself when the data rate becomes higher, [8]. The lack of a built-in mechanism to provide quality of service with IEEE 802.11 based WLANs has triggered the work of a working group on a new standard, known as the IEEE 802.11e which introduces the so-called hybrid coordination function (HCF) for enhanced distributed channel access (EDCA) and HCF controlled channel access (HCCA). As a step in that direction, Cisco recommends to change settings of the contention windows at the Access Point (AP) thus being able to respond to class of service labels of appropriately tagged packets in infrastructure networks, [9]. Banchs and Vollero analyze the delay behaviour of the EDCA mechanism by varying the values of *CWmin, CWmax* and a parameter that determines how long a station has to wait to decrement the backoff counter after a successful transmission, AIFS, [10]. Wang et.al, analyze how to improve network performance, when VoIP traffic is considered, by changing some parameters at the AP of an infrastructure network, [11]. However, these studies consider that parameter settings of all stations as a whole, but do not consider the possibility of individual settings.

The difficulty associated to carry out a theoretical analysis when terminals possibly will be carrying traffic of different nature and may be configured with different parameter values invites to study network performance by means of a simulation model using Network Simulator 2 (ns-2). The aim of this publication is to analyze on how tuning the initial and final contention window settings on the terminals carrying real time traffic will affect delay and throughput in individual and global performance for Ad hoc networks that will carry mixed VoIP and data traffic under congestion.

2 Simulation Scenario

To establish a performance evaluation of the protocol with ns-2 simulator, we consider two kinds of terminals: some running real time applications with small sized packets scheduled for transmission (for example, VoIP, in which case a payload size of 55 bytes may be considered representative) and others transferring large files (for example, 1500 bytes, which is the maximum size of an Ethernet payload) with less stringent delay requirements (videostreaming, or data exchange). The hidden terminal and capture phenomena are avoided by placing terminals at equal distance (2m) from the center of a circle. All terminals transmit packets to one terminal that is placed in the center of the circle, which only receives. This arrangement is a simple means to keep track of all packets that have been received successfully. The network operates in saturation mode, that is, every transmitting terminal has always a packet ready for broadcast in its output buffer.

The ns-2 simulator is furthermore configured with following settings: *WirelessChannel*, *Two Ray Ground* as a radio propagation model, *Wireless physical* interface, *802.11 MAC*, *DropTail/PriQueue* queue management, the maximum queue length is 5 packets, *LL* link layer, omni-directional antennas, *DSDV* routing protocol. We have configured the slot time in 20[μs], SIFS time in 10[μs], *Preamble Length* in 144[bits], *PCLPHeaderLength* 48[bits], *Short Retry Limit* and *Long Retry Limit* are set to 7, unless stated otherwise. The basic rate and *PCLPDataRate* were set to 1[Mbps], *RTS threshold* to 3000 and packets were sent without ARP IP packet header. The physical space of the simulation is a circle with a radius of 500 meters. For each station, we run a CBR agent over UDP protocol. We set the data rate to saturate the network each simulation. We run the simulation for 200 [s] taking out the necessary information of the traces to remove warm up time data.

We setup the following experiments:

1. We set *CWmin* = 32, *CWmax* = 1024 at 6 of 7 stations. We set *CWmin* = 4, and *CWmax* = 4, 8, 16, 32, 64, 128, 256 and 512 in increasing values for each simulation at the trial station. Payload sizes are 1028 bytes for all packets. Transmission rate is 1 Mbps. The aim of this experiment is to determine the sensitivity of the network performance to the variation of the *CWmax* parameter at one station.
2. In the second experiment we try to evaluate the effect of having an increasing number of stations that reduce *CWmax*. We initially set *CWmin* = 32 and *CWmax* = 1024 at all stations, to reduce it to *CWmin* = 4 and *CWmax* = 64 in an increasing number of stations. Since 7 stations are involved, 8 simulations are possible and we number them as we increase the number of stations using a reduced *CWmin, CWmax* setting. Payload packet size is 1028 bytes. Transmission rate is 1 Mbps.
3. The third experiment is aimed to determine the effect of packet and contention window size in a network were all but one station of the network of 8 stations use the default settings of *CWmin* = 31 and *CWmax* = 1024, except the remaining station, that uses *CWmin* = 4 and *CWmax* = 8. The number of retries at all stations is set to 7. Transmission rate is 1 Mbps.
4. Experiment 4 considers two terminals that only transmit payload packets of 55 bytes. We set the default values *CWmin* = 32 and *CWmax* = 1024 for the backoff algorithm of these terminals. Data terminals are added in pairs to the network, transmitting 1500 bytes payload packets with the same default settings of the backoff algorithm. Transmission rate is 1 Mbps. We look for average delay, delay jitter and throughput globally and for each focus group (data and voice). We also look for the standard deviation of these performance measures. The aim of this experiment is to establish how the presence of an increasing number of data terminals affects voice connections when default settings are being used in terminals.
5. Same configurations as in experiment 4, but at 11 Mbps rate. With higher transmission rates, it is to be expected that more bits per second will reach the destination successfully, on the average. However, since control information is transmitted at a lower data rate than user data, more time will

be spent in transmitting control information. We want to make an assessment of how this affects overall performance.

6. In experiment 6 two terminals transmit only VoIP size packets (55 bytes) with the contention window set to *CWmin* = 4, *CWmax* = 16. We add 2 terminals at a time, with default settings of the backoff algorithm parameters (*CWmin* = 32, *CWmax* = 1024), transmitting 1500 bytes packets in pairs. We look for average delay, jitter and throughput globally and for the two focus groups on the average and establish its standard deviation. Transmission rate is 1 Mbps. The aim of this experiment is to see the advantage that can be obtained by reducing the contention window settings of the backoff algorithm to reduce delay of voice traffic, as compared to experiment 4.
7. Same configuration as in experiment 6, but transmissions are at at 11 Mbps rate, so as to compare the effect of the contention window size reduction for voice traffic.

These experiments will provide insight of network performance experiencing congestion.

3 Experiment Outcomes

We here describe the outcomes of the experiments outlined in the previous section. To get these results we program a trace filter in C language to eliminate warm up time and system messages from the *ns-2* simulation. Thereafter we identify packets transmitted by each station and proceed to find the time elapsed from the moment a packet is ready for transmission and acknowledgement reception. We then establish average value, 95% confidence intervals of the average value and standard deviation using Matlab.

Table 1 shows the results of experiment 1, with the first column showing the values of *CWmax* of the single station that varies its backoff algorithm configuration. The second column shows the lower limit of the 95% confidence interval of the average delay, while the third column shows the average delay, the fourth column the upper limit of the 95% confidence interval of the average delay and the fifth column, the standard deviation of that delay for the single station. Columns 6, 7, 8 and 9 are the set of values for the remaining seven stations of the network. Columns 10, 11, 12 and 13 reflect the values of the average delay and standard deviation of the entire network (all 8 stations). Payload sizes of packets are 1028 bytes for all terminals.

From the data displayed in table 1 one may easily conclude that while overall network delay remains approximately the same, the use of low values of *CWmax* in one station reduces considerably its own delay to less than 59% of the delay experienced by the remaining stations, on the average, while *CWmax* of that station is kept below 32. If *CWmax=64* for the single station, delays are still 69% of the average delay experienced by the remaining stations. For values larger than *CWmax* = 64 on the single station, the delay is basically the same for all stations and has no effect on overall performance. This result coincides with a recommendation issued by CISCO for Access Point settings in infrastructure networks, which states that one should avoid setting *CWmax* at delay sensitive stations below *CWmin* of the rest of the stations, so as not to affect overall network performance, [9]. However, if the aim of the adjustment is to reduce time response at connections sensitive to delay, this result clearly indicates the convenience of setting *CWmin* and *CWmax* of that connection at lower values than the rest of the network settings for that purpose.

Table 1. Network performance sensitivity to *CWmax* variations on one station.

1 Mbps	Single station, CWmin = 4 Delay [s]				Remaining stations, CWmin = 32, CWmax = 1024 Delay [s]				Network values Delay [s]			
CWmax of Single Station	Low 95% CI Value	Average	Upper 95% CI Value	Std. Dev.	Low 95% CI Value	Average	Upper 95% CI Value	Std. Dev.	Low 95% CI Value	Average	Upper 95% CI Value	Std. Dev.
4	0.0438	**0.0447**	0.0456	0.0041	0.0808	**0.0826**	0.0841	0.0135	0.0716	**0.0734**	0.0752	0.0236
8	0.0454	**0.0464**	0.0473	0.0043	0.0796	**0.0816**	0.0834	0.0150	0.0716	**0.0734**	0.0752	0.0238
16	0.0482	**0.0494**	0.0505	0.0047	0.0815	**0.0838**	0.0861	0.0187	0.0742	**0.0764**	0.0785	0.0277
32	0.0532	**0.0546**	0.0559	0.0055	0.0778	**0.0797**	0.0815	0.0154	0.0733	**0.0750**	0.0767	0.0216
64	0.0665	**0.0693**	0.0722	0.0101	0.0747	**0.0762**	0.0778	0.0133	0.0739	**0.0754**	0.0768	0.0188
128	0.0677	**0.0712**	0.0748	0.0121	0.0741	**0.0758**	0.0775	0.0146	0.0736	**0.0751**	0.0766	0.0195
256	0.0734	**0.0775**	0.0816	0.0134	0.0730	**0.0746**	0.0762	0.0135	0.0734	**0.0748**	0.0762	0.0183
512	0.0726	**0.0774**	0.0822	0.0156	0.0744	**0.0763**	0.0781	0.0160	0.0746	**0.0762**	0.0779	0.0218
1024	0.0684	**0.0716**	0.0749	0.0108	0.0734	**0.0751**	0.0767	0.0141	0.0733	**0.0747**	0.0761	0.0186

In Table 2 we show the results of experiment 2. The first column the number of stations configured with *CWmin* = 4 and *CWmax* = 64, while the rest of the stations use the default values of *CWmin* = 32 and *CWmax* = 1024. That is, at row 0 the simulation is run with all stations using the default settings for the backoff algorithm, at row 1, one station is set to *CWmin* = 4 and *CWmax* = 64, while the rest maintains the default settings, and so on. The remaining columns have a similar meaning as it was explained in Table 1.

Table 2. Delays when an increasing number of stations reduce *CWmin* and *CWmax*.

1Mbps Number of Stations with reduced CW	Stations with CWmin = 4, CWmax = 64 Delay [s]				Remaining stations, with default CW,CWmin = 32, CWmax = 1024 Delay [s]				Network values Delay [s]			
	Low 95% CI Value	Average	Upper 95% CI Value	Std. Dev.	Low 95% CI Value	Average	Upper 95% CI Value	Std. Dev.	Low 95% CI Value	Average	Upper 95% CI Value	Std. Dev.
0	0.0351	**0.0369**	0.0389	0.0105	0.0351	**0.0360**	0.0369	0.0121	0.0354	**0.0362**	0.0371	0.0124
1	0.0223	**0.0228**	0.0232	0.0034	0.0395	**0.0405**	0.0415	0.0130	0.0354	**0.0363**	0.0373	0.0139
2	0.0244	**0.0249**	0.0254	0.0036	0.0383	**0.0397**	0.0411	0.0178	0.0352	**0.0364**	0.0375	0.0171
3	0.0267	**0.0272**	0.0278	0.0038	0.0385	**0.0401**	0.0417	0.0204	0.0362	**0.0375**	0.0388	0.0190
4	0.0283	**0.0290**	0.0297	0.0044	0.0378	**0.0396**	0.0414	0.0232	0.0360	**0.0375**	0.0390	0.0218
5	0.0328	**0.0336**	0.0344	0.0047	0.0391	**0.0411**	0.0431	0.0261	0.0381	**0.0397**	0.0414	0.0239
6	0.0377	**0.0385**	0.0394	0.0047	0.0402	**0.0416**	0.0430	0.0185	0.0398	**0.0410**	0.0422	0.0166
7	0.0439	**0.0449**	0.0458	0.0050	0.0436	**0.0441**	0.0445	0.0057	0.0438	**0.0442**	0.0446	0.0056

Reading the data of table 2 shows that when less than 4 stations switch to lower values of *CWmin* and *CWmax*, these stations will experiment delay reduction of 73% as compared to the remaining stations running with the default settings of the backoff algorithm. On the other extreme, if 7 stations switch to the lower values of *CWmin* and *CWmax*, the average delay for these stations is worse than for those that use the default values (compare row 0 to row 7) and the overall network delay has increased due to the fact that the number of collisions has increased. This tells us that only a fraction of all stations of a network should be privileged, if deemed necessary, with a reduction of their *CWmin* and *CWmax* values. These stations should be running real time applications. Thus, one may conclude that in a network running VoIP and data connections it seems to be a safe practice to reduce the contention window size of the backoff algorithm of terminals dealing with voice traffic on a regular basis.

Figure 3 reflects the effect of packet and contention window size in a network were all but one station of the network of 8 stations use the default settings of *CWmin* = 31 and *CWmax* = 1024, except the remaining station, that uses *CWmin* = 4 and *CWmax* = 64. The number of retries at all stations is set to 7. Transmission rate is 1 Mbps.

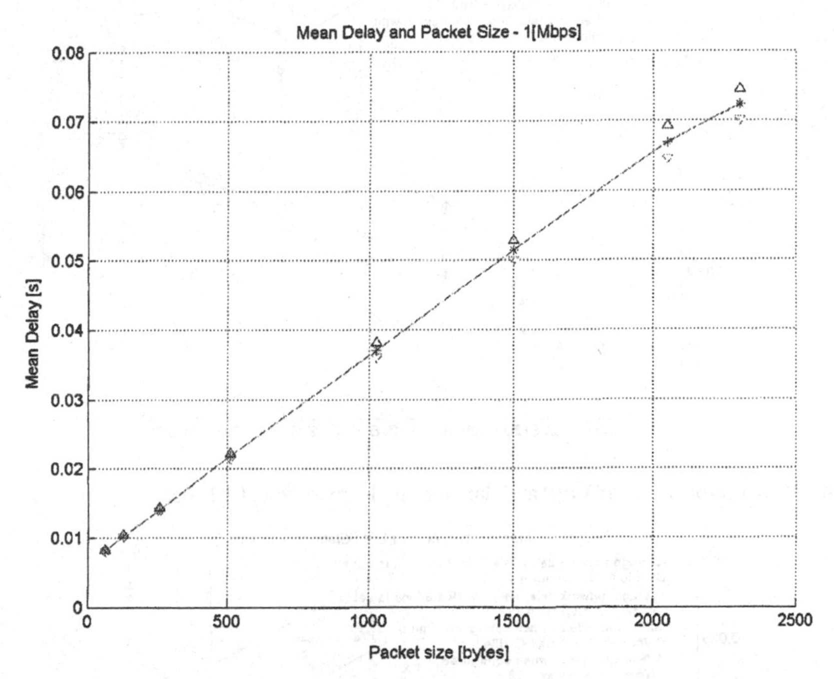

Fig. 3. Effect of backoff algorithm configuration and packet size in network.

From figure 3 one may conclude that at a given transmission rate, if all stations transmit packets of equal size, the delay that each successful transmission experiences is proportional to the packet size, a fact that is intuitively perceived. The fact of having one terminal configured with a lower value of the initial contention window does not seem to affect the overall performance of the network. Therefore, if a terminal is configured to have a lower value of the initial contention window size to reduce its delay when transmitting voice packets and then uses these settings to transmit packets of different sizes, as any other terminal will do, the effects on overall performance are negligible.

Experiment 4, 5, 6 and 7 are an attempt to establish the viability of having a terminal carrying delay sensitive data (VoIP) in a network that otherwise provides a wireless service to data transfers. The voice terminals have been configured with either *CWmin* = 32 and *CWmax* =1024 or *CWmin* = 4 and *CWmax* = 16, while data terminals have been set with *CWmin* = 32 and *CWmax* = 1024, according to the findings of experiment 1. Figure 4 shows the results for a network operating at 1 Mbps. The number of voice stations (VS) and stations sending data packets (DS) are shown on the horizontal axis. Average values of the 95% upper and lower confidence intervals are indicated. Figure 5 exhibits a similar result for network operating at 11 Mbps.

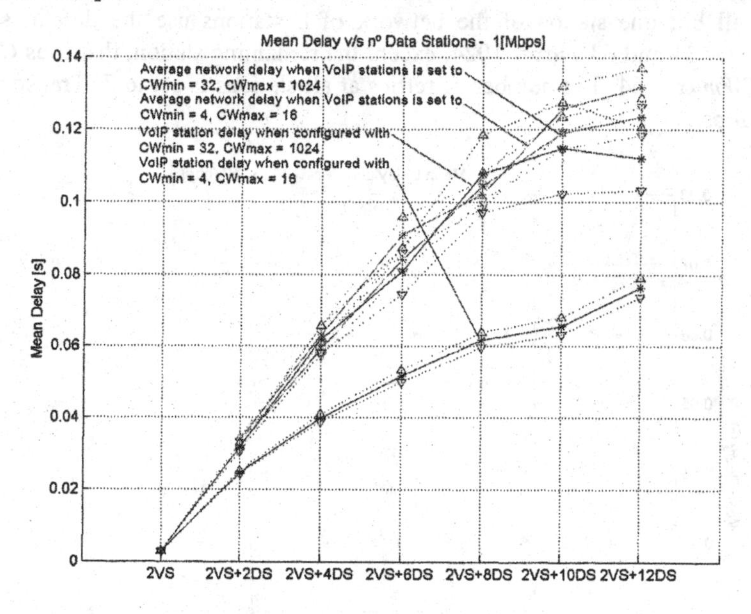

Fig. 4. Delay performance of VoIP and data terminals operating at 1 Mbps.

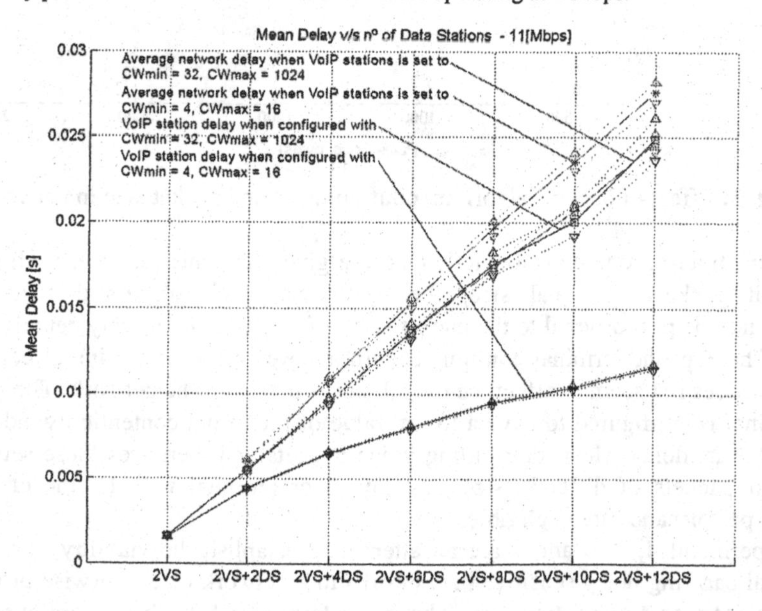

Fig. 5. Delay performance of VoIP and data terminals operating at 11 Mbps.

From figure 4 and 5 it is simple to see that there is a clear advantage for VoIP connections in terms of delay if the initial and maximum contention window values are set to *CWmin* = 4 and *CWmax* = 16, while the rest of the stations maintain the default settings (*CWmin* = 32 and *CWmax* = 1028). One advantage of assigning access privileges to delay sensitive terminals is that not only delay is reduced, but so is its jitter, when the network consists of many terminals. Another advantage is that even though VoIP terminals have improved their performance by having been granted access privileges, the affect on delay and delay jitter on data terminals is almost not perceived. However, these settings do affect overall network performance as can be seen in figure 6. Overall throughput deteriorates due to the increase in collisions as a result of the reduction of the window sizes of the backoff algorithm of the VoIP terminals.

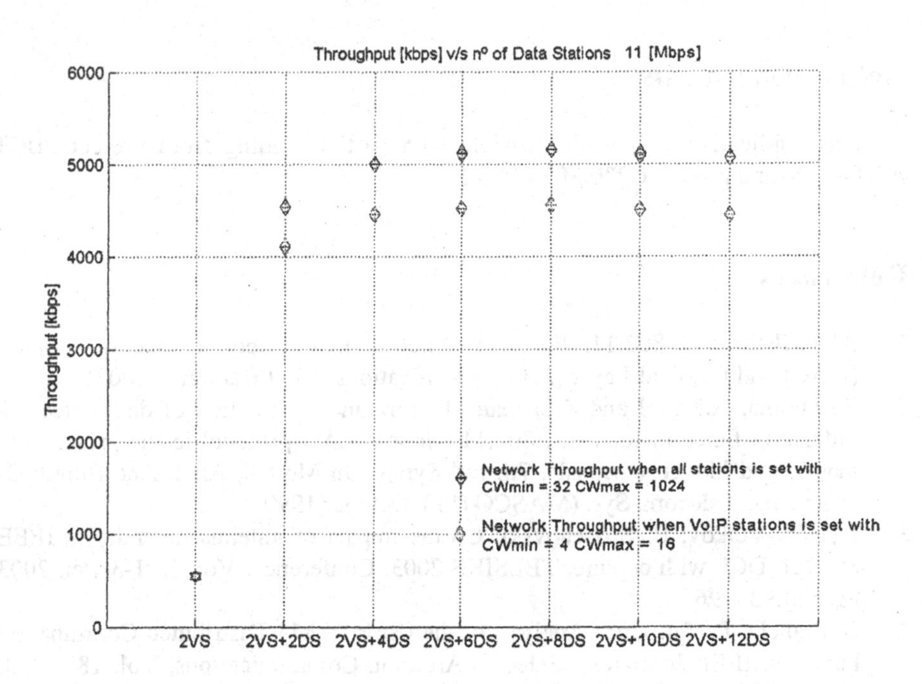

Fig. 6. Throughput as a function of network load and contention window settings.

In figure 6 the upper throughput points are due to a network that has all stations working with the default contention window configuration (*CWmin* = 32, *CWmax* = 1024). The lower values belong to the network where data stations (DS) use the default settings, while the 2 voice stations (VS) have their values set to *CWmin* = 4 and *CWmax* = 16. Clearly, a 10% deterioration is observed due to the overhead of collisions. However, the advantage observed is a 50% reduction of the delay of the time sensitive application running on the voice stations (see figure 5).

Conclusions

We have conducted a set of simulation experiments for wireless Ad Hoc wireless networks using the IEEE 802.11 protocol to be able to establish in which way time sensitive applications may benefit from reducing the contention window settings (*CWmin* and *CWmax*) of the backoff algorithm, thus reducing their delay without affecting the average network delay that much, as long as only a few stations of the network take advantage of this possibility. Throughput degradation may be acceptable under these circumstances as a necessary tradeoff due to the overhead caused by an increase of collisions and increased overhead due to the smaller packet sizes of the voice connection. It is in our best knowledge that no publication has reported this effect so far.

Acknowledgements

This publication was made possible with partial funding from project PBCT ACT-11-04 and project UTFSM 23.05.21.

References

1. ANSI/IEEE Std 802.11, Part 11: Wireless LAN Medium Access, Control (MAC) and Physical Layer (PHY) Specifications, 1999 Edition (R2003)
2. S.Khurana, A.Kahol and K.Srimani, Performance evaluation of distributed co-ordination function for IEEE 802.11 wireless LAN protocol in the presence of mobile and hidden terminals, 7th Intl Symp. On Model., Anal. And Simul. Of Comp. and Telecom. Sys. (MASCOT99), October 1999.
3. Z.Hadzi-Velkov; B. Spasenovski; On the impact of antenna diversity in IEEE 802.11b DCF with capture, TELSIKS 2003. Conference, Vol. 1, 1-3 Oct. 2003 Page(s):93 – 96.
4. G. Bianchi, Performance Analysis of the IEEE 802.11 Distributed Coordination Function, IEEE Journal on Selected Areas on Communications, Vol. 18, N°. 3, March 2000, pp. 535-548.
5. H. Wu, Y. Peng, K. Long y S. Cheng. ``A Simple Model of IEEE 802.11 Wireless LAN". Proc. IEEE Intertational Conferences on Info-Tech and Info-net (ICII), Beijing, vol 2, 514-519, Oct. 2001.
6. H. Wu, Y. Peng, K. Long, S. Cheng, J. Ma, "Performance of Reliable Transport Protocol over IEEE 802.11 Wireless LAN Analysis and Enhancement", IEEE INFOCOM Feb. 2002.
7. E. Ziouva y T. Antonakopoulus, "The Effect of finite population on IEEE802.11 Wireless LANs Thoughput/Delay Performance", Proc 11th IEEE MELECON 2002, pp. 95-99, May 7-9 .
8. Y. Xiao, ``A Simple and Effective Priority Scheme for IEEE 802.11". IEEE Comm. Letters, 7(2): 70-72 Feb 2003

9. http://www.cisco.com/en/US/products/hw/wireless/ps430/prod_technical_reference09186a0080144498.html
10. A. Banchs, L. Vollero, A delay model for IEEE 802.11e EDCA, IEEE Communications Letters, Vol. 9, N° 6, Jun 2005, pp. 508- 510
11. W. Wang, S. Chang, L. Li, Solutions to performance problems in VoIP over a 802.11 wireless LAN, IEEE Trans. on Vehic. Tech., Jan. 2005, Vol. 54, N°: 1, pp. 366- 384

Wireless Networks in industrial environments: State of the art and Issues

Xavier Carcelle, Tuan Dang, Catherine Devic
EDF Research&Development
6, quai Watier – BP 49
78401 Chatou Cedex, France
{xavier.carcelle, tuan.dang, catherine.devic}@edf.fr

***Abstract**. Wireless is everywhere nowadays and WLAN (i.e. 802.11 standard family) has became used by almost any communications devices in the mass market.*
The recent achievements in the fields of modulation techniques, such as Spread Spectrum, coding methods, such as Turbocodes, CDMA2000, and frequencies allocation methods, such as OFDM and Frequency Hopping, has pushed the growing uses of reliable and low-cost wireless technologies. Among them the last standards are: IEEE 802.11 family (i.e. WiFi), HyperLAN and HyperLAN2, IEEE 802.15 (i.e. WPAN), IEEE 802.16 (i.e. WiMAX)...
However, the industrial environments are not taken into consideration in the design of those standards, because its harsh constraints has specific characteristics (reliability, interferences with existing equipments, multi-path propagation, low-power consumption, real-time reconfiguration, security...) that need specific requirements and eventually standards.
This paper will intent to give an overview of the wireless technologies and discusses the current and future possible technologies for the uses in the industrial environments (power plants and stations, factories, industrial buildings, automotive...). Our current works showed us that there is no perfect technology by it-self but the best trade-off solution is a hybrid architecture combining the right wired and wireless technologies.

Please use the following format when citing this chapter:

Carcelle, X., Dang, T., Devic, C., 2006, in International Federation for Information Processing (IFIP), Volume 212, Ad-Hoc Networking, ed. Al Agha, K., (Boston: Springer), pp. 141–156.

1 Introduction

The last past years have been intense in terms of development of wireless standards and wireless applications. Those applications are going from mass market domestic uses including Internet access to industrial usage in the field of wireless sensors networks, wireless interconnection between computer based control devices (DCS, PLC...) and industrial asset management based on pervasive networks indoor or outdoor.

These emerging wireless technologies can give benefits in cost-reduction, and reliability in industrial applications as well as opportunities in improving operational performance. But there is still work in progress to achieve usable technologies which meet industrial requirements. Firstly we will present an overview of the current and future wireless technologies from a standardization point of view. Secondly we will analyze the work to be done in the design and implementation in the industrial environments, such as in the utilities installations (power plants, sub-stations, factories). Finally we will present our current experimentations and future works within hybrid technology networking fields.

2 Overview of wireless communication technologies

2.1 Taxonomy and technical overview

Wireless networking technologies can be divided into three main classes (see Fig). Each class addresses specific requirements and purposes in point-to-point and point-to-multipoint communication.

WPAN addresses Personal Area Network in which most of the time, point-to-point communications are involved. However, point-to-multipoint communications are possible with wireless networks protocols such as PicoNET (based on Bluetooth) or ZigBee (based on IEEE 802.15.4b). The range performances are typically from 1 meter to a few dozens meters. The WPAN are designed for low data rate (usually 100-200 kbps). This family gather the following technologies: ZigBee, Bluetooth and UWB.

WLAN addresses Wireless Local Area Networks where the main uses are inter-connecting high data rate applications (Multimedia streaming, files sharing...), building easy-to-deploy HotSpot-like networks and lately Ad-Hoc enabled networks such as Mesh Networks. The range performances are typically from a few dozens meters indoor to a few hundred meters outdoor. The WLAN are designed for high data rate (usually 1 to 20 Mbps). This family is composed with WiFi and DECT..

Finally WWAN addresses Wireless Wide Area Networks which are mainly focused for long-distance point-to-point high data rate connections. They are designed to link plant sites networks all together with date rate ranging typically over 10Mbps with distance performances over few hundred meters. This long-distance family gathers: WiMAN, WiMAX and GSM.

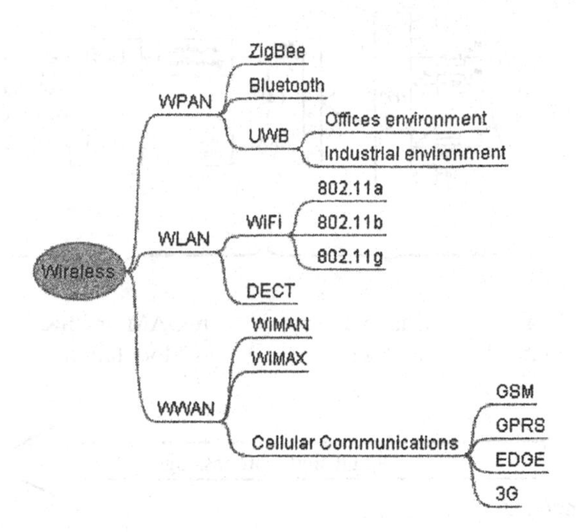

Fig.1. Wireless technologies taxonomy

From a more technical point of view, wireless networks use a lot of underlying mobile communications technologies benefiting from digital signal transmission researches. The following tables present the technical characteristics of the different wireless standards with their respective frequencies and modulation issues. In term of frequency issues, the chapter III will cover the different regulations and the co-existence problems between each wireless technology. It intents to present a brief guideline that may help to make the right choice in industrial applications.

In digital mobile communications systems, the modulation and the multiple access methods are important characteristics that has influence on the efficiency of the channel in terms of: data rate, robustness and power consumption. IEEE describes the robustness [1] as the degree to which a system or component can function correctly in the presence of invalid inputs or stressful environment conditions. Robustness can also be achieved using MIMO systems. In communication theory, MIMO refers to radio links with multiple antennas at the transmitter and the receiver side. Given multiple antennas, the spatial dimension can be exploited to improve the performance of the wireless link. The performance is often measured as the average bit rate (bit/s) the wireless link can provide or as the average bit error rate (BER). Which one has most importance depends on the application.

Most of digital transmission system uses advanced channel coding technique to prevent errors in the transmission and to correct them in the receiver when they happen. Below (see

Fig) is an example [2] of the encoding method for OFDM:

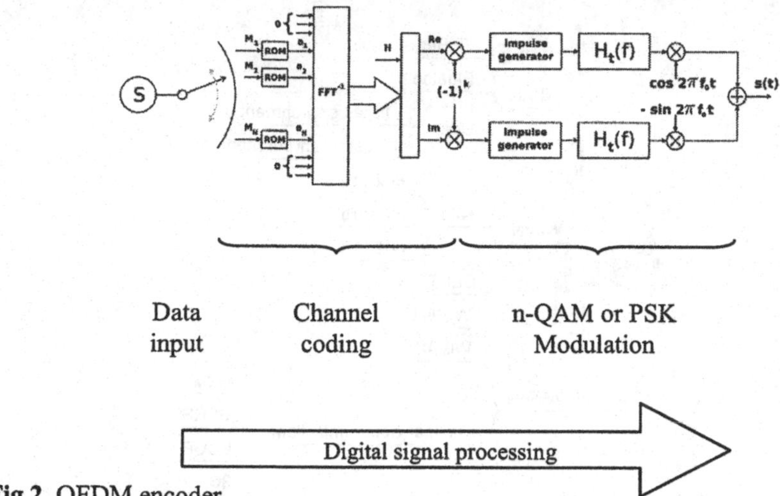

Fig.2. OFDM encoder

OFDM uses the principle of multi-carrier transmission technique that converts a serial high-rate data stream onto multiple parallel low-rate sub-streams. Each sub-stream is modulated on another sub-carrier. Below is an example of multi-carrier modulation with four sub-channels [3].

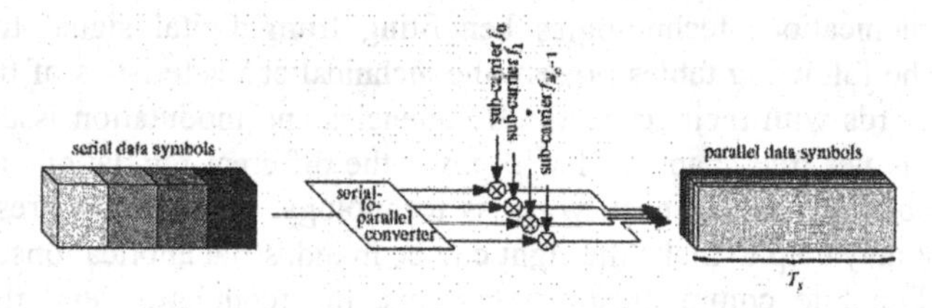

Fig.3. Example of multi-carrier modulation

In Spread Spectrum communication, the baseband signal bandwidth is intentionally spread over a larger bandwidth by injecting a higher-frequency signal. So, energy used in transmitting the signal is spread over a wider bandwidth, and appears as noise. Different Spread Spectrum techniques use different manners of injecting Pseudo Noise sequence (code) to distribute the power of the baseband signal. Below is an illustration of Direct Sequence Spread Spectrum technique [4].

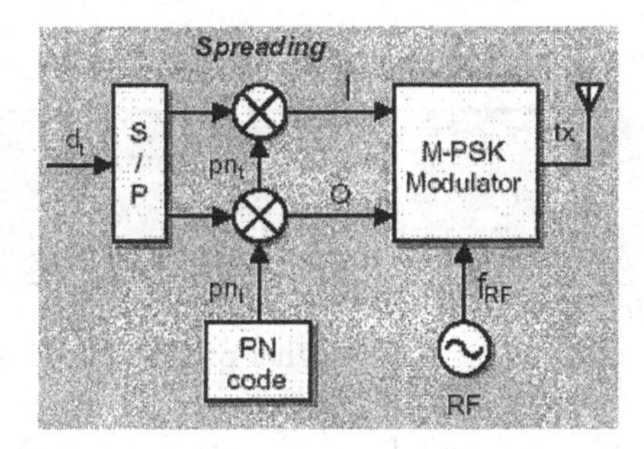

Fig.4. Typical DSSS circuit

Following the standardized OSI model for wireless protocols, the physical (PHY) and the medium access (MAC) layers can be seen as below:

Table 1.. PHY and MAC layers for wireless protocols

<table>
<tr><td rowspan="2">MAC</td><td colspan="5">IEEE 802.3, IEEE 802.13, IEEE 802.15</td></tr>
<tr><td>Multiple Access logic</td><td colspan="4">CSMA/CA</td></tr>
<tr><td rowspan="3">PHY</td><td rowspan="2">Channel coding or decoding</td><td>Spreading, despreading, serial-to-parallel or parallel-to-serial...</td><td rowspan="3">Narrowband technique: OFDM</td><td rowspan="3">Spread-spectrum technique: FHSS, DSSS...</td><td rowspan="3">Ch. multiple access: CDMA, TDMA, FDMA</td></tr>
<tr><td>FEC (block coding, convolutional coding, Turbocode, ...)</td></tr>
<tr><td>Modulation or Demodulation</td><td>n-QAM or FSK or PSK...</td></tr>
</table>

Each digital signal transmission technique has its own advantages and drawbacks. Following is the comparison of the different Multi-Carrier narrowband Transmission and Spread spectrum Techniques:

Table 2. Comparison of different digital signal transmission techniques

Transmission Technique	*Advantages*	*Drawbacks*
FHSS (Bluetooth, DECT)	• robust to interference • strong with jamming	• limited data rate • higher power consumption
DSSS (IEEE 802.11b, ZigBee, GSM)	• support variable data rates • resistance to multi-path • resistant to narrow-band interferences	• sensitive to jamming • limited number of same-cell access points
OFDM (IEEE 802.11g, IEEE 802.11a)	Resistance to • link dispersion • multi-path • frequency interference • burst noise	• higher power consumption • higher CPU needs

In the following paragraphs, we will analyse the characteristics of each class of wireless networking technologies:

2.2 WPAN (Wireless Personal Area Networks)

WPAN technologies are being quite heavily used these past years in the mass market industry but a very few in the industrial environment. The coming years will see a great spread out of these technologies in the factories and the industry in general. For instance the IEEE 802.15.4 working group is leading the technology standardization for such technologies matching the needs and the requirements.

Table 3. WPAN technologies

Wireless comm. technology	Bluetooth	Ultra Wide Band (HDR) (Offices environment)	"ZigBee"	Ultra Wide Band (Industrial environment)
IEEE Standards	802.15.1	802.15.3 (WG a)	802.15.4 (WG b)	802.15.4 (WG a)
Peak data rate	723.2 kbps	480 Mbps	• 20 kbps (868 MHz) • 40 kbps (915 MHz) • 250 kbps (2.4 GHz)	1 Mbps
Frequency range	2402-2480 MHz	3.1-4.8 GHz	• 2.4-2.4835 MHz • 902-928 MHz (US) • 868.3 MHz (Eu)	5.9-10.6 GHz
Channel bandwidth	1 MHz	1.368 GHz or 2.736 GHz or 528 MHz	5MHz	500MHz
Number of channels	79	2 or 13	1 (868 MHz) 10 (915 MHz) 16 (2.4 GHz)	-
Multiple access	TDMA or CDMA	Ternary CDMA or TFI-OFDM	CSMA/CA with FDMA and TDMA	Impulse Radio
Modulation	GFSK	• BPSK/QPSK (DS-SS UWB) • QPSK(MB-OFDM)	• BPSK (868/915 MHz) • OQPSK (2.4GHz)	• TH-PPM • TH-A-PAM
Power-consumption	+++	++	+	+
Range performance	+	+	++	+
Localization performance	++	+++	+	+++
Security	++	+++	+++	+++

2.3 WLAN (Wireless Local Area Networks)

WLAN technologies headed a huge development these pasts years with main applications such as Private LAN (Local Area Networks) and Public Internet Hot-Spots where the WiFi technology is now embedded in any electronic device as one of the main features. DECT has been also extremely used in-the-homes and is now used in industrial environment for voice and data over the private phone system. For wide industrial environment, such as big factories, storage areas, docks or power plants, DECT might be a good to have a reliable, robust wireless private phone system but also add to this system data communications and emergency alarms using the worldwide ISM bands. The backbone linking the DECT base stations is usually wired.

Table 4. WLAN technologies

Wireless comm. technology	WiFi			DECT
Standards	IEEE 802.11a	IEEE 802.11b	IEEE 802.11g	ETSI
Peak data rate	54Mbps	11Mbps	54Mbps	100kbps
Frequency range	• 5.15-5.35 GHz (US) • 5.470-5.725 GHz (Eu) • 5.725-5.825 GHz (US/China)	• 2.4-2.4835 GHz (US/Eu) • 2.471-2.497 GHz (Japan) • 2.4465-2.4835 GHz (Fr) • 2.445-2.475 GHz(Sp)	2.4-2.4835 GHz	• 1880-1900 MHz (Europe) • 1880-1990 MHz (Worldwide)
Channel bandwidth	20MHz	20MHz	20MHz	1.728MHz
Number of channels	12	3 (non overlapping)	3 (on overlapping)	10 (12 users per channel)
Multiple access	CSMA/CA	CSMA/CA	CSMA/CA	FDMA/ TDMA
Modulation	• BPSK,QPSK • 16QAM, 64QAM	• BPSK,DQPSK (Header) • BPSK,QPSK(Payload) • CCK, PBCC	• BPQK, QPSK, • 16-64QAM	GFSK
Power-consumption	++	++	++	+
Range performance	+++	++	++	++
Security	++	++	++	++

2.4 WWAN (Wireless Wide Area Networks)

WWAN technologies is used mainly for two applications nowadays is cellular phone communications and wide range IP-networks such as inter-cities point to point links. The WiMAN technology for instance is high-data rate with range performances up-to several kilometers and no mobility. Whereas the cellular communications for data transfer are usually low-to-fair data rate with complete mobility in the covered areas with GPRS services. From an industrial point of view, the two cases can be found as applications. A far remote power plant can be connected to the corporate backbone using a long-distance IP-based connection like a 802.16 link retrieving data from a sensors. Also a GPRS modem can help to regularly access a remote sensors or enabling a power plant staff to stay connected to the corporate backbone while off-site for a manual metering or a measurement task.

Table 5. WWAN technologies

Wireless comm. technology	WiMAN	WiMAX	Cellular Communications
Standards	IEEE 802.16	IEEE 802.16a	GPRS
Peak data rate	134Mbps	a:75Mbps e:15Mbps	100kbps
Frequency range	10-66GHz	a:2-16GHz e:2-6GHz	GSM bands
Channel bandwidth	20Mhz 25MHz(US) 28MHz(Eu)	a:1.5-20MHz e:>5MHz	usually 1.25MHz
Number of channels	-	a:1.5-20MHz e: under definition	depends on service
Multiple access	TDMA	OFDM	CDMA
Modulation	QPSK, 16QAM,	QPSK, 16QAM, 64QAM	QPSK, HPSK
Power-consumption	+++	+++	++
Range performance	+++	+++	+++
Localization performance	+	+	++
Security	+++	+++	+++

3 Frequency regulations and co-existence issues

3.1Frequency regulations issues

These below tables present a brief overview of the different frequency regulations for the wireless technologies discussed in the previous chapter:

3.1.1 WPAN

Table 6. WPAN frequency regulations

Region	Bluetooth	UWB (office environment)	ZigBee	UWB (industrial environment)
North America	ISM 2.4 GHz	ISM	ISM 2.4GHz, 916MHz	FCC 15.209 and FCC 2002
Europe	ISM 2.4 GHz	ECC/DECC/(06)AA	ISM 2.4GHz, 868MHz	CEPT/ECC/TG3 -41dBm/MHz
Japan	ISM 2.4 GHz	-41dBm/MHz	ISM 2.4GHz 868MHz	-41dBm/MHz

3.1.2 WLAN

Table 7. WLAN frequency regulations

Region	802.11a	802.11b	802.11g	DECT
North America	ISM	ISM	ISM	ISM
Europe	ISM	ISM	ISM	ISM
Japan	ISM	ISM	ISM	ISM

3.1.3 WWAN

Table 8. WWAN frequency regulations

Region	802.16	802.16e	Cellular
North America	Licenses	Licenses	Licenses
Europe	Licenses	Licenses	Licenses
Japan	Licenses	Licenses	Licenses

3.2 Coexistence issues in the 2.4GHz

The Steinbeis-Transfer Centre [5] has been testing the interference between ZigBee data communications (channel 11 to 26) and the other 2.4 GHz technologies. The below table summarizes the main results:

Table 9. Steinbeis-Transfer Centre coexistence tests

Technology	Packet loss results (IEEE 802.15 frames lost)
WiFi (802.11b/f=2437 MHz)	92% lost
Bluetooth	10 % lost
Microwave	1% lost

We can see both the 802.11b and the 802.15.4 are DSSS technologies that can interfere a lot between each other compared to other transmission technique in the same band.

Another test of coexistence has been led by the company Crossbow [6] measuring the perturbations of a data communications system with ZigBee technology receiving interferences from Wi-Fi radio frequencies using the 802.11b technology and namely the channel 3 at the frequency of 2.422MHz:

Table 10. Crossbow coexistence tests

802.15.4 channel	11 2.405GHz	14 2.420GHz	15 2.425GHz	20 2.450GHz	26 2.480GHz
Packet loss	0%	5%	2%	0.01%	0.01%

The results show that the nearest is affected by quite an important packet loss that can affect the reliability of a data communications system. This implies the best trade-off between the transmission method chosen and the frequency channel used.

4 What needs to be done to implement industrial wireless solutions?

4.1 The environment

The industrial environments present some specific issues and requirements. For example, the I&C domain concerns instrumentation, supervisory and control of the processes. I&C focuses mainly on three levels that can be represented as below:

Table 11. Typical I&C architecture

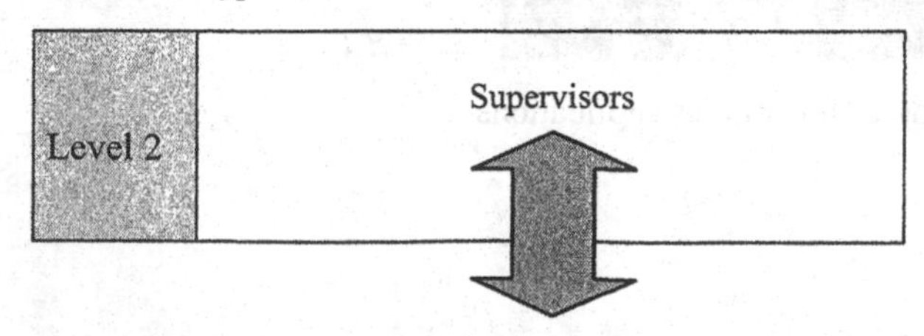

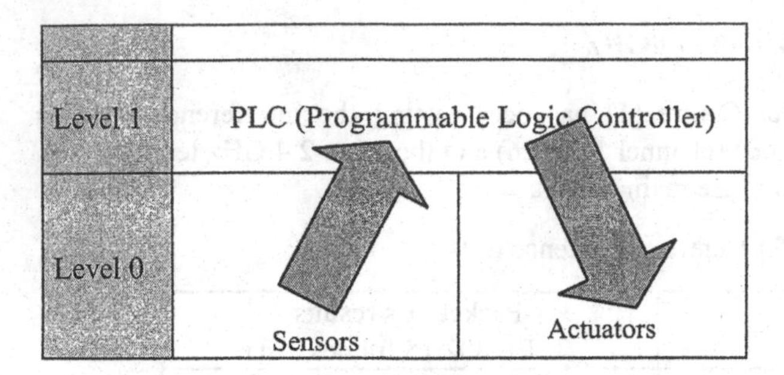

This functional architecture has several level-to-level interfaces requirements that need to be achieved by the communications network. These requirements are:

- Level 0 to level 1: real-time control (persistent stable duplex communications links), deterministic data transfer (robustness of the LLC stack), short ranges communications, always-connected, lower data rate communications.
- Level 1 to level 2: wide range communications, hybrid-type physical medium, not-always connected, higher data rate communications, possible data aggregation.

4.2 The benefits from going wireless

The benefits one can expect from going wireless for a sensor network in the I&C domain can be listed:

- cables cost reduction
- mobile points of acquisition
- self-healing communications architecture
- low-power consumption
- adaptable topology (star, tree, mesh)
- ad-hoc communications
- harsh wiring conditions and difficult environment
- hand-over between WPAN cells and between WPAN and WLAN architecture (typical uses of wireless networks are shown in in the E.D.F. – Electricité De France - environment)

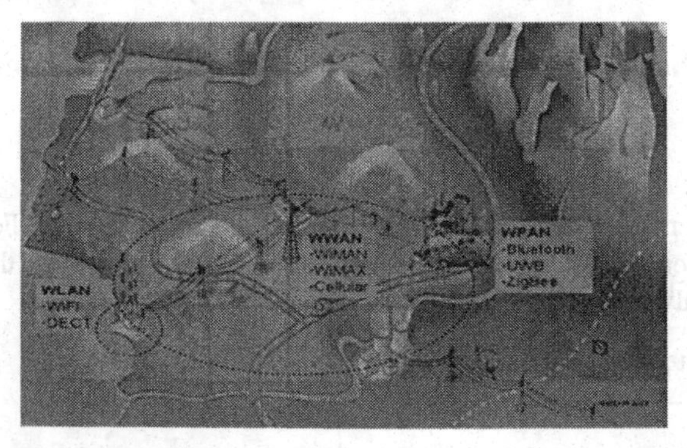

Fig. 5. Wireless technologies for utilities applications

4.3 What needs to be done?

These benefits can be obtained if the following challenges are fulfilled:

- Electro-Magnetic Compatibility satisfied despite persistent EMI (Electro Magnetic Interference) from electric welding/motors, transformers, lightning, switches, ovens, mid and high-voltage lines…
- Possible interference from same-band RF devices turned on accidentally or maliciously
- Worse large scale path-loss
- Worse fading (multipart)
- Optimised radio cell distribution
- Advanced networks protocols

The following table proposes some suggested solutions and optimizations:

Table 12. Suggested solutions and optimizations

	Challenges	Solutions	Optimizations
1	EMI	FHSS, retransmission, UWB	Notches, wide band protocols
2	Same-band RF devices	OFDM, CSMA	Random retransmission
3	Path-loss	DSSS, MIMO	Multiple antennas
4	Fading	Repeaters, smart antennas	Power regulations
5	Radio cell	RF expertise, hybrid fixed and mobile bas stations	Radio environment modeling tool
6	Network protocols	Proactive and On-demand routing protocol	Energy oriented adaptative protocol, payload balance between nodes

5 The right solutions for the right applications

Once we have gathered all these requirements and technical characteristics of the wireless technologies, one is ready to start designing the right solutions for the right applications. For instance, none technology is perfectly matching the needs of the applications and being aware of the bottlenecks of each one helps the network architect to deploy the optimized solution.

At E.D.F., we have different applications cases of wireless networks in an industrial environment such as:

- wireless tele-dosimetry
- mobile handheld devices for I&C patrols

- telecontrol of far-remote power plant sites
- geo-localization of biohazard products

The typical applications requirements in the I&C domain can be summarized into these tables:

5.1 Control applications

Table 13. Controls applications Vs wireless solutions

Constraints		*Range*		
Real-time	Yes	WPAN	WLAN	WWAN (rarely)
Harsh RF	Yes			
Battery life	No	Short-to-mid range non-beacon WiFi		
Mobility	No			GPRS
Data rate	No			
Ad-hoc	No			802.16
Security	Yes			

5.2 Measure applications

Table 14. Measures applications Vs wireless solutions

Constraints		*Range*		
Real-time	No	WPAN	WLAN	WPAN
Harsh RF	Yes			
Battery life	Yes			
Mobility	Yes	Bluetooth ZigBee	802.11b	GPRS
Data rate	No			
			802.11g	802.16

	Yes	UWB			
Ad-hoc	Yes				
Security	Yes				

Sometimes, we are able to find complete wireless solutions for controls or measures applications. For instance, the EDF R&D EMC laboratory specifies that wireless can interfere with old analog electronic boards.

To overcome such a barrier, we need to hybrid the technologies combining wireless and wired solutions. Concerning the wired solutions, PLC (Power Line Communications) networks can also reduce the cable cost and achieve the needed network requirements by using standardized interfaces.

5.3 Hybrid networks: wireless and power line networks

In the past years, PLC (Power Line Communications) technologies have reached a level of maturity in terms of data rate, standardization, inter-operability with the generalization of IEEE 802.3 standard and security.

That maturity allows its use in the industrial environments, such as power plants and sub-stations, by implementing the last developments in PLC networks.

Nowadays PLC Networks technologies can be described by several industrial standard-like:

Table 15. PLC Technologies

Data rate	*PLC technology*
Low	X10 LonWorks CEBus Homeplug Control and Command (2006)
High	Homeplug 1.0, AV DS2 Spidcom

Besides this list of PLC technologies, we don't look after using Homeplug BPL for industrial applications.

Finally, the cutting-edge industrial networks equipment could be a mix between:

- Zigbee and Homeplug Command and Control
- 802.11 and Homeplug AV
- UWB and Homeplug Command and Control

6 Conclusion and future works

The general feedback from our experimentation and test cases in utilities industrial environment is as follows:

- For Process Controls applications, IEEE-802.11 family standard needs to be implemented/deployed in one hand with WIPS (Wireless Intrusion Prevention System) and WIDS (Wireless Intrusion Detection System), and in the other hand with non-beacon transmission mode to reduce latency. Moreover, interference with existing analog electronic control devices is a real issue that needs to be carefully detected before any deployment. Thus, we believe that an hybrid communication architecture combining Power Line Communication technology with the IEEE-802.11 family represents a cost-effective and interesting alternative.
- For Wireless Measures applications, WPAN technologies like Zigbee and UWB are the technologies of choice as a lot of researches have been done in the area of power consumption optimisation control routing protocol [7]. Of course, careful wireless sensor network design is particularly important in terms of power conservative performance. This is an area we continue to investigate in terms of network modelling, design and deployment engineering tools that must take into account the industrial installations characteristics.

References

[1] Institute of Electrical and Electronics Engineers. IEEE Standard Computer Dictionary: A Compilation of IEEE Standard Computer Glossaries. New York, NY: 1990.

[2] http://www.wikipedia.org/WIKI/ofdm.

[3] K. Fazel and S. Kaiser, "Multi-Carrier and Spread Spectrum Systems", Wiley Editor, 2003.

[4] J. Meel's (De Nayer Institute), "SS Introduction", October 1999.

[5] http://www.ba-loerrach.de/stzedn

[6] http://www.xbow.com/Products/Product_pdf_files/Wireless_pdf/ZigBeeandWiFiInterference.pdf

[7] Ya Xu, John Hedeimann, Deborah Estrin, "Adaptive Energy-Conserving Routing for Multihop Ad hoc Networks", USC/ISI Research report 527, October 2000.

[8] J. Karedal et al, "Statistical Analysis of the UWB Channel in an Industrial Environment", IEEE Vehicular Technology Conference, pp. 81-85, December 2004

[9] M. Andersson, "IEEE 802.11b and Bluetooth in an Industrial Environment", connectBlue AB, May 2001.

[10] Qixin Wang, Xue Liu, Weiqun Chen*, Wenbo He, and Marco Caccamo, Real-Time Systems Lab, CS Dept., UIUC, *ECECS, Univ. of Cincinnati "Building Robust Wireless LAN for Industrial Control with DSSS-CDMA Cellphone Network Paradigm" IEEE RTSS 2005

DHT-based Functionalities Using Hypercubes

José I. Alvarez-Hamelin[1]*, Aline C. Viana[2], and Marcelo D. de Amorim[3]

[1] Universidad de Buenos Aires, Argentina
[2] IRISA/INRIA-Rennes, France
[3] CNRS/LIP6 – Université Pierre et Marie Curie – Paris VI, France

Abstract. Decoupling the permanent identifier of a node from the node's topology-dependent address is a promising approach toward completely scalable self-organizing networks. Existing solutions use a logical tree-like structure that, although allowing for simple address assignment and management, lead to low route selection flexibility. This clearly results in low routing performance and poor resilience to failures. In this paper, we propose to increase the number of candidate paths by using incomplete hypercubes. We will see that this solution can cover a wide range of applications by adapting to the dynamics of the network.

Key words: Self-organizing networks, indirect routing, DHT, hypercubes.

1 Introduction

A scalable location (lookup) service is one of the main design blocks of a completely self-organizing architecture for spontaneous networks. In traditional wired networks, location information can be easily embedded into the topological-dependent node address, which also uniquely identifies the node in the network. In self-organizing networks, however, a source only knows the destination's *identifier*, and this identifier does not give any clue of the destination's *address*. There is no static relation between the node's location and the node's identifier as a consequence of the spontaneity and adaptability of the network.

In response to these requirements, distributed hash tables (DHT) can be adopted as a scalable substrate to provide location-independent node identification [1, 2, 3, 4]. The functionalities of decoupling identification from location, and of providing a general mapping between them, have made the DHT abstraction an interesting principle to be integrated at network layer – this technique is called *indirect routing*. The main advantage of such systems is that they offer powerful and flexible rendezvous-based communication abstraction [2, 3, 4, 5, 6, 7].

A number of works have already proposed to use DHTs in routing protocols. These works can be classified in two main groups, which differ in the way

* Contact author: `Ignacio.Alvarez-hamelin@th.u-psud.fr`. This work was performed while José Ignacio Alvarez-Hamelin was a researcher scientist at LPT/CNRS, University of Paris XI, France.

Please use the following format when citing this chapter:

Alvarez-Hamelin, J.I., Viana, A.C., de Amorim, M.D., 2006, in International Federation for Information Processing (IFIP), Volume 212, Ad-Hoc Networking, ed. Al Agha, K., (Boston: Springer), pp. 157–176.

the DHT structure is deployed [8]. In the first group, the addressing and the lookup models are completely independent and routing is performed at the designed addressing structure. A DHT structure is defined to distribute and locate information among the nodes in the addressing structure. Examples of proposals in the literature that implement this approach are: Terminodes [2, 9, 10], Grid [3, 11], and DLM [4]. Most of them assume, however, that nodes know their geographic coordinates through some positioning system (*e.g.*, GPS). In the second group classification, the same structure deployed to address nodes and consequently to perform routing, is also used by the lookup model. This model describes a coherent sharing of the addressing space among the nodes, which determines the consistency of the routing protocol. Tribe [7], PeerNet [6, 12], Landmark [13, 14], and L+ [5] are examples of such protocols.

The proposals that fall in the second group proved that it is possible to build a logical and mathematical structure from mere connectivity between nodes. Routing using this mathematical space gives the exact behavior of the routing mechanism in the physical layer. Nevertheless, they lack of robustness since their space sharing mechanism follows a tree structure. Although simple to implement, a tree offers low flexibility in route selection. Furthermore, tree structures are not robust to node mobility, since a node departure causes the breakage of the tree.

Motivated by these observations, in this paper, we propose to use incomplete hypercubes instead of trees. Contrary to trees, hypercubes allow the establishment of multiple paths between any two nodes, which increases the robustness of the topology to mobility. Indeed, according its literal concept, a tree not allows nodes, in its subtree, to be connected to nodes in others subtrees. Moreover, a tree is a 2-dimensional structure. Otherwise, in a hypercube nodes can communicate in a d-dimensional space, which allows multiple paths among nodes. We expect then to represent at least a part of the broadcast nature of wireless scenarios through the multiple dimensions of a hypercube. In wireless environments, the connectivity is controlled by the density and communication range of nodes, which can be relatively large.

Our contributions are twofold. First, we propose a proactive routing approach, where routes are determined *a priori*. Second, we propose a reactive protocol that establishes routes on an on demand basis. While the proactive approach is more adapted to quasi static networks, the reactive protocol is indicated to mobile networks. We show through a number of examples that our proposals are promising and are more robust to dynamic networks than the existent related tree-like approaches.

The remainder of the paper is organized as follows. In Section 2, we present the indirect routing model approach with related work and the proposed architecture. We introduce the hypercube used as addressing space in Section 3. Section 4 presents our approach and discusses routing-specific issues. Some cases of study are addressed in Section 5. Finally, Section 6 discusses the applicability of our proposal and Section 7 conlude this paper and discusses future researches.

2 Indirect routing strategy

As well described by works found in the literature [2, 3, 4, 5, 6, 7], the indirect service model is instantiated as a rendezvous-based communication abstraction. Nodes called *rendezvous nodes* are responsible for storing the location information of others nodes in the topology. Routing is performed indirectly and the rendezvous nodes translate a node's identifier into its location-dependent address in the topology. We briefly describe here how indirect routing is performed by the use of DHT abstraction. More details can be found in the referred works.

Routing is performed through a topology-dependent technique. Every node is identified by its position in the topology, which is translated into a topology-dependent address. It is important to underline that the only way of routing is by using this address. In the general case, every node has three identifiers. The first one, called universal identifier, U, is supposed to be known by any other node that are supposed to communicate with the node. This identifier is independent of any network-level characteristics. It can be a word, a numerical value, or even an IP-like address. The second identifier, the virtual address V, is a translation of U into the virtual addressing space, $\mathcal{V}$. This translation is performed through a classical linear congruential hash function $f(U') = V = aU' + (b \bmod p)$. The virtual address V is used to name the correspondent rendezvous node. The last identifier, the relative address E, is the current topology-dependent address of the node. Observe that the relative address changes if the node moves, but both the universal and virtual identifiers remain unchanged. Fig. 1 illustrates the steps of the routing procedure and the use of the described identifiers.

When source s wants to communicate with destination d and has no idea of d's relative address, it first contacts the node responsible for storing the relative address of node d (arrow 1). Call this node T_d. Thus, the message sent by s will travel in the network until it is received by T_d, the node whose managed subspace contains the required address. Note that node s does not know E_d, but it knows V_d (obtained from U_d). Node T_d knows the relative address E_d because node d has previously informed T_d about its current address. The rendezvous node T_d plays the role of a "rendezvous" point where the location of node d is stored. The particularity of this approach is that the rendezvous point is virtually identified and can be any physical node in the network. Rendezvous nodes are distributed and depend only on the nodes' identifiers. When contacted by s, T_d responds with a message containing the relative address of node d, E_d (arrow 2). Node s can now communicate directly with d (arrow 3).

2.1 Related work

In the traditional Internet model, routing information is embedded into the topological-dependent node address, *i.e.* IP addresses have been defined for both *identifying* and *locating* a node in the network. This does not work

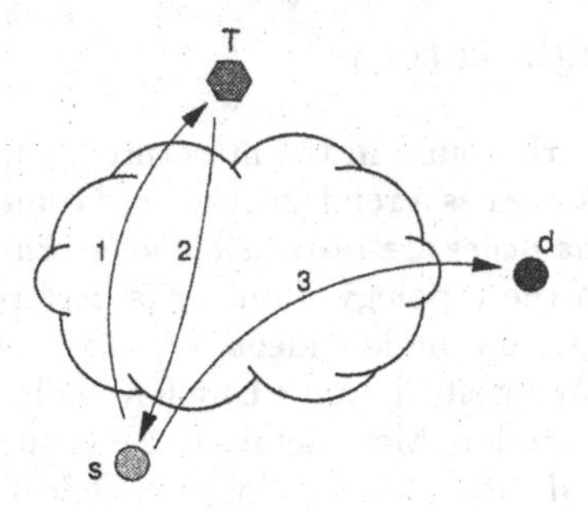

Fig. 1. Lookup (arrows 1 and 2) and direct communication (arrow 3) phases in a DHT-based routing procedure

well in mobile networks (even if they are not self-organized networks), because permanent node addresses cannot include dynamic location information, which invalidates topology information. More recently, a number of flooding-based protocols have been used to address this problem in the specific case of ad hoc networks. Nevertheless, it has been observed that these architectures do not scale well beyond a few hundred nodes [15, 16]. For instance, in sensor or wireless mesh networks, where the potential number of addressable nodes may be in the order of thousands, current solutions cannot be used.

Most proposed routing algorithms for self-organizing networks distribute the topology information to all nodes in the network. Thus, following the idea of indirection routing, the *i*3 [17] proposes an overlays-based infrastructure that offers a rendezvous based communication abstraction. *i*3 decouples the act of sending from the act of receiving: sources send packets to a logical identifier and receives express interest in packets sent to this identifier. *i*3 uses a set of servers that store identifiers and map packets with these identifiers to *i*3 nodes interested in receiving the packets. This approach combines the generality of IP-layer solutions with the versatility of overlay solutions. Our proposition uses a similar concept of indirect routing, however, it is not based in an overlay infrastructure and is independent of IP-layer.

L+ [5] proposes an improved version of Landmark [13, 14] routing, which is better suited to large ad hoc wireless networks. This protocol describes a more scalable address lookup service and algorithm improvements that react better to node mobility. An L+ node updates one location server for each level in the landmark hierarchy. L+ uses a routing algorithm similar to DSDV [18] and keeps more than just the shortest route to each destination. Nevertheless, L+ and Landmark creates a tree-based hierarchical topology where nodes are placed, offering a low flexibility in route selection.

Tribe [7] is a rendezvous-based routing protocol for self-organizing networks. By managing regions of a logical addressing space, Tribe nodes route in a hop-by-hop basis with small amount of information and communication cost. Nodes that are physically close in the network also manage close regions in the Tribe addressing space. Thus, the main component of Tribe is its proposed simple manageable addressing space used to assign addresses to nodes. Nevertheless, this space is also a tree-like structure, which limits paths by the hierarchical structure of a tree – there is only one path between any two nodes.

Similarly to Tribe, PeerNet [12] is a peer-to-peer based network layer for dynamic and large networks. The address reflects the node's location in the network and is registered with the respective identifier in the distributed node lookup service. In PeerNet, the addresses are organized as leaves of a binary tree – the address tree. PeerNet routing is a recursive procedure descending through the address tree. Thus, in contrast to Tribe, PeerNet routing disseminates information about the global state of the network, and nodes maintain a routing table that has $l = \log N$ entries, *i.e.* $O(\log N)$ per-node state (N is a number of nodes in the network). Because of the address tree organization, a node movement may require the assignment of new addresses to several nodes in PeerNet structure, which implicitly generates many updates in lookup entries.

2.2 Increasing the number of paths connections

The design of a self-organized network architecture requires an efficient combination of robustness and complexity. The resilience of existent proposals and, consequently, the performance of the routing protocols are strongly related to the complexity of the deployed addressing structure. On the one hand, tree-like structures (*e.g.*, L+ [5], Tribe [7], and PeerNet [6]) lead to simple manageable spaces. Nevertheless, they have low route selection flexibility, which results in low routing performance and poor resilience to failures/mobility. Their low complexity is obtained at the cost of some loss of robustness. On the other hand, more complex structures, like multidimensional Cartesian spaces, improve the resilience and routing performance due to the flexibility in route selection. The associated addressing and location models, however, become more complex and require a tight association between the logical and physical planes. In this paper, we propose to increase the number of paths connections through hypercubes.

Hypercubes have the inherent property of multiple paths between any couple of nodes, given a good and interesting logical-topological mapping. This possibility gives the following improvements. First, traffic can be well balanced, in contrast to what occurs in a tree, where the root is heavily charged. This characteristic allows using more efficiently the bandwidth. Another important improvement is that distances in the DHT hypercube-like structure are closer to geographic distances in the network than in the DHT tree-like structures (*e.g.*, L+ [5], Tribe [7], and PeerNet [6]). This makes communications shorter. Finally, a hypercube allows using different routing methods thanks to its logical-topological mapping (proactive and reactive routing), *i.e.* the network could have a routing schema adapted to the dynamics of the network.

In the following sections, we present our addressing system and explain how hypercube representation allows the specification of a logical structure where

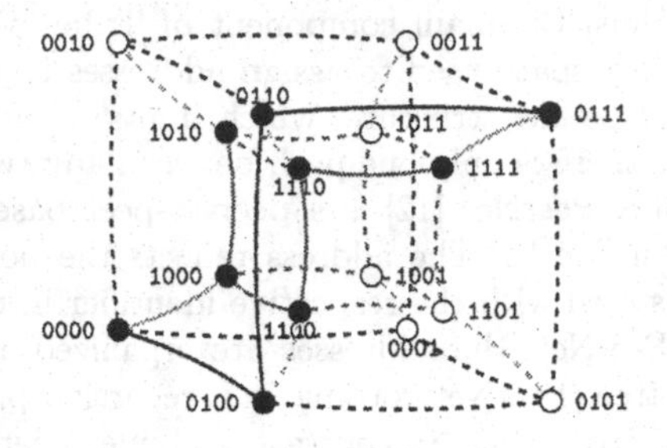

Fig. 2. Hypercube of dimension $d = 4$

proactive/reactive routing approaches can be exploited while the lookup service is performed in a simple way.

3 Address Spaces based on hypercubes

In this section, we describe how to implement a virtual addressing space based on a hypercube structure.

3.1 A very brief overview of hypercubes

The hypercube is a generalization of a 3-dimensional cube to an arbitrary number of dimensions d [19]. Each node of the d-hypercube has coordinates 0 or 1 for each dimension, covering all the combinations. This implies that the total number of nodes is 2^d. Each node is linked to all nodes whose coordinates differ only in one dimension. For example, the cube has a node at coordinates $(0, 0, 0)$, or simply 000, which is connected with nodes at coordinates 001, 010 and 100, which differ only in one of their dimensions. Thus, the degree, or the number of edges of each node is equal to the dimension d.

The most important property of the hypercube is the adjacency of nodes generated by its construction. Fig. 2 shows a hypercube of dimension $d = 4$. We can use the coordinates of a node as its network address, then the length of the address is d. It easy to see that the distance between two nodes is measured by XORing the two addresses. For example, the distance between nodes 0100 and 0111 is 2 (there are two different bits between these nodes), *e.g.*, a route could be 0100 -> 0110 -> 0111.

We find interesting examples of hypercube use in: parallel computing [20, 21], peer-to-peer networks [22], genetic codes [23], fault-tolerant and redundant systems [24], message stability detection in distributed systems [25], parallel multiprocessor systems [26], data communication [19].

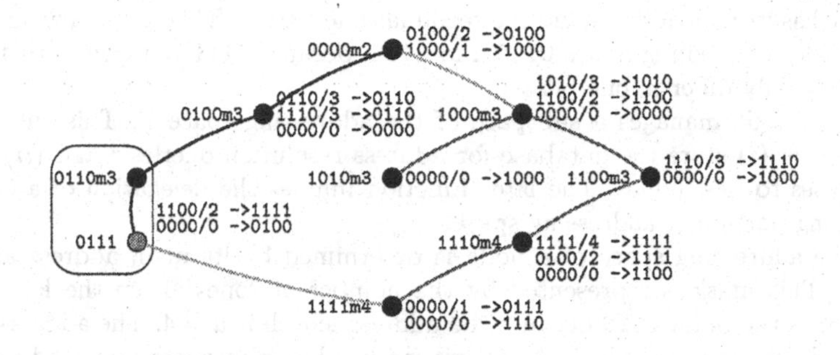

Fig. 3. Spontaneous network: physical position of nodes

3.2 The network layer

Using node coordinates in the hypercube as its relative address E, it is possible to map a physical network into a logical one. For an arbitrary physical network, the corresponding mapping produces an incomplete hypercube, because the number of nodes present is less than 2^d, and their physical connection possibilities do not necessarily correspond to all edges of the hypercube. We show an arbitrary network in Fig. 3 and its representation on the hypercube in Fig. 2, where physical nodes are represented by black circles. Fig. 3 also has a possible routing table at the right side of each node.

We have considered that nodes in Fig. 3 have a circular coverage radius. The hypercube in Fig. 3 does not represent all neighborhood connections. For example, node 0100 has a physical connection with node 1010, but their addresses differ in more than one bit and consequently, they are not connected in the hypercube structure. We say then that the hypercube is incomplete. Nevertheless, even loosing some connections, the network can take advantage of the hypercube adjacency for routing.

One way to improve this mapping and to make more physical connections become edges in the hypercube, is by assigning multiple addresses to some nodes. Since two nodes may not be neighbors in the hypercube although being physically connected, this allows us better representing physical adjacencies.

The information stored in each node is composed of the main address, the secondary addresses and its addressing space. The main address corresponds to a network or relative address E, which is given during the connection process. When a new node joins the network, the main address is selected by itself from the addresses proposed by its neighbors (already connected to the network). After obtaining the main address, the new node can chose one or more secondary addresses. This is done if it were connected to other physical neighbor nodes which are not adjacent in the hypercube, *i.e.* their network addresses E_i are not adjacent to the new node's main address. For example the node 0110m3 in

Fig. 3, has it main address and the secondary one: 0111. This secondary address is used for connecting nodes 0110 and 1111, because 0111 is adjacent to 1111, *i.e.* they only differ in one bit.

Each node manages a subspace of the addressing space $\mathcal{V}$. This subspace is used to: (*i*) store the database for address resolution queries,[2] and (*ii*) give addresses to new nodes. The later function implies the delegation of a corresponding portion of addressing space.

The addressing space of a node is determined by its main address and a mask. This mask is represented by the number of "ones" from the left side, *e.g.*, m3 is the mask 1110 because the address length is $d = 4$. The address and its mask (doing bitwise logic AND) gives the addressing space managed by the node. This method is very similar to IP subnet masks, because the part with zeros corresponds to the addressing space managed by the node. For instance, node 0000m2 in Fig. 3 manages addresses 0000 (its main address), 0010, 0001, and 0011.

The first parameter to fix is the dimension d of the hypercube, which is known *a priori* by all the participants of the network. On the one hand, this parameter limits the maximum number of nodes, but on the other hand, it gives more flexibility to connecting nodes due to secondary addresses. The problem is that each new node should be adjacent to a maximum number of nodes, ideally to all nodes within its radio coverage, in order to be strongly connected. Intuitively, the larger the addressing space, the richer the nodes' choice. We address this issue in detail in Section 5.1.

3.3 Indirect routing in the hypercube

Recall that using an indirect routing technique means that there are two phases for forwarding information: (*i*) the source asks, to the rendezvous node, the destination's address using its universal identifier, (*ii*) the source sends the messages to the destination. This mechanism presupposes that there exists a method to find the rendezvous node, because the only available information is the destination's rendezvous address V which is managed by a certain node.

As previously seen, the main address and the addressing space are given by already connected nodes. When a node gives an address, it also delegates a portion of its used addressing space (generally the upper half of it) to a new incoming node. For example, in Fig. 3 the node 0000m2 would give the main address and addressing space 0010m3 to a new node, causing the change in the 0000 mask: from m2 to m3, and it sends all the address resolution information stored for this addressing space. This means that the main address of a new node is 0010, and it manage the addresses 0010 and 0011. The utilization of this method for all the nodes causes a tree distribution of the network addresses, which we call $\mathcal{T}$ in the remainder of this paper. Fig. 3 presents a real topology,

[2] The rendezvous node stores the $U \rightarrow E$ entry.

where cutting the link between nodes 0111 and 1111, we can observe an example of the $\mathcal{T}$ tree.

Therefore, for a given rendezvous address V, we should find all the possible nodes which can manage it in their addressing space. This task might be very simple using the $\mathcal{T}$ tree. In this case, it is enough to move through the tree following the match of the rendezvous address V's prefix. Again, this search is trivial for the complete hypercube, but in an incomplete case one needs to find the $\mathcal{T}$ tree. In a normal operation, $\mathcal{T}$ always exists. We handle different cases in Section 5.

4 Design issues: Proactive or reactive?

We present two routing methods in this paper: proactive and reactive. The first builds and maintains the routing tables all the time, and assures a route for every node in a network. The second method finds a route on demand, and maintains the route for a given period of time. Clearly, the proactive approach is very useful for quite stable networks, (*i.e.* where node mobility is low and nodes' lifetime is long). For highly dynamic networks, where nodes are joining and leaving all the time, the reactive method is more appropriate.

4.1 Case 1: Proactive routing protocol

In a complete hypercube, there is no problem for routing, because all nodes and edges exist, then it is possible to use the adjacency properties of the hypercube. In a general case, we should propose a routing table composed of a combination of default entries and some other routing entries. The default entries take advantage of the address assignment method (the $\mathcal{T}$ tree). The other entries consist in a set of routes for other connections which do not belong to $\mathcal{T}$, represented by the secondary addresses. In other words, we put one entry in a routing table for each connection of the node, and also for the shortest advised routes. Because the address assignment method, each node v has a parent node and it may also has some children nodes, noted by

- *Parent node*: P_v is the node that assigns a main address to node v. The parent node also delegates a portion of its addressing space to node v.
- *Child node*: C_v^i is the node that has node v as parent node, *i.e.* $P_{C_v^i} = v$, $1 \leq i \leq k$, being k the number of v children nodes.
- *Children set*: represented by $\mathbf{C}_v = \{C_v^1, \ldots, C_v^k\}$, is the set of children nodes.

The address assignment method is formalized as follows. The main address of node v is p_0 m b, where p is the prefix of the v address, _0 is the zeros which completes the address length, and b is the number of bits from the left. The prefix is obtained by doing v AND M_v, where $M_v = \sum_{j=b}^{d-1} 2^j$. Thus, the node v assigns an address as following

$$p_v\_0 \text{ m } b_v \xrightarrow{\texttt{address\_assignament}} \begin{cases} p_v\_0 \text{ m } (b_v + 1) \\ p_v\_0 + 2^{d-b_v-1} \text{ m } (b_v + 1) \end{cases} \quad (1)$$

The parent node P_v has always the main address $p_v\_0 - 2^{d-\beta_v}$, where β_v is the first value of b_v, *i.e.* when the main address of v was assigned. Each child C_v^i in the children set $\mathbf{C}_v$, when they exist, has as main address $p_v\_0 + 2^{(d-1)-x_i}$, $\forall x_i \in \{\beta_v, \beta_v + 1, \cdots, d-1\}$. Note that the child index is defined as $i = x_i - \beta_v + 1$.

Each entry in a routing table is composed of a prefix, a mask, and a next hop. The masks have the same form as in the IP case, *i.e.* the number of ones from the left side.

As mentioned before, there are two types of entries:

- the entries of $\mathcal{T}$ tree, *e.g.*, $0\_0/0 \rightarrow p_v\_0 - 2^{d-b}$ for the parent node P_v, and $p_v\_0 + 2^{d-1-x_i} \ / \ x_i \rightarrow p_v\_0 + 2^{d-1-x_i}$ for each child node $C_v^{x_i-\beta_v+1}$;
- the entries for a neighbor t (*i.e.* w, u, and z in the example) which does not belong to the $\mathcal{T}$ tree is $p_t\_0/a_t^v \rightarrow t$, where p_t_0 is the prefix obtained applying the mask defined by a_t^v, as $M_t = \sum_{j=a_t^v}^{d-1} 2^j$.

The entries at v's routing table are

$$\begin{array}{|c|} \hline p_w\_0 \ / \ a_w^v \rightarrow w \\ p_v\_0 + 2^{d-1-x_n} \ / \ x_n \rightarrow p_v\_0 + 2^{d-1-x_n} \\ \vdots \quad \vdots \quad \rightarrow \vdots \\ p_u\_0 \ / \ a_u^v \rightarrow u \\ p_v\_0 + 2^{(d-1)-x_1} \ / \ x_1 \rightarrow p_v\_0 + 2^{(d-1)-x_1} \\ p_z\_0 \ / \ a_z^v \rightarrow z \\ 0\_0 \ / \ 0 \rightarrow p_v\_0 - 2^{d-b} \\ \hline \end{array}$$

where $a_w^v \geq x_n \geq \cdots \geq a_u^v \geq x_1 \geq a_z^v > 0$, and x_i is the number of bits from the left, obtained after the $i^{\text{th}} = x_i - \beta_v + 1$ child (C_v^i and $x_i \in \{\beta_v, \beta_v + 1, \cdots, d-1\}$). The order is very important because the first matching is used for routing.

These entries are determined by Algorithm 0.1 when a local node v is connected to $u \notin \mathbf{C}_v$. The first step computes the node y which is in the middle of the path from v to u in the tree $\mathcal{T}$. Then, it computes s, which is the length of the matching prefix, either of v or of u, because y is ancestor o v or u. Finally, a message advertising the new route is sent to all neighbors. Then, once receiving the message each neighbor u executes the Algorithm 0.2 to add and resend the new received routes when necessary. In this algorithm, $d_H(\cdot, \cdot)$ is the distance in the hypercube.

We should consider also the case when a node v lost the connection with its parent node P_v. In this case it sends a message $\mathcal{M}$ to its neighbors, in order to find a connection with the $\mathcal{T}$ tree. This message $\mathcal{M}$ is resent by each node until

Algorithm 0.1 Routing tables construction at node v

1 Reach a node y, such that $d(y,x) \leq d(v,y) \leq d(y,x) + 1$, where $d(\cdot,\cdot)$ is the distance on the default tree $\mathcal{T}$.
2 Set the entry $y/s\text{->}x$ in v's routing table, where s is the number of unchanged bits between y and, x if it is a y's descendant in a $\mathcal{T}$, else v is a y's descendant.
3 Send a message to all neighbors, except x, with $y/s\text{->}v$.

Algorithm 0.2 Forwarding routing tables messages

1 Node u receives $\{y/s\text{->}v\}$ from neighbor v
2 **If** the $d(y,u) \leq d_H(y,v) + 1$ **then**
3   Add the entry $y/s\text{->}v$
4   Send a message to all the neighbors, except v, with $\{y/s\text{->}u\}$.

one, *e.g.* w, which is connected to its parent node P_w and the prefix P_v of the first node v is not contained in P_w. Then, node w resends a message reply to v which confirms and sets the default route of v: $0/0 \rightarrow u$, such as u is the v's neighbor having a path to w. The node w also sends a message, following the $\mathcal{T}$ tree, to reach P_v or its closer ancestor, we call this node $\mathcal{P}_v$. The objective is to establish a route from $\mathcal{P}_v$ to v passing by w, restoring the $\mathcal{T}$ tree. In this way the $\mathcal{T}$ tree is reconnected, assuring the default route for nodes v and C_v^i.

4.2 Case 2: Reactive routing protocol

In our case, the logical topology is built following adjacent addresses, hence there is a coherent mapping between the physical positions and the logical addresses.

There are two complementary methods for routing: the first is for address resolution messages and the second is for other messages.

Let us begin with the second case. This method considers that the hypercube is complete, and routes the message by sending it to neighbors whose addresses are closer to the destination. When a message is blocked, *i.e.* there is no route, the message goes backwards and it is sent through a different route, leaving a mark on the unsuccessful route. Algorithm 0.3 presents the method used to forward a message at node v, received of node w, when the source is x and the destination is z. Fig. 4 shows an example where there is no route from v to z. The number over the arrows corresponds to step number of the algorithm. The curved arrows are the sent message $\mathcal{M}$ and the right arrows is the return of the message $\mathcal{M}$. The special case of arrows with 6.1 and 6.2 correspond to the first and second iteration of the loop, respectively.

Remember that $d_H(\cdot,\cdot)$ is the distance in the hypercube, and $\mathcal{T}$ is the initial tree used for distributing the addressing space. This algorithm favors the exploration of farther regions from the root of $\mathcal{T}$. If it does not find a route

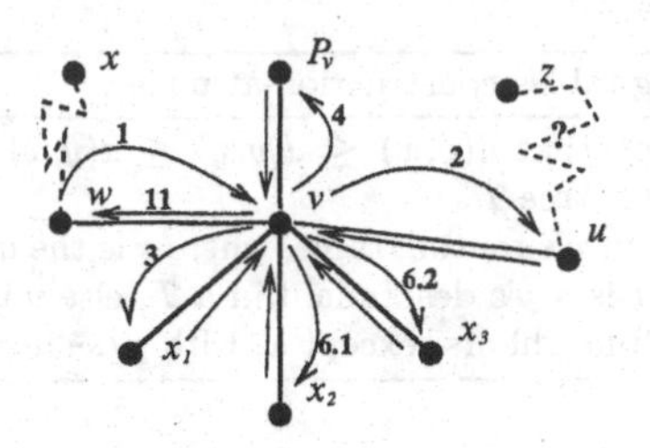

Fig. 4. Execution of Algorithm 0.3

Algorithm 0.3 Forwarding in reactive routing at node v

---

1 v receives a message $\mathcal{M}(x,z)$ form neighbor w.
2 v sends the message to a neighbor $u \neq \{P_v, w\}$, such that u minimizes $d_H(u,z)$
3 **If** there is no route from u **then** mark this route and resend the message to other neighbor $\neq \{P_v, w\}$.
4 **If** the message is returned again **then** send the message to its parent P_v in $\mathcal{T}$ and mark all the remaining neighbors as unexplored.
5 **If** the message returns **then** do
  until all neighbors are explored:
6   send the message to a neighbor marked as unexplored
7   **if** the message returns **then** mark this neighbor as blocked, and return to step 5.
8 **If** there is no route **then**
9   **If** the original sender is the local node v:
10   **then** *no_route_to_host* := *true*.
11   **else** resend the message $\mathcal{M}(x,z)$ to the neighbor sender w.

---

then it sends the message towards the root, and finally if it still does not find a route, it performs an exhaustive exploration. A timer is used by resetting the marks in unsuccessful routes, but they can also reset by an update message. The value of this timer is long, and is only used to give a robust behavior, *i.e.* when an update message is lost.

The update messages are sent when new topological connections are made. When a node v has been connected with another node w, node v sends update messages with its address and the new neighbor address w to all its neighbors (w does not consider this message). Other case is when v receives an update message from a neighbor u, then v clears the blocked routes in the u corresponding interface.

The first routing case, which corresponds to a resolution request, uses a variation of Algorithm 0.3. This variation consist in, firstly to change of step 2, and secondly to eliminate the step 3. The elimination of step 3 is motivated to give more priority, to address resolution messages, to reach their destination.

It is clear that the number of address resolution messages [3] are lower than the data messages, and then they have less contribution to the congestion of the $\mathcal{T}$'s root. The step 2 of Algorithm 0.3 is replaced by

---

2 v sends the message to a neighbor $u \neq w$, such that
u minimizes $d_{\mathcal{T}}(u, p_z\_0)\ \forall\ s\ /\ p_z\_0 = z$ AND $\sum_{i=s}^{d-1} 2^i$.

That is, it finds the neighbor which minimizes the distant to one of the possible prefixes of the virtual address in the $\mathcal{T}$ tree. The reason is that the virtual address is contained in the managed addressing space of a certain node, because the $\mathcal{T}$ tree distribution method.

5 Practical considerations and case studies

In this section we will consider the application of our architecture in different scenarios. Then, we present two examples for each routing method.

5.1 Choosing the dimension d

One important issue of hypercubes is the addressing space, because it defines multiple possibilities of connection and routing. We consider two cases: sparse and dense networks. Given a fixed d, nodes are connected until their radio neighbors have not any available addresses. In sparse case, nodes are mainly connected augmenting the diameter of the logical graph. Dense networks, however, are susceptible to have a lot of connections per node, increasing the number of secondary addresses, consuming a lot of address per node, and given a small diameter of the logical graph. Therefore, there is a trade-off between the radio coverage and the maximum size of the network for choosing the dimension.

More precisely, the extreme case on sparse network is when a node has only two neighbors, this results in a linear chain with $2d$ nodes because the address distribution method follows a $\mathcal{T}$ tree. In general, the maximum number of nodes $n_{\max}$ that can join a sparse network with k neighbors is

$$n_{\max} = \sum_{i=1}^{k} s(d-i,k)\ , \quad \forall\, 2 < k < d$$

where d is the dimension of the hypercube, and $s(\cdot,\cdot)$ is the following recursive function

$$s(h,k) = \begin{cases} \sum_{j=1}^{k-1} s(h-j,k)\ , & \forall\, h > k \\ 2^h\ , & \forall\, h \leq k \end{cases}$$

[3] Discovered addresses are stored in a local cache table and associated to a timeout. Resolution messages are sent one time for the first communication, and then, when the timeout of the corresponding cache table's entry has expired.

For dense networks, the number of addresses in each node depends on the number of physical neighbors, considering that all nodes could be obtained from a compatible secondary address with their neighbors. Therefore, a high percentage of neighbors of a node are connected among them, which means that the network has a lot of triangles. If the percentage is denoted by $c < 1$, k is the number of neighbors, and d is the number of dimensions, then, for each $c \cdot k$ nodes there is a clique[4]. Consequently, if $n_{\max}$ is the number of nodes that can join a dense network, there are $n_{\max}/(c \cdot k)$ cliques and $\frac{c \cdot k(c \cdot k-1)}{2}$ number of connections, *i.e.* secondary addresses, for each clique. Then,

$$\begin{aligned} \frac{n_{\max}}{c \cdot k} \cdot \frac{c \cdot k(c \cdot k - 1)}{2} &\leq 2^d \\ n_{\max}(c \cdot k - 1) &\leq 2^{d+1} \\ n_{\max} &\leq \frac{2^{d+1}}{c \cdot k - 1} \ , \end{aligned}$$

where 2^d is the total number of nodes in a d-dimensional hypercube.

A useful approximation of maximum path length, for both cases, is the following. Considering $n(\ell)$ the number of total neighbors up-to distance ℓ for a node in a k regular network (*i.e.*, each node has k neighbors). Then, for $\ell = 2$ we have $n(\ell) = (k-1)^2 + 1$, because the neighbors at distance 1 are k, and each of these neighbors has other $k - 1$ different neighbors. The maximum path length $\ell_{\max}$ for a network with n nodes is

$$\begin{aligned} n &= n(\ell_{\max}) \\ n &= (k-1)^{\ell_{\max}} + 1 \\ \log_{k-1} n &\simeq \ell_{\max} \ , \end{aligned}$$

which is valid for $k < d/2$. The main difference of $\ell_{\max}$ between sparse and dense networks is the value of k, because dense networks has a higher k than sparse ones, thus the maximum path distance will be smaller in dense networks.

Therefore, considering the general purpose case, where the addresses are not too long and where it is also possible to obtain some secondary addresses, an empirical choice of d could be $n_{\max} = 2^{4d/5}$. That is, we propose to increase the addressing space by 20% of the address length, allowing up to $2^{d/5}$ secondary addresses per node.

5.2 An example of the proactive protocol

[4] In a clique of n nodes each node is connected to all nodes, and the total number of connections is $n(n-1)/2$.

We present here examples of the routing table construction, communication between two nodes, and address resolution.

For the proactive method, each node has a pre-established table. Consider Fig. 3 and the routing table of node 1000m3:

destination	next hop
1010/3	-> 1010
1100/2	-> 1100
0000/0	-> 0000

The first entry means that all messages addressed to destinations whose most significant bits are 101 must be sent through node 1010 (one of its children). The second line is for addresses attained through the child 1100. It is worth noting here the strict relationship between the addressing space of a child and the destination entry in the table at the time the child was connected, *e.g.*, the entry 1100/2 and its first child 1100m2. Currently, node 1100 has mask m3 because it has already assigned an address to a new node (but its mask was m2 before the arrival of the new node). We call the addressing space of a node at the time it joins the network the *initial addressing space* of the node.

Finally, the last line is the default route to its parent node 0000. (Note that "/0" means the first "0" most significant bits.) The default route is represented by 0000/0 because it matches all nodes.

It is important to stress that the order of the lines in the routing table is important. The first line is the most constraining entry, because the 3rd most significant bits must match (due to "/3"). The last line is the least constraining entry, hence, the default route entry. The first node in the network does not have a default route, because it has no parent and it is the parent of all nodes. However, it has entries for its children, then all the possible addresses in the hypercube are represented.

There are others types of entries in order to represent a connection that does not follow the tree structure. This is the goal of our proposal. For example, Fig. 3 displays the connection between nodes 1111 and 0111, and the corresponding routing tables. In this scenario, node 1111 has the following routing table:

destination	next hop
0000/1	-> 0111
0000/0	-> 1110

The default route is through the node's parent, and the other route means that all the addresses whose most significant bit is 0 can be reached through node 0111. This entry, at local node v =1111, can be determined by Algorithm 0.1 after the connection with u =0111.

Now we illustrate a case where a node exchanges data. Consider that node 1110 sends a message to node 0110. The first entry in the routing table of 1110 is 1111/4 ->1111. This means that the comparison is done using the four most significant bits (because of "/4") of the destination node 0110. We observe that the final destination is different to the entry at routing table, *i.e.* 0110≠1111, and therefore the matching fails. The second line is 0100/2 ->1111, the two most significant bits of the destination are 01, and they equal the two most significant bits of 0100/2. Therefore, this entry matches and the packet is forwarded to node 1111. The first entry of the routing table of 1111 is 0000/1 ->0111 and the most significant bit of destination is 0 – this entry matches and the packet is forwarded to 0111. As 0111 is a secondary address, the packet is now at node 0110, which is the final destination address.

Finally, we present an address resolution request. This kind of message is routed in the same form as data messages. The only difference is that the destination, *i.e.* the rendezvous address, may or may not be the main address of a node. If it is not the main address, the message will arrive at the node which manages this address. Therefore, before applying the routing algorithm, each node must verify if the destination belongs to addresses that it manages. For example, node 0110 wants to know which is the network address of a particular identifier U. Then it applies the hash function to know the rendezvous address, that is $hash(U)$ =1101. Because this address is not managed by the local node 0110m3, it sends the message to 1101. The first entry in 0110's routing table is 1100/2 ->1111, and it matches because the two most significant bits of 1101 are 11. Then the request message is sent to node 1111. This node does not manage the address in the request either, so it forwards the message using its routing table. The first entry is 0000/1 ->0111, which does not match. The second is 0000/0 ->1110, which matches because it is the default routing entry, and the message is forwarded to node 1110. Since this node has a m4 mask, it does not manage the address into the request, so it will forward the message. The first entry in its routing table is 1111/4 ->1111, which does not match, and the second one is 0100/2 ->1111 which does not match either. Finally, the last entry matches because it is the default route. The node 1100 receives the request for the server resolution of address 1101, and the addresses managed by 1100m3 are 1100 and 1101. This node looks up the network address E corresponding to node U, and sends a reply to the source node 0110 with the network address E. The source can then directly communicate to the node whose address is E.

5.3 An example of the reactive protocol

In the reactive case, there are no routing tables, but some information concerning temporary path recently used by each node. This information is created in a communication step, storing the unsuccessful paths. In this section we present two communication cases and an address resolution procedure.

Because this method starts with no *a priori* knowledge of how complete the hypercube is, it uses standard routing in hypercubes. This means that routing is done by changing the different bits one by one, *i.e.* sending to neighbors closer to the destination (recall that a node is a neighbor if their addresses differ on one bit). For example, if node 0100 sends a message to 1111, it does

(0100 XOR 1111)=1011, that is the first, third, and fourth bits change. Then node 0100 can send the message to one of the following neighbors: 1100, 0110 or 0101, because they differ, from 0100, in only one bit. The only node present in the network is 0110 (see Fig. 3), therefore the message is forwarded to this node. At node 0110, XOR is applied again, which results in 1001. The only existing neighbor is 0111, which corresponds its secondary address. Finally, the result of XOR is 0001, and the neighbor 1111 is the last step.

We illustrate a more complicated case with the following example. Node 1000 sends a message to node 0110, then (1000 XOR 0110) = 1110, and the possible forwarders in the network are 1010 and 1100. Node 1000 sends then the message through 1010. Candidate forwarder neighbors of node 1010 are 1110 and 0010, because (1010 XOR 0110) = 1100. But 0010 does not exist in the network and 1110 is not connected to it. Node 1010 sends the message backwards, and node 1000 sets a temporary entry because now it knows that there exists no path. Of course, this entry should be removed after a timeout, or if the node becomes connected to other nodes. Finally, the message is forwarded to node 1100. At this node, the result of (1100 XOR 0110) is 1010, then a possible forwarder, present in the network, is 1110. This latter receives the message and computes (1110 XOR 0110) = 1000, but the nodes 1110 and 0110 are not interconnected. In this case, it is better to take a new path in the opposite way. Then, the message is sent to node 1111. This node computes (1111 XOR 0110) = 1001, and the possible forwarder is 0111. As 0111 is a secondary address and its primary address is 0110, the message has arrived to the final destination.

For the address resolution case, we use the modified Algorithm 0.3. Suppose that node 1110 wants to send a message to node with universal address U, then it obtains $hash(U)$ =0101 (the rendezvous address). The node who minimize $d_{\mathcal{T}}(1110, 0101)$ is its parent node P_v = 1100. Since the other nodes are in a similar situation, the message is forwarded to consecutive parent nodes until it reaches 0000. Because the first most significant bit is the same as the desired address 0101, the actual node checks if this address belongs to its managed space. The result is negative and the message is sent to the neighbor 0100 which is the closest to 0101. This node has in its managed space the addresses 0100 and 0101 (because its mask is m3). Therefore, node 0100 looks up the virtual address and sends it to 1110 in a response message. The communication was then done using the $\mathcal{T}$ tree. If the $\mathcal{T}$ tree is disconnected, the message is sent backwards until a route is found, as in the data communication case.

6 Discussion

The most effective protocol to self-organization networks is a combination of a good physical-to-logical mapping with a simple and robust routing protocol, and small routing tables based principally on the adjacencies. The geographical routing could be the most promising, but the reception of GPS can not be enough, *e.g.*, inside of a building. Moreover, the GPS error, which depends also the reception quality, is too large for some dense networks. Next candidates are those that use indirect routing and build a logical and mathematical structure from mere connectivity between nodes. Up to now, this protocols propose a logical tree for connecting nodes [5, 6, 7, 12, 13, 14].

In the deployment of self-organized systems, flexibility in route selection is an important issue to be considered, which affects the performance in terms of path length, traffic concentration, and resilience to failures. In this context, the organization of the addressing structure has a strong influence. In the tree-based structures, paths are limited by the hierarchical structure of a tree – there is only one path between any two nodes. A tree offers low flexibility in route selection, contrary to the greater flexibility offered by the multi-dimensional approaches. Our hypercube approach offers multiple links options that get the path closer to the physical distance.

A spontaneous network could have a well balanced traffic only when the distance between two nodes is closer to their physical distance. In a case that the logical structure is a tree, is very difficult to fill this condition, mainly because the connection order. Even, following the optimal connection order, when the density of nodes is high, a message sent to a physical neighbor should pass to other node before to arrive at the destination. Instead, the incomplete hypercube is better because it allows multiple links, even for far nodes, giving more privilege to the neighbors' connections. This also makes a more coherent physical-to-logical mapping, given similar physical and logical distances. Therefore, using the hypercube as underling logical structure, coupled with indirect routing, we provide redundant connections, a better load distribution. These characteristics permit to cover a wide range of applications according to their mobility characteristics.

Although the greater flexibility in route selection offered by the multi-dimensional approaches, their associated addressing and location models are more complex, contrarily to simple manageable structures offered by tree-like structures. The main problem with the incomplete hypercubes could be their relative complexity, but evidently there exist a trade-off between the simplicity and the robustness. Our proposal provides the advantages of a good physical-to-logical mapping and multiples paths which gives a robust behavior.

7 Conclusion

Decoupling the permanent identifier of a node from the node's topology-dependent address is a promising approach toward completely scalable self-organizing networks. A group of proposals that have adopted such an approach use the same structure to: address nodes, perform routing, and implement location service. In this way, the consistency of the routing protocol relies on the coherent sharing of the addressing space among all nodes in the network. Such proposals use a logical tree-like structure where routes in this space correspond to routes in the physical level. The advantage of tree-like spaces is that it allows for simple address assignment and management. Nevertheless, it has low route selection flexibility, which results in low routing performance and poor resilience to failures. In this paper, we propose to increase the number of paths using incomplete hypercubes. The design of more complex structures, like multi-dimensional Cartesian spaces, improves the resilience and routing performance due to the flexibility in route selection. We present a framework for using hypercubes to implement indirect routing. This framework allows to give a solution adapted to the dynamics of the network, providing a proactive and reactive routing protocols, our major contributions.

Future research includes a complete evaluation of the proposed protocol under fixed and mobile environments. Some optimization mechanisms and implementation issues for improving robustness in terms of location information availability, load balancing, and failures are also interesting to analyze.

References

1. I. Stoica, R. Morris, D. Liben-Nowell, D. R. Karger, M. F. Kaashoek, F. Dabek, and H. Balakrishnan, "Chord: a scalable peer-to-peer lookup protocol for internet applications," *IEEE/ACM Transactions on Networking*, vol. 11, no. 1, pp. 17–32, Feb. 2003.
2. L. Blazevic, L. Buttyan, S. G. S. Capkun, J. P. Hubaux, and J. Y. L. Boudec, "Self-organization in mobile ad-hoc networks: the approach of terminodes," *IEEE Computer Communications Magazine*, June 2001.
3. J. Li, J. Jannotti, D. S. J. D. Couto, D. R. Karger, and R. Morris, "A scalable location service for geographic ad hoc routing," in *Proceedings of ACM MOBICOM'00*, Aug. 2000.
4. Y. Xue, B. Li, and K. Nahrstedt, "A scalable location management scheme in mobile ad-hoc networks," in *Proceedings of IEEE Conference on Local Computer Networks (LCN)*, (Tampa, FL, USA), Nov. 2001.
5. B. Chen and R. Morris, "L+: Scalable landmark routing and address lookup for multi-hop wireless networks," tech. rep., Massachusetts Institute of Technology, Cambridge, Massachusetts - MIT LCS Technical Report 837 (MIT-LCS-TR-837), Mar. 2002.
6. J. Eriksson, M. Faloutsos, and S. Krishnamurthy, "Scalable ad hoc routing: The case for dynamic addressing," in *Proceedings of IEEE INFOCOM'04*, (Hong Kong), Mar. 2004.
7. A. C. Viana, M. D. Amorim, S. Fdida, and J. F. Rezende, "Indirect routing using distributed location information," *ACM Wireless Networks*, vol. 10, no. 6, pp. 747–758, Dec. 2004.
8. A. C. Viana, M. D. Amorim, S. Fdida, and J. F. Rezende, "Self-organization in spontaneous networks: the approach of dht-based routing protocols." to appear in Ad Hoc Networks Journal, 2005.

9. J. P. Hubaux, T. Gross, J. Y. L. Boudec, and M. Vetterli, "Towards self-organized mobile ad hoc networks: the terminodes project," *IEEE Communications Magazine*, vol. 39, no. 1, pp. 118–124, Jan. 2001.
10. Terminodes Project. `http://www.terminodes.com/`.
11. Grid Project. `http://www.pdos.lcs.mit.edu/grid/`.
12. J. Eriksson, M. Faloutsos, and S. Krishnamurthy, "Peernet: Pushing peer-to-peer down the stack," *Proceedings of International Workshop on Peer-To-Peer Systems (IPTPS'03)*, Feb. 2003.
13. P. F. Tsuchiya, "The landmark hierarchy: a new hierarchy for routing in very large networks," in *Proceedings of ACM SIGCOMM'88*, Aug. 1988.
14. P. F. Tsuchiya, "Landmark routing: Architecture, algorithms and issues," tech. rep., MTR-87W00174, MITRE Corporation, Sept. 1987.
15. J. Broch, D. A. Maltz, D. B. Johnson, Y. Hu, and J. Jetcheva, "A performance comparison of multi-hop wireless ad hoc network routing protocols," in *Proceedings of ACM MOBICOM'98*, Oct. 1998.
16. S. Ni, Y. Tseng, Y. Chen, and J. Sheu, "The broadcast storm problem in a mobile ad hoc network," in *Proceedings of ACM MOBICOM'99*, pp. 152–162, Aug. 1999.
17. I. Stoica, D. Adkins, S. Zhuang, S. Shenker, and S. Surana, "Internet indirection infrastructure," in *Proceedings of ACM SIGCOMM'02*, Aug. 2002.
18. C. E. Perkins and P. Bhagwat, "Highly dynamic destination sequenced distance-vector routing (dsdv) for mobile computers," in *Proceedings of ACM SIGCOMM'94*, Oct. 1994.
19. Y. Saad, "Data communication in hypercubes," tech. rep., Research Report 428, Department of Computer Science, Yale University, New Haven, CT, 1985.
20. F. T. Leighton, *Introduction to parallel algorithms and architectures: array, trees, hypercubes.* Morgan Kaufmann Publishers Inc. San Francisco, CA, US, 1991.
21. E. Oh and J. Chen, "Parallel routing in hypercube networks with faulty nodes," in *IEEE International Conference on Parallel and Distributed Systems (ICPADS '01)*, pp. 338–345, July 2001.
22. M. Schlosser, M. Sintek, S. Decker, and W. Nejdl, "Hypercup - hypercubes, ontologies, and efficient search on peer-to-peer networks," in *Agents and Peer-to-Peer Computing: A Promising Combination of Paradigms, LNCS 2530*, pp. 112–124, July 2003.
23. M. A. Jimenez-Montano, C. R. de la Mora-Basanez, and T. Poeschel, "On the hypercube structure of the genetic code," in *Proceedings of Bioinformatics and Genome Research*, pp. 445–459, Oct. 1994.
24. D. Wang, "A low-cost fault-tolerant structure for the hypercube," *Journal of Supercomputing*, vol. 20, no. 3, Nov. 2001.
25. R. Friedman, S. Manor, and K. Guo, "Scalable stability detection using logical hypercube," tech. rep., Technion, Department of Computer Science Technical Report 0960, May 1999.
26. J. Slack, "Visualization of embedded binary trees in the hypercube," tech. rep., Final Report of the Project for Information Visualization, Department of Computer Science, University of British Columbia, Apr. 2003.

ADMP: An Adaptive Multicast Routing Protocol for Mobile Ad Hoc Networks*

Rolando Menchaca-Mendez[1], Ricardo Menchaca-Mendez[1], and J. J. Garcia-Luna-Aceves[12]

1 Dept. of Computer Engineering, University of California, Santa Cruz
1156 High Street, Santa Cruz, CA 95064, U.S.A.
{menchaca, rmenchaca, jj}@soe.ucsc.edu
WWW home page: http://www.soe.ucsc.edu/ research/ccrg/home.html
2 Palo Alto Research Center (PARC), 3333 Coyote Hill Road
Palo Alto, CA 94304, U.S.A.
WWW home page: http://www.parc.xerox.com

Abstract. We present ADMP, the adaptive mesh-based multicast routing protocol, in which nodes are able to independently tune the amount of redundancy used to transmit data packets with the goal of improving the overall packet delivery ratio while keeping the retransmission overhead as low as possible. ADMP is based on a novel distributed algorithm for computing connected dominating sets. ADMP uses a single type of control packet, called multicast announcement, which is used to build the meshes of multicast groups, elect the core of each mesh and obtain two-hop neighborhood information. Using detailed simulations for different scenarios, we show that ADMP achieves similar or better reliability than two mesh-based multicast protocols that are very resilient (ODMRP and PUMA) while inducing low packet retransmission overhead.

1 Introduction

Mobile Ad Hoc Networks (or MANETs) are highly dynamic and do not rely on a fixed infrastructure. MANETs are well suited to applications where rapid deployment and dynamic reconfiguration are necessary. Examples of such scenarios are: military battlefield, emergency search and rescue, conference and conventions. The objective of a multicast routing protocol for MANETs is to enable

* This work was supported in part by the Mexican National Council for Science and Technology (CONACyT), by the Mexican National Polytechnic Institute (IPN), by the National Science Foundation under Grant CNS-0435522, and by the Baskin Chair of Computer Engineering at the University of California, Santa Cruz.

Please use the following format when citing this chapter:

Menchaca-Mendez, R., Menchaca-Mendez, R., Garcia-Luna-Aceves, J.J., 2006, in International Federation for Information Processing (IFIP), Volume 212, Ad-Hoc Networking, ed. Al Agha, K., (Boston: Springer), pp. 177–188.

communication between one or more senders and a group of receivers in a network where nodes are mobile and may not be within direct wireless transmission range of each other. These protocols must use the available bandwidth and nodes' energy very efficiently, given that they are scarce resources in MANETs and do so when nodes may be highly mobile.

Several MANET multicast protocols have been proposed recently (e.g. [1-8]). In general, the approaches taken up to date can be classified by the way they support the routing structure they maintain; namely tree-based and mesh-based protocols.

A tree-based multicast routing protocol constructs and maintains either a shared multicast routing tree or multiple multicast trees. Recent examples of tree-based multicast routing protocols are the Multicast Ad hoc On-demand Distance Vector Protocol (MAODV) [1] and the Adaptive Demand-driven Multicast Routing Protocol (ADMR) [2]. The tree-based approach has adequate performance in wired networks [9]; however, establishing and maintaining a tree or a set of trees in MANETs incurs substantial communication overhead as the branches break due to node mobility, which has a negative impact in the overall performance of the protocol [3].

On the other hand, a mesh-based multicast routing protocol maintains a mesh for each multicast group consisting of a connected sub-graph of the network that includes all receivers of a particular group and the relays needed to maintain connectivity with all the receivers in the group. Maintaining a connected component is far less complicated than maintaining a tree and hence mesh-based protocols tend to be simpler and more robust. However, as we will see in Section 4, in situations with high mobility or high channel-contention, mesh-based multicast protocols can also have poor performance when too many redundant relays are used to forward multicast traffic. Two well-know representatives of mesh-based protocols are the Core Assisted Mesh Protocol (CAMP) [4] and the On-Demand Multicast Routing Protocol (ODMRP) [5].

In this paper we present the Adaptive Dominant Multicast Protocol (ADMP), a protocol that further improves the reliability and efficiency of its direct predecessors PUMA [6] and DPUMA [3]. ADMP makes use of a novel distributed algorithm that computes connected dominating sets to provide high delivery ratios under high node-mobility and high channel-contention. The main idea that ADMP borrows from PUMA is that a single control packet (a multicast announcement) is flooded periodically to build the mesh for one or multiple multicast groups, elect the core of each mesh and collect two-hop neighborhood information. When forwarding a packet, ADMP dynamically computes the connected dominating set of the current mesh using a utility function that takes into account relative mobility of nodes and channel contention. Depending on the local node conditions, a node adjusts the amount of redundancy used to cover these two-hop neighbors that are also mesh members of a given multicast group.

The remaining of this paper is organized as follows. Section 2 summarizes related work on multicast routing protocols for MANETs and the distributed computation of connected dominating sets. Section 3 presents ADMP and the General Augmented Greedy Set Cover (GAGSC) algorithm. As we will explain in more detail in Sub-section 3.2, GAGSC is able to compute connected dominating sets taking into account two-hop information regarding channel contention and nodes' mobility in order to compute a dominating set whose size reflects the amount of redundancy used to forward a multicast data packet. In section 4 we show a series of performance comparisons among ODMRP, PUMA, DPUMA, and ADMP over different scenarios. Finally, in Section 5 we present concluding remarks and current work.

2 Related Work

2.1 Multicast Routing Protocols

ODMRP is a representative of the state of the art in mesh-based multicast routing protocols. In order to establish the mesh, ODMRP requires cooperation of nodes wishing to send data to a multicast group. Senders periodically flood a Join Query packet throughout the network. These periodic transmissions are used to update the routes. Each multicast group member after receiving a Join Query, broadcasts a Join Table to all its neighbors in order to establish a forwarding group. Senders broadcast data packets to all its neighbors. Members of the forwarding group forward the packet. Using ODMRP, multiple routes from a sender to a multicast receiver may exits due to the mesh structure created by the forwarding group members. The limitations of ODMRP are the need for network-wide packet floods and the sender initiated construction of the mesh. This method of mesh construction results in a mesh that includes many more nodes that there are needed in a multicast routing tree, as well as numerous unnecessary transmissions of data packets compared to a receiver initiated approach. DCMP [7] is an extension to ODMRP that designates certain senders as cores and reduces the number of senders performing flooding. NSMP [8] is another extension to ODMRP aiming to restrict the flood of control packets to a subset of the entire network. However, DCMP and NSMP fail to eliminate entirely ODMRP's drawback of multiple control packet floods per group.

CAMP avoids the need for network-wide floods from each source to maintain multicast meshes by using one or more cores per multicast group. A receiver-initiated approach is used for receivers to join a multicast group by sending unicast join requests towards a core of the desired group. The drawbacks of CAMP are that it needs the pre-assignment of cores to groups and a unicast routing protocol to maintain routing information about the cores. This later characteristic may induce considerable overhead in a large ad hoc network.

PUMA supports the IP multicast service model of allowing any source to send multicast packets addressed to a given multicast group, without having to know the constituency of the group. Furthermore, sources need not join a multicast group in order to send data packets to the group. Like CAMP, PUMA uses a receiver initiated approach in which receivers join a multicast group using the address of a special node (core in CAMP), without the need for network-wide flooding of control or data packets from all the sources of a group. PUMA implements a distributed algorithm to elect one of the receivers of a group as the core of the group, and to inform each router in the network of at least one next-hop to the elected core of each group (mesh establishment). The election algorithm used in PUMA is essentially the same as the spanning tree algorithm introduced by Perlman for internetworks of transparent bridges [10]. Within a finite time proportional to the time needed to reach the router farthest away from the eventual core of a group, each router has one or multiple paths to the elected core.

Hence a receiver can connect to the elected core along all shortest paths between the receiver and the core. All nodes on shortest paths between any receiver and the core collectively form the mesh of the multicast group. This is the case given that all nodes in the network receive multicast announcements for every active multicast group stating the core of the group. Hence a sender node can send packets to the multicast group by encapsulating them in unicast packets to the core along any of the paths to the core. PUMA uses a single control packet for all its functions, the multicast announcement. Each multicast announcement specifies a sequence number, the address of the group, the address of the core, the distance to the core, a mesh member flag that is set when the sending node belongs to the mesh, a parent field that states the preferred neighbor to reach the core, and a list of neighbors who are mesh members. With the information contained in such announcements, nodes elect cores, determine routes for sources outside a multicast group to unicast multicast data packets towards the group, notify others about joining or leaving a group's mesh, maintain the mesh and get two-hop information of nodes belonging to each multicast group.

In the basic PUMA protocol, once a multicast message reaches a mesh member, it is flooded across the whole mesh. This can lead to unnecessary overhead because a given node can be covered by more than one neighbor and hence receive a multicast message more than once. In order to reduce this overhead, DPUMA incorporates the concept of connected dominating sets to dynamically determine a subset of one-hop nodes such that if these nodes broadcast the packet, it will be received by all mesh members in a two-hop neighborhood and eventually by all members in the mesh.

2.2 Distributed Computation of Connected Dominating Sets

For the distributed computation of connected dominating sets, we use a simple graph $G = (V,E)$ to represent an ad hoc wireless network, where V represents a set of wireless mobile nodes and E a communication link between two nodes. An edge (u,v) indicates that both nodes u and v are within each other's transmission range. Such graph is also called *unit disk graph* [11]. It is easy to see that the topology of this type of graphs vary over time due to node mobility.

For a given undirected graph $G = (V, E)$, a connected dominating set (CDS) in the graph is any set of connected vertices $V' \subseteq V$ such that each $v \in V - V'$ is adjacent to some vertex in V'. The problem of determining the minimum connected dominating set (MCDS) is known to be NP-complete. Therefore, only distributed approximated algorithms running in polynomial-time are practical for MANETs.

If we compute a connected dominating set V' of a given network, only those nodes belonging to V' have to broadcast a packet in order to reach every node in the network, with the corresponding savings of V- V' messages. It is important to note that distributed approximations that run in polynomial-time do not compute the minimum dominating set; however, in the context of MANETs, computing a larger dominating set is actually desirable to augment the reliability with which a packet is delivered.

Lim and Kim [12] showed that the *minimum connected dominating set* (MCDS) problem can be reduced to the problem of building a *minimum cost flooding tree* (MCFT) and they proposed a set of heuristics for flooding trees that lead to two algorithms: *self-pruning* and *dominant pruning* (DP). They also showed that both algorithms perform better than *blind flooding*, in which each node broadcast a packet to its neighbors whenever it receives the packet along the shortest path from the source node, and that DP outperforms self-pruning. Since then, many other approaches have been purposed to compute CDS and to improve communication protocols applying CDS. For example, enhancements to dominant pruning have been reported by Lou and Wu [11] who describe the *total dominant pruning* (TDP) algorithm and the *partial dominant pruning* (PDP) algorithm, and by Spohn and Garcia-Luna-Aceves [13] who presented the *enhanced dominant pruning* (EDP) algorithm which improves DP's performance. All these algorithms utilize two-hop neighborhood information.

In this work we propose a generalization to the approach used by Lim and Kim in their dominating pruning algorithm [12]. Their approach uses a greedy set cover (GSC) strategy in order to compute the dominating set of each two-hop neighborhood of the nodes involved in the diffusion of a packet.

3 Adaptive Dominant Multicast Protocol (ADMP)

In [3] we demonstrate how DPUMA effectively increase the delivery ratio of PUMA while incurring far less retransmission overhead. However, as it is shown in Figure 4, this is not longer true for scenarios where nodes have high mobility. The reason for this behavior is that, in general, the performance of protocols that rely on the freshness of topological information is strongly impacted by the relative mobility among nodes. It would be desirable to have an approach capable of delivering the reliability achieved by PUMA under light loads or high node mobility, and the one achieved by DPUMA under high loads with low mobility.

The first step towards such a protocol is to get an accurate view of the instantaneous levels of relative mobility and contention, so that; nodes were able to select the operation mode that performs best under each condition. The next section describes two simple mechanisms to detect the degree of relative mobility and the degree of local contention.

3.1 Detection of Relative Mobility and Contention Levels

To compute the level of relative mobility, each node keeps track of how its one-hop neighborhood has changed between two consecutive sampling periods, then, nodes compute an exponential weighted moving average to avoid reacting too fast to changes in their perceived relative mobility.

We define instantaneous relative mobility m as $[d/(r+d)]/s_p$, where s_p is the length of the sampling period, d is the number of new or missing one-hop neighbors detected in the current sampling period with respect to the neighbors detected in the previous sampling period, and r is the number of neighbors that did not change from the previous sampling period with respect to the current sampling period. The degree of relative mobility υ_n during sampling period n is:

$$v_n = (\alpha - 1)v_{n-1} + \alpha m \quad (1)$$

Where α is a constant used to assign weight to the previous (υ_{n-1}) and newly calculated values (m) of the degree of relative mobility.

Another aspect that has a strong influence over the performance of protocols that use contention-based medium access control (MAC) protocols is traffic load. To measure one-hop contention we propose a simple and very intuitive metric that is based on the ratio between the number of received signals with errors and the total number of received signals during a fixed period of time. This ratio tries to approximate the current probability of a successful transmission. Then, as in the previous case, we use an exponential weighted moving average to cope with sudden and short term variations. We define the instantaneous contention level c as $(e/t)/s_p$, where e is the number of signals with errors received during the sampling period, and t is the total number of signals received during the sampling period. The *degree of contention* γ during sampling period n is defined as:

$$\gamma_n = (\beta - 1)\gamma_{n-1} + \beta c \quad (2)$$

Analogously to the previous case, β is a constant used to assign weight to the previous (γ_{n-1}) and newly calculated values (c) of the degree of contention.

The current default value for α and β is 0.2. However, our results show that the performance of ADMP is not very sensitive to these parameters.

3.2 General Augmented Greedy Set Cover (GAGSC)

In the case of DPUMA, since nodes already interchange one-hop topology information, they can, almost for free, gather information about contention and mobility of the nodes that belong to their two-hop neighborhood. Here we present a novel algorithm that takes advantage of this information, and that makes more fine-grained decisions when selecting the amount of redundancy used to relay a packet.

Our algorithm, which we have called General Augmented Greedy Set Cover (GAGSC), has two main phases. In the first phase, based on their local contention and relative mobility degree, two-hop neighbors are assigned with a coverage value which reflects the amount of redundancy that will be used to cover that node, or in other words, the number of one-hop neighbors that the algorithm will try to use to cover (or to dominate) that particular two-hop neighbor. In the second phase, the algorithm uses a greedy strategy by selecting one-hop neighbors with the highest value in a utility function f_u. $f_u(\cdot)$ of a given one-hop neighbor b is proportional to number of two-hop neighbors (nn) which are covered by b, and inversely proportional to the exponential of b's contention (cd) and relative mobility degrees (md). By using this utility function, GAGSC tend to favor one-hop neighbors with lower local contention and mobility degrees over nodes which might cover more two-hop neighbors but that have larger values for these metrics.

In particular, our current implementation of ADMP uses the following utility function.

$$f_u = nn \cdot e^{-1.5cd-1.5md} \quad (3)$$

Figure 1 shows a partial plot of the utility function that only considers the contention and relative mobility degrees. From the plot of the function, it is easy to see how nodes with low contention and mobility degrees will tend to be selected first than nodes with larger values in these metrics.

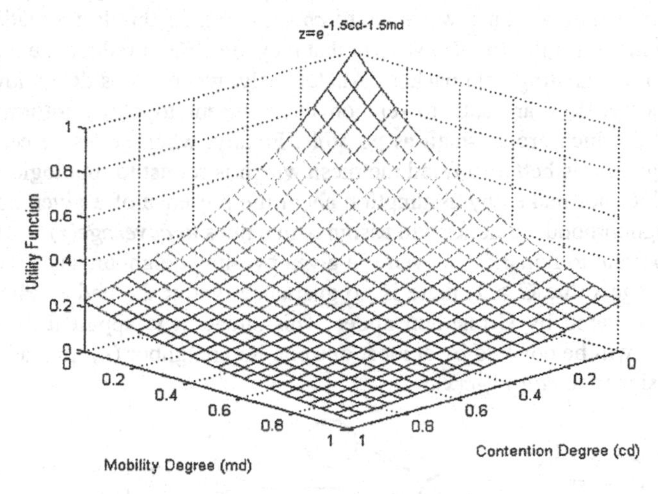

Fig. 1. Plot of the utility function used to select one-hop neighbors

Now, we are ready to make a more formal description of the GAGSC algorithm. As in [12] we use N(u) to represent the neighbor set of a given node u (including u) and N(N(u)) to represent the neighbor set of N(u) (i.e., the set of nodes that are within two hops from u). When a mesh member v receives a data packet from u, it selects a number of forwarding nodes that can cover (with the adequate redundancy) all the nodes in N(N(v)). u is the previous relaying node, hence nodes in N(u) have already received the packet, and nodes in N(v) will receive the packet after v rebroadcast it. Therefore, v just needs to determine its forwarding list $F(u,v)$ from $B(u,v) = N(v) - N(u)$ to cover all nodes in $U(u,v) = N(N(v)) - N(u) - N(v)$.

The GAST algorithm works as follows.

Phase 1: For all two-hop neighbor node $x \in U(u,v)$, let *coverage*(x) be its corresponding coverage value, i.e., the number of one-hop neighbors that the algorithm will try to use to cover (or dominate) that particular node. Now, using rules like "*if v's contention is low and v's mobility is low and x's contention is low and x's mobility is low then set coverage(x) equal to 3*" or "*if v's contention is high and v's mobility is low and x's contention is high and x's mobility is low then set coverage(x) equal to 1*". Nodes use two threshold values to decide whether their current contention and relative mobility degrees are low or high. GAGSC employs 16 rules that correspond to all possible combinations of high and low contention and mobility degrees for the two-hop node x under consideration and the node v which is computing its forwarding list.

The intuition behind these rules is as follows. When nodes detect low contention degree in the channel, they are safe to use high redundancy during the dissemination of data, or in other words, they can assign a high value to *coverage*(x), so that nodes will try to cover (or dominate) their two-hop neighbors with as many one-hop neighbors as possible. This mode of operation is similar to PUMA where data packets are flooded within the mesh. On the other hand, when high degrees of contention are detected, nodes will try to compute a CDS which is as small as possible; hence they assign low values to *coverage*(x). In this last situation, nodes operate in a mode similar to DPUMA, so that they are able to reduce the redundancy used when disseminating data packets. Analogously, when nodes detect low relative mobility degree, they are safe to rely on their current topology information and compute CDS which are as small as possible. Finally, when nodes perceive a high mobility degree, it is better to flood the mesh which is robust to topological changes because it does not make any assumption about the presence of a given node in the one-hop neighborhood, so nodes will assign high values to *coverage*(x).

It is important to remark that even if a given two-hop neighbor, say x, is assigned with a coverage value $C > 1$, there is no guarantee that at the end of Phase 2, x is going to be covered by C one-hop nodes. This situation is apparent on Figure 2, where node x will be covered by at most one one-hop neighbor (a) no matter what is the value assigned to *coverage*(x).

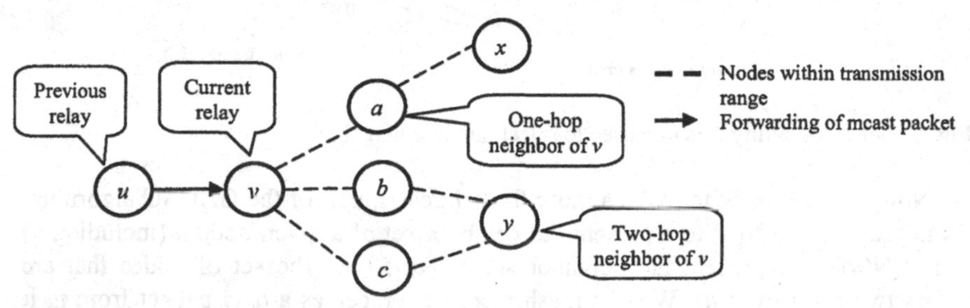

Fig. 2. Two-hop neighborhood of node v that has not been covered so far when receiving a multicast data packet from node u

Phase 2: Compute: $F(u,v)$.

Let $F(u,v)$ be the forwarding list to be computed, Z be the set of nodes that have been covered up to the current iteration which is initially empty, $S_i = N(v_i) \cap U(u,v)$ be the set of two-hop nodes that can be covered by node v_i, $K = \bigcup S_i$ be the set of nodes that have to be covered at the end of the execution of the algorithm, and $mob(v_i)$ be the relative mobility degree of v_i, and $con(v_i)$ be the contention degree of v_i for all $v_i \in B(u,v)$.

1. Find the 1-hop node v_m whose $f_u(|S_m|, con(v_m), mob(v_m))$ is a maximum
2. For all node $x \in S_m$ make $coverage(x) = coverage(x) - 1$ in all S_i
3. For all S_i, make
   - $E_i = \{x \mid x \in S_i \text{ and } coverage(x) = 0\}$,
   - $S_i = S_i - E_i$, $Z = Z \cup E_i$, $S_m = \phi$ and

- o $F(u,v) = F(u,v) \cup \{v_m\}$

4. Stop if $Z=K$ or if $F(u,v) = B(u,v)$; otherwise, goto step 1
5. If $F(u,v) = B(u,v)$ then $F(u,v) = \varphi$ where φ is an special marker used to denote that every one-hop neighbor (if it has not done that before) has to retransmit the data packet

It is important to note that, in order to mimic the behavior of PUMA and achieve its resilience to continuous topological changes it is not enough to designate all one-hop neighbors as forwarders. We also need a way to specify that any mesh member, that happens to be in the one-hop neighborhood, has to retransmit a packet, even if the current forwarding node has not perceived it yet. In the specification of our algorithm, the φ marker introduced in Step 5 plays this role.

3.3 Forwarding Data Packets Within The Mesh

Finally, to complete the description of the GAGSC algorithm, we present how it is used in the context of disseminating a data packet within a mesh.

- o When a mesh member v receives a multicast data packet from its transport layer, it determines its forwarding list $F(\text{-},v)$ using GAGSC, then the node piggybacks $F(\text{-},v)$ in the data packet and transmits it.
- o When v receives a multicast data packet from a mesh member u
  - o If $v \in F(*,u)$ or $F(*,u)$ equals φ, it uses GAGSC to determine its forwarding list $F(u,v)$, piggybacks $F(u,v)$ in the data packet and retransmit it.
  - o If $v \notin F(*,u)$, it just accepts the packet
- o When v receives a multicast data packet from a non-mesh member u, v computes the forwarding list $F(\text{-},v)$, piggybacks $F(\text{-},v)$ in the data packet and retransmit it. In this case, u can be a sender or a next hop in the path from the sender to the core.

4 Experimental Results

We compared the performance of ADMP against the performance of PUMA, DPUMA and ODMRP. We used the discrete event simulator Qualnet version 3.5. The distribution of Qualnet itself has the ODMRP code. Each simulation was run for five different seed values with the exception of the mobility scenario which uses 20 seeds. This is necessary to obtain representative results because a given seed can generate very different mobility traces for different protocols. To have meaningful comparisons, all timer values (i.e., interval for sending JOIN requests and JOIN tables in ODMRP and the interval for sending multicast announcements in the PUMA family) were set to 3 seconds. Unless other values are specified, Table 1 lists the details about the simulation environment. The metrics used are packet delivery ratio and average number of data packets relayed.

In our first experiment we varied the packet size from 64 to 1024 bytes. There are two senders and one group composed of 30 nodes. Only one sender belongs to the multicast group. From Figure 3 we can observe how PUMA performs very well for small packet sizes but as the packet size increases, its packet delivery ratio drops dramatically.

Table 1. Simulation environment

Simulation Environment			
Total Nodes	50	Simulation time	100s
Node Placement	Random	Simulation area	1300×1300m
Mobility Model	Random Waypoint	Channel Capacity	2000000 bps
Pause Time	10s	MAC protocol	IEEE 802.11
Min-Max Vel.	0 – 10 m/s	Data Source	MCBR
Transmission Power	15 dbm		
Number of packets sent per source			1000

This experiment shows how for medium to large packet sizes those protocols that compute dominating sets (DPUMA, and ADMP) achieve higher delivery ratios than protocols like PUMA that use much more redundancy. From Figure 3 we can also observe how ADMP performs very close to the best case of the base protocols, namely, close to PUMA for small packets and close to DPUMA for large packets. This is a strong indication that ADMP nodes effectively detect their current conditions on the channel and select the appropriate mode of operation.

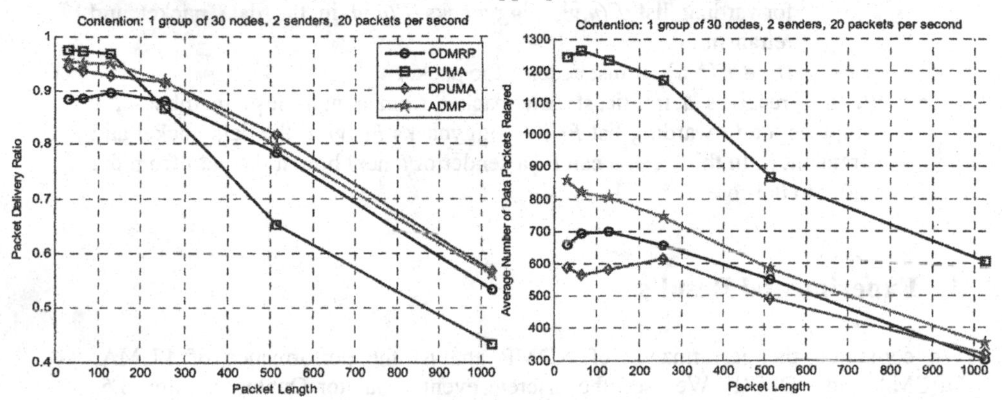

Fig. 3. Packet delivery ratio and average number of retransmission when varying the packet size

In our second experiment we varied from 1 to 50m/s the nodes' speed (with a pause time of 0 seconds). In this experiment we show how effective is the proposed metric to detect relative mobility, and how this information is used by the nodes to autonomously decide which mode of operation has to be used. As it can be seen on Figure 4, ADMP performs similar or better than the best of the base options of the family of PUMA protocols (PUMA, DPUMA). Again, this is a strong indication that ADMP nodes effectively detect the current mobility condition and select the appropriate mode of operation.

A very interesting situation is that for speeds between 10m/s and 30m/s, ADMP performs even better than the base protocols. The reason is that nodes can independently select the current "best strategy", so nodes which are in different regions of the MANET can use the operation mode that best fit that particular region.

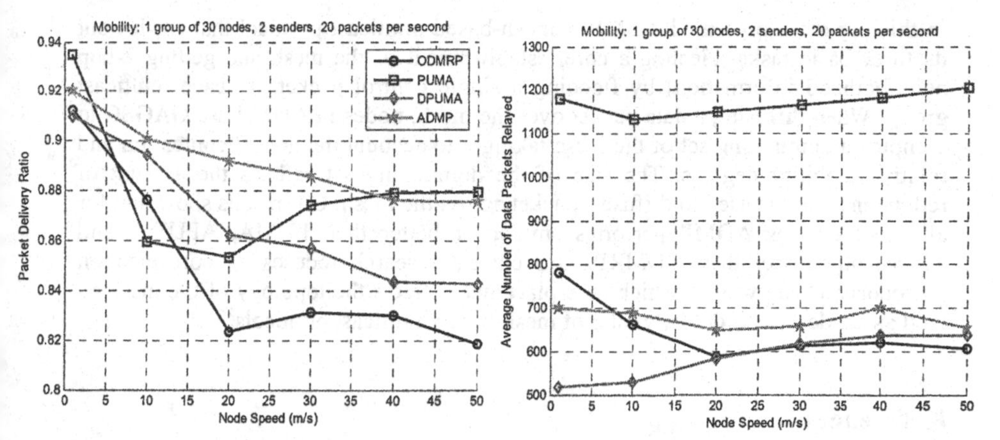

Fig. 4. Packet delivery ratio and average number of retransmission when varying the speed of the nodes

Finally, Figure 5 shows the behavior of the degree of relative mobility of a given node for different values of the speed of the nodes. From the figure we can observe that as the speed of the nodes increases, the height of the peaks in the graphs also increases. The peaks in the graphs correspond to the time when a multicast announcement is flooded across the MANET. This is also the time when the all the topology information is updated.

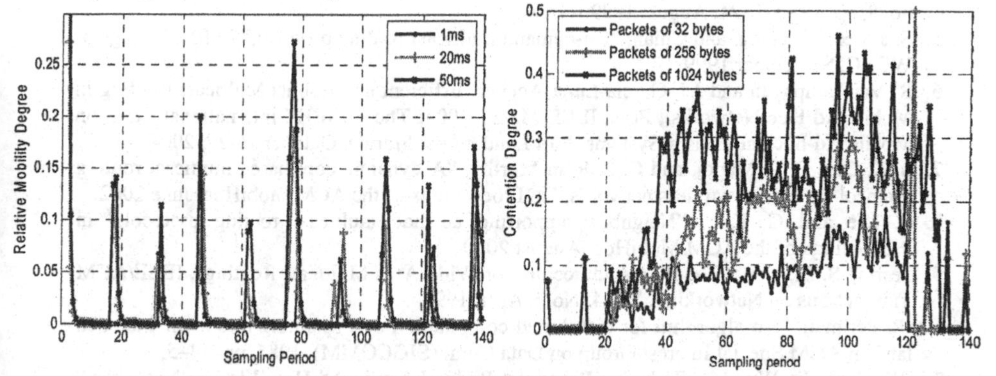

Fig. 5. Values taken by the Relative Mobility and Contention Degree metrics for different values of the speed of the nodes and packet length

Figure 5 also shows the behavior of the contention degree perceived by a given node for different values of the length of the data packets. As well as in the case of the relative mobility degree, we can observe a good correlation between the proposed metrics and the conditions in the network. As we saw in the previous paragraphs, our protocols take advantage of this information to tune the amount of redundancy used to transmit data packets.

5 Conclusions

In this paper we presented ADMP, a mesh-based multicast protocol that carries out its three basic tasks (electing a core, establishment of the mesh and getting 2-hop neighborhood information) by flooding a single control packet per each multicast group. When diffusing a data packet over the mesh, nodes in ADMP use GAGSC to compute a dominating set of the mesh taking into account the nodes' contention and relative mobility degrees. The size of the dominating set reflects the amount of redundancy that is used to diffuse a packet across the mesh. Our results show that for all the scenarios ADMP performs similar or better than PUMA, APUMA and consistently better than ODMRP. Our current research focuses on core election protocols and the way in which core placement affects the topology of the mesh as well as the delay and delivery ratio of mesh-based multicast protocols.

References

1. E. Royer and C. Perkins, "Multicast operation of the ad hoc on-demand distance vector routing protocol," in Proceedings of Mobicom, August 1999
2. L. Ji and M. S. Corson, "A lightweight adaptive multicast algorithm", in Proceedings of IEEE GLOBECOM 1998, December 1998, pp. 1036–1042
3. R. Menchaca-Mendez, R. Vaishampayan, J. J. Garcia-Luna-Aceves, K. Obraczka, "DPUMA: A Highly Efficient Multicast Routing Protocol for Mobile Ad Hoc Networks," ADHOC-NOW 2005: 178-191
4. J. J. Garcia-Luna-Aceves and E.L. Madruga, "The core assisted mesh protocol," IEEE Journal on Selected Areas in Communications, Special Issue on Ad-Hoc Networks, vol. 17, no. 8, pp. 1380–1394, August 1999
5. S. J. Lee, M. Gerla, and Chian, "On-demand multicast routing protocol," in Proceedings of WCNC, September 1999
6. R. Vaishampayan and J.J. Garcia-Luna-Aceves, Efficient and Robust Multicast Routing in Mobile Ad Hoc Networks , Proc. IEEE MASS 2004: The 1st IEEE International Conf. on Mobile Ad-hoc and Sensor Systems, Fort Lauderdale, Florida, October 25-27, 2004
7. S. K. Das, B. S. Manoj, and C. S. Ram Murthy, "A dynamic core based multicast routing protocol for ad hoc wireless networks," in Proceedings of the ACM MobiHoc, June 2002
8. S. Lee and C. Kim, "Neighbor supporting ad hoc multicast routing protocol," in Proceedings of the ACM MobiHoc, August 2000
9. Deering S. E., et-al, "The PIM Architecture for Wide-Area Multicast Routing", IEEE/ACM Transactions on Networking, Vol.4, No.2, April 1996
10. R. Perlman, "An algorithm for distributed computation of a spanning tree in an extended lan," in ACM Special Interest Group on Data Com. (SIGCOMM), 1985, pp. 44–53
11. Wei Lou, Jie Wu, "On Reducing Broadcast Redundancy in Ad Hoc Wireless Networks," IEEE Transactions on Mobile Computing, Vol. 1, Issue 2 (April 2002), Pages: 111 – 123
12. H. Lim and C. Kim, "Flooding in wireless ad hoc networks," Computer Communications, vol. 24, February 2001
13. M.A. Spohn and J.J. Garcia-Luna-Aceves, "Enhanced Dominant Pruning Applied to The Route Discovery Process of On-demand Routing Protocols," Proc. IEEE IC3N 03: Twelfth Int. Conf. on Computer Com. and Networks, Dallas, Texas, October 20 - 22, 2003